Rugby League Annual Re

2007

Edited by Dave Farrar and Peter Lush

London League Publications Ltd

Rugby League Annual Review 2007

A CIP catalogue record for this book is available from the British Library.

First published in Great Britain in April 2007 by:
London League Publications Ltd, P.O. Box 10441, London E14 8WR

ISBN: 978-1903659-31-1

Cover design by: Stephen McCarthy Graphic Design
                             46, Clarence Road, London N15 5BB

Layout: Peter Lush

Printed and bound by: Biddles Ltd
                             King's Lynn, Great Britain

Contents

A new rugby league publication

After seven years of publishing our twice-yearly magazine *Our Game*, we have decided to switch to an annual review. There were some administrative reasons for this – the amount of time taken to run a subscription based publication and the difficulty of producing the summer edition when we are busy working on books for the autumn high among them. However, the main reason was that we felt we could offer a more interesting publication for our readers in book format.

We hope that you will agree. The breadth and scope of articles in this publication probably covers what would have been in four editions of *Our Game*. We can now say to authors that if they want 4,000 to 5,000 words to develop their ideas the space is available for them.

We still want to have different points of view put forward. We want to be able to continue to examine the sport's history from different angles. We want to be able to offer comprehensive book reviews and fulsome obituaries. Both these areas are at times neglected by parts of the sport's trade press.

We hope to include fiction and even poetry in future editions. We will retain an international outlook that we believe is fundamental to the future of rugby league. And we have retained our sense of humour, with our cartoon Grubber continuing in this publication.

Thank you to everyone who contributed to *Our Game* over the past seven years, to our subscribers and other readers. And thank you to everyone who has contributed to this new publication. Without those prepared to give up their time to research and write articles, this publication would not exist.

Feedback is very welcome. However, at present our plans are to continue with an annual review published in the spring near the start of the season. There are already two other annuals published in the autumn, and we believe that this publication offers something different to the reader from those books.

And we hope that this new publication will offer the same as *Our Game:*

Rugby League Analysis, History and Vision.

Dave Farrar and Peter Lush
Joint Editors, *Rugby League Annual Review 2007*

Editorial Board: Giovanni Cinque, Tony Collins, Robert Gate, Phil Melling, Michael O'Hare and Huw Richards.

Closed shop Super League and the soul of the game

David Hinchliffe looks at promotion and relegation.

I fully appreciate that the idea of a Wakefield Trinity supporter arguing for the retention of promotion and relegation will, for some, seem the equivalent of a turkey actively campaigning for Christmas. But the prospect of a Super League closed shop in the very near future seems to me, as a life-long follower of rugby league, to be against the best traditions and philosophy of the game.

Of course, I totally understand the arguments put forward by those who are behind this quite profound change, but I believe their proposals are short-sighted and a superficial response to various problems within our sport which have been identified for some time. They see, in particular, the threat of relegation from Super League as a destabilising factor for those clubs that are possible candidates for the drop. They argue that it leads to short term thinking within the clubs concerned, whose sole objective becomes simply the avoidance of going down. This manifests itself, in particular, in teams being filled by short-term import players, with the development of home grown talent being largely ignored, to the detriment of the long term future of both the club concerned and this country's international prospects.

I certainly recognise these symptoms of a malaise that does indeed need a cure. I wasn't entirely oblivious to the fact that during Wakefield Trinity's dramatic fight for survival during the 2006 season, the seventeen turning out in the famous red, white and blue frequently contained a mere handful of British-born players.

And, knowing personally many of those at Trinity whose jobs and prospects were genuinely on the line until the last match of the season, I am also very sensitive to the argument that relegation is unfair to players, coaching staff and others employed at clubs who, with their families, faced very uncertain futures. Mortgages have to be paid and the prospect of entire families being unsettled and uprooted is, I accept, a matter of serious concern to all of us who believe that the wellbeing of those who play the game is essential to the wellbeing of the game itself.

But those identifying each of these problems as being endemic within a system of promotion and relegation seem to ignore some fairly obvious solutions. Firstly, the fear of relegation is predicated upon a belief that what exists below the level of Super League is manifestly inferior. Rugby league has allowed the hype around the Super League product to leave a prevailing impression of the National Leagues being distinctly second class. The game has, in the main, allowed its broadcasting partners to concentrate on Super League and, with the abysmal coverage rugby league as a whole receives in the national media, sports fans can be forgiven for having no knowledge whatsoever of the existence of the game beyond its top level. The casual spectator is unlikely to be attracted to matches and competitions they know absolutely nothing about.

The fact that the fear of relegation is such a problem for players and clubs is a consequence of the game's collective failure to champion the relevance, importance and quality of the lower leagues. In the National League matches I have seen there is some outstanding talent on display and if such players were able to move into a full-time environment their full potential would be realised to great effect within the game.

We have had some full-time squads within National League One and I believe the game should be aiming to create an environment within that League where it would be possible for all the competing clubs to move in that direction. It is inevitable that there will always be a gap between Super League and the National Leagues but we need to develop an active strategy to ensure that this gap is markedly narrowed. Pulling up the drawbridge and leaving the National League clubs to sink or swim simply isn't the answer. We need to positively discriminate in the direction of the National Leagues to bring about a situation where relegation is no longer viewed as the end of civilisation as we know it.

I'm not just talking about improving the so-called 'parachute payments' to clubs to ease the financial consequences of relegation. What I want to see is the game of rugby league championing the National League competitions in a fundamentally more assertive way than has been the case so far. They should be marketed alongside Super League and, if the sponsors of our premier competition have reservations, it should be put to them that the Super League product with which they are associated would have much more merit and meaning within British sport if it was generally understood to be at the apex of a much larger championship structure. Surely the status of Super League is enhanced if it is widely recognised that this elite competition is the subject of a vigorous ongoing battle among the National League clubs who have a right to be promoted to the top echelons of the game if they triumph on the field and meet the other criteria required of our top clubs.

And in addressing the 'short termism' of potential relegation candidates, let us not forget that when Wakefield Trinity were fielding, during the 2006 season, teams almost entirely consisting of imports, they were doing so wholly within the existing rules. We need to introduce and enforce rules which substantially reduce our dependence on foreign players. As well as impacting upon the development of British players at club level and the competitiveness of our international squads, this will enhance the career prospects of players in the National Leagues whose ability to progress to full-time contracts – and fully develop their potential – is severely limited by the short-term signing of overseas players who are not infrequently of only moderate ability.

The proponents of a closed shop Super League also, I believe, ignore at their peril the fact that the drama of promotion and relegation is surely integral to attracting media and public interest in any sport. I have numerous great memories of watching Wakefield Trinity over the past 50 years but some of the richest are from matches where the club's future was genuinely on a knife-edge.

I won't forget, for example, the dramatic match at Huddersfield when Trinity beat Featherstone in the 1998 Division One Final to enter Super League. Rovers' fans I know are still disputing some of the refereeing decisions of that day. Similarly, the dramatic end to the 2001 Super League is etched in my memory when, on the last day of the season, relegation faced either Huddersfield or Trinity who were playing away to Salford at the Willows. The electronic scoreboard told the more than 2,000 Wakefield fans at the game that Huddersfield, with an earlier kick off time, were easily beating London while Trinity were at that point 24-14 down. In a quite incredible second half, which saw Salford reduced to 11 men and Wakefield to 12, Trinity eventually pulled in front to win 32-24 and relegate the Giants.

I find it hard to believe that anyone who followed the remarkable relegation tussle of the 2006 Super League could argue for the closed shop. The evidence of the spectator and media interest generated by the relegation fight is blatantly obvious. Look at the crowds Wigan were pulling in when they seemed almost certain for the drop. Look at the media coverage for the relegation decider between Trinity and Castleford which was unprecedented. My family and I were on holiday in the far north of Scotland during the week before this match, but I was reading daily feature articles about the contest up there in various national newspapers. And Belle Vue had its biggest crowd in donkeys' years for the match. I cannot remember the last time I saw people turned away from the ground because it was sold out or sitting on rooftops to see the game, even though it was being broadcast live nationally on Sky Television.

Such matches and memories are the stuff of sport. They're what it's really all about, and taking away the drama and excitement that promotion and relegation generate would significantly reduce the interest in rugby league as well as further damage its credibility with the sizeable group of followers of the sport who still remain alienated by the circumstances in which Super League was created in the first place.

I still meet life-long supporters of clubs which were left out of the inaugural Super League in 1996, who remain bitter and angry at what to them seemed the arbitrary and unfair decisions taken at its inception. We need to understand that there is a quite widely held view, even among some who have championed our game, (and writers such as Harry Edgar and Ian Clayton are prime examples) that rugby league lost some of its integrity at that point in its history. It is vital that we do not add to their grievances by distancing our elite clubs even further from the National and amateur leagues. We should learn from the various mistakes made over a decade ago and not compound them, losing even more support for the game in the process.

One of the reasons I have been involved in rugby league, one way or another all my life, is a respect for that integrity. The game's basic values have – throughout most of its history – reflected inclusiveness, decency and fairness. Those from the humblest of origins have been welcomed in the game, regardless of class, colour or creed. Adopting a big-city franchise approach, which some have favoured since the Super League revolution over a decade ago, and appearing to cast aside the smaller town clubs and communities which have been a key part of our game for generations would strike at the very soul of rugby league.

Closing the Super League door to the rest of the game may not result in the marches and protests that heralded the advent of the competition because, sadly, many of those involved in the game then have abandoned it, feeling disillusioned and betrayed. The ridiculous club merger proposals which incensed so many at that time are unlikely to be repeated, so the start of closed shop Super League will probably not be accompanied by public outpourings of anger. Nevertheless, it will represent a further departure from the inclusiveness which has been at the core of the game for a very long time. The sense of 'them and us', which undoubtedly exists among those with affiliations outside Super League, will without doubt increase.

But it is certainly not too late to avoid this further polarisation within our great sport. Under Richard Lewis's leadership, in most other respects, rugby league has made very encouraging progress and I believe that he has shown on many occasions that he has a vision for the sport which stretches far beyond just our top teams. I hope that he and others charged with plotting the future direction of rugby league will come to recognise that proposals to end promotion to and relegation from Super League may tackle the symptoms of some of our current problems, but they certainly don't address the underlying causes.

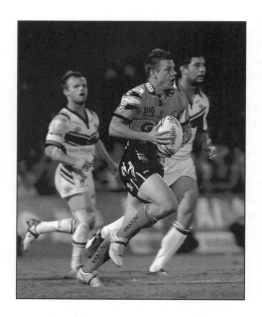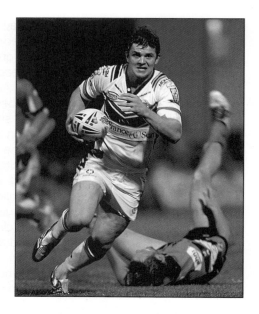

Wakefield versus Castleford: The 2006 relegation decider.
Top left: Castleford's Ryan McGoldrick; top right: Wakefield's Jamie Rooney.
Bottom: Castleford fans facing life in NL1.
(All photos: David Williams, rlphotos.com)

Promotion and Relegation seasons

Peter Lush looks at two books that record successful and traumatic 2006 seasons for the clubs involved: Hull Kingston Rovers and Castleford Tigers.

'We are Hull KR' – Back from Oblivion by Mike Sterriker and
It's Not The Size of the Tiger in the Fight but The Size of the Fight in the Tiger
by Mark Hudson

Hull Kingston Rovers are one of the great names and traditional clubs in rugby league. When I started watching the game in 1980, Hull was the capital of the British rugby league world, with both Rovers and Hull FC winning trophies and drawing large crowds. Both teams gradually declined during the 1980s, and by the time Super League started, neither Hull team could claim a place among the game's elite clubs.

Hull FC returned to the top flight first, albeit through a merger with Gateshead that set back the development of the game in the north east for at least a decade. Hull KR, meanwhile have had to rebuild and battle their way up through the National League structures to rejoin the top flight.

The main focus of the book is a match-by-match account of Hull KR's season. Clearly dominant in National League 1, there is always the worry that a place in Super League will be decided by 80 minutes in the end of season Grand Final. An early warning is sounded when the Northern Rail Cup Final results in a defeat against Leigh by 22-18. But Rovers recovered, and did not allow a 50-0 defeat in the Challenge Cup semi-final against St Helens to deflect them from their goal – the prized place in Super League.

Having won through in the play-offs, Rovers faced Widnes on 8 October at Warrington's Halliwell Jones Stadium in the Grand Final. Although a final score of 29-16 implies a close match, Rovers had the match won by half-time with a 22-4 lead. The goal of Super League had been achieved.

Giant-killing in the Challenge Cup has become less and less common in the modern game. The Super League clubs are full-time and pitches are better, so defeat on a mud-heap is rare. However, one of the most exciting Challenge Cup matches in the 2006 season is covered in the book, Rovers' victory over Warrington.

The book also includes an analysis of the development of Super League from a Hull KR point of view, and interviews with club chairman Neil Hudgell and coach Justin Morgan. Both recognise the enormous challenge that Super League will be for the club.

As one team rises, another falls. Castleford Tigers, one of the great names of the modern era, had hit hard times and been relegated in 2004. 'Classy Cas' had fought their way out of NL1 in 2005, and returned to Super League in 2006. A new coach, Australian Terry Matterson, had been recruited. So could they survive?

Mark Hudson's entertaining book is part autobiography as well as providing a supporters' view of Castleford's dramatic 2006 season, and is well worth reading. The first part of the book outlines his life and background up to that date, with some interesting insights into what sport means to people.

It would not be unreasonable to argue that the real interest in Super League in 2006 was the lower half of the table. It was clear that St Helens were going to finish top of the table, although even if they were runners-up it didn't really matter that much.

The spoils were decided at the Grand Final. There was some interest in the battle for sixth place, but the team finishing sixth have not usually made much impression on the play-offs anyway.

But for the last two months of the season, there were six teams who all could have gone down. Harlequins only secured safety with one match left, and the relegation issue came down to a 'winner takes all' match on the final day: Wakefield Trinity versus Castleford Tigers. The fact that it was a local derby, and the two teams had originally in 1995 been proposed to become part of a merged 'Calder' team in Super League raised the stakes even higher. Of course, the pressure on the fight to avoid relegation had been even greater because Super League had agreed that Catalan Dragons could not be relegated, even if they finished bottom of the table.

The ups and downs and moments of elation and disappointment are all graphically outlined by Mark Hudson. On 2 July, Cas beat Warrington 52-26, had 15 points and were seventh in the table. Mark notes that no team had ever been relegated with 15 points. But Catalans' relegation exemption moved the goalposts, and a better check may have been what teams finishing 11th had amassed in the past. But the next week saw a crucial defeat, 24-16, in London to Harlequins, and after that, Cas only won two more matches, one a dramatic 31-30 win over Leeds.

With one game left, Castleford were 10th, a point clear of Wakefield. 'Judgement day' saw the Tigers take an early 11-2 lead, but they could not hold on and eventually went down 29-17.

From the experience of these two teams it can be argued that British rugby league will be less interesting if there is no relegation to and from Super League. Sport is not just about winning; a fight against relegation is part of the British tradition in winter team sports, unlike in America or Australia. And what will happen to clubs like Castleford or Hull KR if they are not in Super League. Will their supporters accept what they will see as 'second class' rugby league?

Of course, it is a broader question. The game needs to expand – South Wales and in the slightly longer term Dublin are both ripe for Super League clubs. Maybe the solution is two 'conferences' of 12 to 14 clubs each, which would mean recognising that some of the smaller 'heartland' clubs will never have the resources or support to play at the top level. A closed shop of franchises may not be the answer in the longer term.

It's Not The Size of the Tiger in the Fight but The Size of the Fight in the Tiger: Published in 2006 by Grosvenor House Publishing at £9.99. ISBN: 1905529783.
'We are Hull KR': Published in 2006 by Riverhead Publishing at £10.99. ISBN: 0955023726.

Photo: Hull KR's James Webster with the National League 1 trophy (David Williams, rlphotos.com)

Wembley and the Challenge Cup

Michael O'Hare looks at the return of the Challenge Cup Final to Wembley this year, and a personal dilemma over the 2006 final.

Since 2000, on the back of some excellent weekends in Edinburgh and the Welsh capital since the Final was forced to up sticks and vacate Wembley, there have been sporadic calls for the big match to be kept permanently away from north London. Both the Scottish and Welsh capitals have proved welcoming and hospitable venues far removed from the famous stadium on an industrial estate by London Underground's Metropolitan Line. Those wishing for the final to have a lasting presence either in Cardiff or as a travelling roadshow may have a point but, nonetheless, rugby league's most famous match will return to Wembley in 2007.

However, the mild controversy surrounding this decision is nothing at the side of that generated in 1928 when taking the Final to London was first mooted by Welshman John Leake at the RFL's annual conference at the Marine Hotel, Llandudno. While Leake was possibly only giving voice to others who saw the benefits of a move to the capital, it is no less ironic that it took a Welshman to highlight the opportunities of such an action, despite the furious debate his proposal engendered.

As we hear so often today, the critics complained that rugby league was a game of the north. Crowds in London would be far lower than any that could be generated in a northern stadium. The RFL would bankrupt itself. With hindsight, the reactionaries have been proved incorrect, but Leake's proposal, seconded by Walter Waide of Hunslet, won by only a slender margin of 13 votes to 10.

The Final is more popular now than it has ever been. It is televised nationally and is one of a number of listed British sporting events that the government insists is shown only on free terrestrial television. Would that have been the case if it were still played in Rochdale or Wigan? It was huge attendances at Challenge Cup Final venues such as these in the 1920s that had forced the RFL to look elsewhere to accommodate the numbers that wished to see the match. In total, 10 venues had been used since the first final at Leeds in 1897 and attendances had grown in number with each subsequent year. The police had difficulty handling the crowds at these smaller northern venues and the authorities realised that an alternative, preferably a permanent one, was needed quickly. Odsal Stadium in Bradford, which would house a record crowd of 102,569 for the 1954 Challenge Cup Final replay, had not then been built. Was there anywhere that would fit the bill?

Well, yes there was more than one venue to choose from. But they were all in London, where rugby league was virtually unknown. Remember, this was in the days before television; it was even in the days before the failed professional rugby league club ventures of the 1930s at London Highfield, Streatham & Mitcham and Acton & Willesden. Yet London did have three stadiums that could fit the bill – White City, Crystal Palace and Wembley, the newly built home of football's FA Cup Final. After White City – home to the 1908 Olympic Games – was dropped because the RFL considered its facilities inferior – League secretary John Wilson visited the capital, along with RFL chairman Fred Kennedy, to check out the remaining two. They had the full backing of the RFL which, at a full meeting of its Council on 3 October 1928, had ratified Leake's proposal from earlier in the year. Of course, the RFL was keen to see a whole new audience for the sport grow up in the capital, but it was – first and foremost – in search of a venue capable of holding safely a decent-sized crowd.

Wilson was bearing in mind the RFL's insistence that the venue should "make it easy in a financial sense and convenient from a travelling point of view to get there". This was immediately to mitigate against south-of-the-Thames Crystal Palace for most supporters would be travelling from the north of England, but Wilson's mind was made up when the stadium's owners demanded one-third of all gate money plus 100 per cent of any taken before noon on the day of the match. Figuring that many supporters would travel immediately to Crystal Palace after reaching London and would arrive before midday, Wilson quickly turned his attention to north London and Wembley.

Sir Arthur Elvin, proprietor of Wembley Stadium, had more favourable terms in mind and Wilson was pleased to report back to the RFL that the stadium was available for 7.5 per cent of the gate money taken (although the figure is reported in some quarters as 15 per cent, still significantly less than one-third). In the end the decision was a straightforward one, although not without further opposition. Some said it was illogical to stage the final in an area where no professional rugby league was played, and that it served no purpose. They saw no benefit in taking the game to the nation's biggest stage, however much that might present the sport to a wider audience. These are arguments still heard today in connection with any attempt to increase the geographical spread of rugby league, yet how many people would argue 75 years on against the Final being played in one of Britain's capital cities? London, Edinburgh and Cardiff are all far from League's heartlands, yet the only debate now seems to be over which venue of these to select. Nobody would actually opine today that it should return to Headingley or Salford. Back in 1929, however, many people failed to realise the impact that a major game in the nation's premier stadium could have on Britain's sporting public.

Entry to the stadium ranged from 2 shillings (10p) to 10 shillings and sixpence (52½p) and vindication of the RFL's stance was to follow a bold advertising campaign. Bravely, the RFL printed 15,000 flyers which were handed out at England's Twickenham rugby union internationals against Wales and Ireland. An extensive poster campaign followed and the reward was ticket applications from all over the country including London and the south-east, the south-west, the Midlands and Wales.

Naturally, the RFL was delighted with the response, as was shrewd entrepreneur Arthur Elvin. He knew that if – as he expected – the RFL drew a significant crowd, it would be keen to return and so, although he offered excellent terms for the first Final, his cut would increase in subsequent years in line with the contract he offered the RFL. In 1930, he was set to receive 25 per cent of the gate. Nonetheless, it showed the faith that Elvin had in league. He fully expected to make a decent return from the sport and his attitude contrasted starkly with those who purported to be its supporters.

That Wigan defeated Dewsbury 13-2 in Wembley's first Challenge Cup Final before a crowd of almost 42,000 generating £5,614 - £2,000 more than any previous Final – was almost an irrelevance. More important was that a precedent had been set. Rugby league could survive and thrive on the nation's biggest stage and the critics had to eat their words as the popularity of the final grew with each passing year. Would the Challenge Cup Final be so widely known throughout the nation today if it was still played in Rochdale?

In the end, perhaps typically when one considers rugby league's historical habit of keeping one eye on the purse strings, it was fortuitous expedience that won the day. Had there been a stadium in the north capable of holding the kinds of crowds the

Challenge Cup Final was beginning to generate, the RFL might not have taken the bold step that took the match to Wembley. The chance to generate money, in the end, played a far bigger part in the decision than a desire to introduce the game to the rest of the nation. Yet had mucky brass not forced the hand of the RFL, who can say whether today there would be two professional rugby league clubs in London, 101 different teams within the Greater London area, large numbers of schoolchildren learning the sport, or a Rugby League Conference with clubs from the southern counties of England playing a major part? It certainly can't have been to their detriment.

Bibliography:
A People's Game: The Official History of Rugby League by Geoffrey Moorhouse (Hodder & Stoughton, 1995)
The Rugby League Challenge Cup by John Huxley (Guinness, 1992)

A Fartown Final

In autumn 2003 I had a life-changing moment. History records that Australia whitewashed Great Britain in that November's Ashes series. But that bare statistic does not convey how close the Lions came to ending one of international sport's longest losing streaks. A 3-0 loss could so easily have been a 3-0 triumph. It was devastating watching those last-minute British collapses wasn't it? Well, wasn't it? Erm, actually, no... no it wasn't...

About three-quarters of the way through the second test at Hull, with Britain leading by the potentially match-winning score of 20-12, it began to dawn on me that one of my life's great purposes could well be removed. Although I was around the last time Great Britain won the Ashes in 1970, I was only six and it happened in the years before mass media. I had no idea it had taken place. I guess I only became aware of the existence of Great Britain's ever-growing roll of dishonour at the hands of the Kangaroos around 1982 when the touring Invincibles so destroyed the home team that it seemed as though another 12 years would pass before Britain could match Australia in the international arena. Time has shown that it was double that... and counting. So I had grown up with the notion of defeat to Australia. It was the default position, the status quo. And because it had dragged on for so long with no sign of respite, it had become part of my 'who I was'. Nothing could exceed the thrill of beating Australia in an Ashes series, except perhaps Huddersfield winning the Challenge Cup. Both were pinnacles to aspire to, they would be the culmination of my years of following rugby league. But... but, what if they were no longer there?

As Great Britain continued to attack Australia on that November evening at Hull, I realised that, if they were to win the series, that one of life's dreams would have been removed... the aspiration would have been achieved... and then what? Win it again? But would that feel anything like as good? How could it, because fear would replace pleasure – the fear of losing would be the only motivation? Ask Wigan supporters how the fifth, or the seventh, or the eighth consecutive Challenge Cup victory felt in the late1980s and early 1990s... not as good as the first, surely? And was the fear of finally losing, a decent substitute to the anticipation of winning that very first time?

Wembley 1953: St Helens winger Steve Llewellyn evades Huddersfield's Johnny Hunter. Duggie Greenall and Lance Todd Trophy winner Peter Ramsden are in the background.
(Photo: Courtesy Denis Whittle)

So once Britain had beaten Australia in the Ashes, could I ever again expect to appreciate the thrill of anticipating the victory? Of course not... A huge chunk of my life would have been expunged.

A friend of mine is an open water swimmer. She insists that self-denial is the essence of pleasure. She's the kind of person who trains in Finnish lakes in February so that the average race around Flamborough Head seems like a splash in a warm bath. Because climbing out of an agonising and wintry Finnish lake is so utterly pleasurable she stays in because the anticipation of respite is even sweeter...

It's the blind date syndrome... the thought is so much better than the outcome. The quest is the purpose, not the fulfilment. I can only thank God that Britain contrived to lose the Ashes series in 2003. I still have raison d'etre... the pleasure of being the perennial loser.

However, the events of 2006 have certainly led me to reappraise this stance. Sitting on an aeroplane to Lake Balaton in Hungary on 22 August, four days before Huddersfield – the team I have supported for my entire life – were set to play in their first Challenge Cup Final since I was born, had my head buzzing with migraine's-worth of conflicting emotions.

It all seemed so simple back in January. What better time was there than to break a 24-year uninterrupted sequence of Challenge Cup Final attendances? The match was at Twickenham, home of the enemy, I'd been there in 2001 and hardly enjoyed the experience. I could make a political point and have a cheap holiday. Those Ryanair flights to Hungary at £6 a pop looked mighty tempting. As I pressed the 'Confirm' button my wife said "You do know this means Huddersfield will get to the final don't you?"

So Fartown supporters the world over can thank me for their good fortune in 2006. And I can suffer, in perpetuity, the thought that I wasn't there. It wasn't meant to be this way. In my Challenge Cup Final mental picture I painted my face claret and gold, I put my son in his 1953 'Peter Ramsden Lance Todd Trophy Winner's' shirt, I blubbed as they played *Abide With Me*, my wife told me not to hyperventilate as the players came out of the tunnel, and I sank to my feet in despair as Huddersfield went 30 points down by half-time. So many things were meant to go wrong that day but the one nailed on certainty, was that I'd be there.

Yet I wasn't. The foiled terrorist plot of 10 August scuppered any chance of flying back from Budapest for the match. Frantic searches of obscure flights via Bucharest and Pecs told me what I expected. I'd be on a Hungarian lakeside beach while Huddersfield took on Saints. But already I'd begun to embrace, yet again, the comfort of unfulfilled destiny. So often I've thought of how that day would be – how I'd react, what it would be like to have my team playing in the big match. I'd seen the Wigan and Saints supporters, the Bulls and Rhinos. I'd even seen the Sheffield supporters with incredulity written across their faces as they defeated Wigan in 1998. And I thought that one day it would happen to me.

But if it had, would I feel a part of me had gone forever? I know I'd felt it that evening at Hull in 2003. And I'm pretty certain I'd have felt it again at Twickenham. My team struggling is an essential part of who I am. My dad actually stopped watching Huddersfield in the late 1980s because they started winning a few matches. It perturbed him markedly. And it seems it's clearly hereditary. Not being in a play-off final, let alone a Challenge Cup Final is all I know, even though Huddersfield have spent seasons in Super League. My desire to get there is far more important than any fulfilment of that dream. I had waited 41 years for Huddersfield to play in a Cup Final. Imagine if they'd won? What would have been left? Far better to wait another 41 years.

And as my swimming friend insisted, when finally, after numerous failures, she sat on a French beach after fulfilling a dream to be a Channel swimmer she felt only misery, not elation. What else was there for her to do now? What was the point of even climbing back into the water again?

And thus it was with Huddersfield. Something I had desired for 41 years I missed. Through my own stupidity. But my dream lives on... seeing Fartown in the Challenge Cup Final. How wonderful is that? I am still whole. Nothing has changed.

Rugby league and the media

Michael Wall examines the game's coverage in the press; **Keith Macklin** reflects on the importance of local radio and **Geoff Lee** outlines his work as a novelist, using the game as a background for his book.

Time to move beyond the myths?

Firstly, congratulations to St Helens RLFC for picking up Sports Team of the Year at the recent *BBC Sports Personality of the Year Awards* (1), this was well deserved given their clear dominance of British rugby league in 2006. The team's record speaks for itself; they won 31 from 35 competitive games played, with none of the four losses incurring a losing margin greater than four points, a remarkable achievement.

However, if the sound of champagne corks being popped in honour of the St Helens team was music to the ears of rugby league fans then the sound of dummies being spat by certain sections of the London centric media was an unwanted bonus track. Some rugby league fans would find it predictable if not even inevitable that the usual clique of hacks who dislike rugby league would find their noses put out of joint by St Helens carrying off the prize rather than their preferred choice, the Ryder Cup team. There are of course whole volumes written about rugby league's uneasy relationship with the London centric media(2), not to mention an undercurrent of antagonism emanating from certain commentators, aloof with barely disguised snobbery, who've never quite forgiven rugby league for not knowing its place.

The crux of the current braying appears to be that the Ryder Cup golf team didn't get any recognition for winning a one off golf event which they've dominated in recent years(3) (they did actually win the award in 2002 when their current period of dominance began). One bone of contention for this clique appears to be the decision of the BBC to decide the award by a public vote, or more specifically a mobile phone text vote based on a shortlist (one vote per phone number) (4), given they're convinced (well they've convinced themselves) that rugby league has no fans, or if it does they're all flat cap wearing, whippet keeping, pigeon fancying stereotypes from the North of England, who are not allowed to have mobile phones, something dodgy must have gone on, mustn't it? It's obvious that a review is needed, isn't it?

The absence of votes for the Ryder Cup team seems to be of less concern for these commentators, perhaps it never crossed their minds that while golf is a phenomenally popular pastime, it's one that has its strength in participation rather than viewing? How many people go to watch a golf tournament regularly, or tune in to television coverage? Is there any factual evidence that golf as a spectator sport is actually more popular than rugby league as a spectator sport? Maybe what they think is needed is a more democratic system than a public vote, perhaps a system where only votes from a clique of sports hacks favouring nice middle class sports should get counted? Yes, I can see that form of democracy being extremely popular with some people.

To be honest, while it's easy to point and laugh at idiots throwing toys out of their prams, it does highlight the more serious long-term problem of media animosity, something that unfortunately shows little sign of abating with time. It's no great controversy to suggest that the London centric media tend to favour the other rugby code, rugby union, that's not to say there are no rugby league fans amongst the fourth estate, or indeed that there aren't fans of both codes who perhaps lean towards one or the other; the problem is that the general trend appears to be skewed disproportionately against rugby league. Nobody doubts that the rugby league is the smaller of the two codes; the question is whether or not it's as small as the (lack of) media coverage suggests? In my opinion the answer to that question is no!

The mythology of those in the media that don't like rugby league is that it's only watched in the North of England yet according to the Rugby Football League website's facts & figures section 50 percent of the audience for rugby league on Sky Sports is based in the South of England (5). Similar claims about the Super League being restricted to Lancashire and Yorkshire are also somewhat wide of the mark unless those counties now extend as far as the South of France or Greater London. It is true that average attendance figures for Guinness Premiership matches have matched the Super League in recent years. How does this justify the disparity in media coverage of both competitions?

While I take issue with the outright lie that nobody watches rugby league outside of the North of England and hence why it gets such weak coverage from the London centric media, I would have no issues if they simply came out and admitted that the disproportionate coverage has a socio-demographic explanation. My significant professional experience of marketing analysis has taught me that people from the higher socio-demographic groups (traditionally thought of as upper-middle and upper class) are often the people who are the hardest to reach by marketing yet are also an extremely lucrative consumer segment in terms of disposable income. They are also the kind of people who hold positions of influence throughout the establishment, industry and commerce. I also don't think it would be too controversial to suggest that rugby union is one of the most popular sports among these socio-demographic groups (6) and as a result the media which is aimed at them or controlled by them is more likely to be biased towards their tastes. A half-baked counter argument about the volume of media coverage and marketing expenditure aimed at football could be flagged, but any such argument would have to ignore the sheer scale of football's domination of British sport.

It's a cheap and easy tactic to dismiss rugby league fans who complain about media bias as having a chip on their shoulder, while some of them undoubtedly do, it's fallacious to use it as an excuse to dismiss what it often a valid point. What's needed is a closer look at the situation, and that's precisely what we don't get from hacks whose grasp of 'facts' tends more towards speculative opinion and hearsay than real facts of the sort that come from actual research into viewing figures, attendances and objective analysis of trends both on and off the field. Regurgitating crude and out of date stereotypes about rugby league only being played and watched in the North of England, despite what real evidence says, is as equally pathetic and superficial as suggesting that rugby union sides were only interested in rugby league coaches for their defensive drills.

In my opinion perhaps the worst example of a journalist behaving churlishly with regards to the St Helens win was Mick Cleary, rugby union correspondent for the *Daily Telegraph*, who I thought didn't even bother to pretend that a piece on the subject in his official blog wasn't a hatchet job, in fact he actually queued up a series of crude and outdated stereotypes rather than bothering with anything as tiresome as a serious analysis (7). A day later Mr Cleary was forced into a rethink (8) when his piece was systematically deconstructed and debunked; that's the problem when the modern media lazily resorts to using outdated stereotypes or skips even the most cursory of research, somebody somewhere will spot the holes and pull your argument apart, a process that's all the more easy if your argument is more holes than substance to start with.

It would be wrong of me to suggest that no animosity remains between the respective supporters of rugby union and rugby league, but I don't think I'm wrong in suggesting that any genuine animosity lies at the fringes, the bulk of fans either have a passing interest in the other code or have no interest whatsoever. Since rugby union progressed from its so-called 'shamateur' era into the open era, the two codes have actually achieved some great synergies by working together. Ambitious rugby union teams reaped the benefits of recruiting professionally trained coaches from rugby league, some of them former rugby union players who they'd formerly shunned. Players like Jonathan Davies, John Bentley, David Young, and Alan Tait who had previously been barred for switching to rugby league were welcomed back to provide professional experience to a sport entering a period of culture shock.

The new found free movement between the codes has been far from a one-way street, for years rugby league was largely pinned into its northern heartlands, but with rugby union entering its open era the establishment prejudice that had restricted the game started to wane. Anybody who doesn't believe there was prejudice on the behalf of the establishment should consider why rugby league was absent from the armed forces for so long or from universities, then they need to think about how other 'British' sports spread around the world and then finally think back to the socio-demographic profile of those people who tend to control huge marketing budgets or even hold high-ranking positions in the media. This waning of the establishment prejudice was one of the catalysts behind the formation of the Rugby League Conference (9) arguably the biggest development in grassroots rugby league since the foundation of BARLA in 1973, a development that also helped reinvigorate other competitions like the London ARL

In the last 10 years many new grassroots clubs have emerged in areas well outside of the traditional rugby league heartlands, often partnering with local amateur union sides who were quick to see the benefits of playing rugby league in summer and rugby union in winter. Commercially the financial contribution from sharing club facilities with a rugby league club makes sound business sense, whether through direct ground usage charges or simply extra bar takings. On the rugby side of things the link-ups benefit the union club if its players decide to develop their skills through trying rugby league.

Prior to rugby union's open era there were plenty of players who had an interest in rugby league, but they either had no realistic opportunity to try the game, or were put off by the potential consequences of taking the chance. Now a union player who wants to try rugby league can do so, safe in the knowledge that there is nothing to lose, if they don't like it they can still go back to playing union, just as they can play both codes if they choose to. Just as newly professional rugby union sides saw the advantages of bringing in rugby league coaches so amateur union players could see that getting access to amateur rugby league coaching and playing may improve their individual skills.

I've already acknowledged that rugby union is clearly the bigger of the two codes and one area where rugby league appears to be a long way behind is player numbers. This is a controversial area for both codes, because a variety of ways are used to calculate those numbers, and that's before the somewhat pointless argument of accounting for players who enjoy participation in both codes but may see themselves as principally attached to one rather than the other. Counting school children as players is also a debatable practice because they may play either code as one of the sports catered for at their school but still have no real interest in the game. That isn't to say that number and geographic spread of schools where the game is played is not an important development metric, particularly for rugby league which has recently seen rapid growth in schools development programmes outside of traditional areas; in fact that particular metric has crucial long-term implications on both audiences and participators.

In terms of adult player numbers rugby union again clearly has a bigger player pool, but this is inflated by a large volume of players who involved in 'social' rugby union. This to me suggests that the playing pool of adults participating at a level which can be considered genuinely competitive is unlikely to be as wide as simply comparing the total volume of adult players claimed by either side, something which is actually rather important when it comes to the development and flow of players up to elite level.

The concept of social rugby union is one from which the code as a whole draws great strength, allowing players who cannot play at a competitive level to continue participating beyond the point where they would have to retire from rugby. The greater cardiovascular demands of rugby league have traditionally meant that players who have been unable to maintain fitness for competitive participation possibly due to age or other commitments have been forced to give up. In recent years there have been some efforts within rugby league to develop a social playing scene via tag rugby tournaments such as IMBRL (10) but it's clear that more can be done to copy this successful aspect of rugby union. Keeping people more closely involved in the club for longer is not only financially rewarding but helps to maintain a long-term structure around the club as players introduce their children or other family members into the club over time.

It's clear to me that rugby league and rugby union have gained far more from working together than they ever did when estranged completely; it is therefore disappointing that an attitude permeates certain sections of the London centric media which causes them to be biased against rugby league, especially when such views are representative only of a small niche. In some sense it would even represent progress if those who demonstrate the bias were even a little more honest about their motivations rather than resorting to cliché, but of course real progress would be more balanced representation reflecting the actual situation. Admittedly the leaders of rugby league may need to do more to try and bring the media on board, even if some sections of the media will never change their opinions of the code no matter how out of touch with reality they are. The realist in me suspects that it will be some time before attitudes move on to a more enlightened stage, but I'm sure it is possible and rugby league has never been in a better position to achieve this goal. However, the cynic in me will always expect the annual 'rugby league is dying' stories around the start of a new season.

Michael Wall

References
(1) http://news.bbc.co.uk/sport1/hi/front_page/6220542.stm
(2) *The Petition – Rugby League fans say "enough is enough"* by Ray Gent (Parrs Wood Press 2002
(3) http://www.dailymail.co.uk/pages/live/articles/columnists/columnists.html?in_article_id=422040&in_page_id=1951
(4) http://sport.guardian.co.uk/news/story/0,,1969869,00.html
(5) http://www.therfl.co.uk/ABOUT/facts.php
(6) http://www.ft.com/cms/s/b20a9968-8985-11db-a876-0000779e2340.html
(7) http://blogs.telegraph.co.uk/sport/mickcleary/dec2006/leagueofitsown.htm
(8) http://blogs.telegraph.co.uk/sport/mickcleary/dec2006/rugbyleague.htm
(9) http://www.rugbyleagueconference.co.uk/home/ See also *Beyond the Heartlands – The history of the Rugby League Conference* by Julian Harrison (London League Publications Ltd)
(10) http://www.imbrl.com/forum/

Rugby league and local radio

Whenever, as frequently happens, rugby league conversations turn to the often vexed question of media coverage, the emphasis is largely on television, and the perceived saturation coverage by Sky TV at weekends. To this three-day milking of the best Super League fixtures, admittedly at a generous fee and with excellent coverage, can be added the BBC's double headers when the Challenge Cup comes around.

No one argues nowadays, as they did in the pioneer television days of the 1950s and 1960s with Eddie Waring, that attendances may be affected, particularly those at the slightly less significant matches. The amount of money going into Super League clubs' coffers is enough to stifle such protests at birth, and in fairness the top games usually command good attendances regardless of the presence of television.

Likewise rugby league fans have learned to live with matches on Friday, Saturday and occasionally Sunday at variable and sometimes bizarre times to suit the Sky schedules. Televised rugby is a fact of life, and both financially and in terms of profile, the game needs television just as the Sky schedulers need good rugby league games.

However, while the big battalions of television cherry-pick the top matches and Challenge Cup ties, insufficient credit is given to the medium which has kept the XIII-a-side code alive for decades, and contributed greatly to its survival in its most struggling times, local radio.

While television does an excellent job of producing glossy and exciting packages with a huge battery of cameras, technical gadgetry and enthusiastic commentary, it is completely orientated towards Super League. Until this season, the National Leagues and the busy amateur game might just as well not have existed except when Grand Finals and cup finals come along to get token coverage. Now some National League games will be shown on Sky on Thursday evenings.

The truth is that while Sky, the B.B.C. and the Super League run a mutually agreeable cartel, the lower leagues have relied on local radio programmes and coverage to keep them in the public eye, and to let fans know that the broader game outside the confines of Super League is still alive, and determined to keep kicking whatever the drawbacks and setbacks.

From their inception in the late 1960s and early 1970s BBC local radio stations, later joined by a handful of commercial stations, have given full coverage within their areas not merely to the glamour clubs, but to every local club under the umbrella of their sports departments. Putting them in alphabetical order rather than in size and listenership BBC Cumbria, Humberside, Leeds, Merseyside and Manchester formerly GMR, have for nearly four decades given detailed commentary and coverage outside the glamour clubs of each era. In fairness it must be said that commercial stations like Piccadilly in Manchester, Aire in Leeds, City in Liverpool and West Yorkshire in Bradford, have sporadically launched rugby league programmes. Wish in Wigan and St Helens and Wire in Warrington and Widnes continue to fly the commercial flag and Wish's coverage is as comprehensive as that of any BBC. station, with Leigh sharing airtime with the giants Wigan and Saints. In London, the BBC's local station regularly covers rugby league.

Ray French and Gerry Burrows were early standard bearers on Merseyside; GMR had the likes of Malcolm Lord and Ron Marlor; Leeds had John Helm, Jack Wainwright and later John Boyd and Ron Hill. On Humberside a former playing favourite David Doyle-

Davidson established himself as a commentator, and in the far North West, in Cumbria, the airwaves were enriched by the voices of ex-players like the late duo of Ron Morgan and Ivor Kelland.

In recent years Manchester area listeners have made favourites of Jack Dearden and Trevor Hunt, at Merseyside Alan Rooney and Steve Roberts have become household names alongside Ray French. John Helm, now more widely known as a football commentator, was for a time the central figure in Radio Leeds' rugby league, and still retains his contacts and enthusiasm for the game in occasional TV specials like *Rugby League Raw*.

Without these and other enthusiastic reporters at games outside the top flight, the game would have shrunk and narrowed to a narrow elite of wealthy top clubs, themselves kept in business by transfusions of television cash. Clubs like Leigh, Swinton, Oldham, Rochdale, Barrow, Workington, Whitehaven, Keighley, York, Featherstone, Batley, Dewsbury, Sheffield and Doncaster, and some sides who have flitted in and out of Super League, might have given up the unequal struggle long ago but for the stimulus to survive and the continued support with the oxygen of publicity given by local radio. Without the coverage given to their games, including interviews with hard-pressed directors, coaches and players, many still surviving clubs, including historic and once-successful clubs like Oldham, would have thrown in the towel. Money has not been thrown at them, as in Super League, but encouragement and, particularly, exposure and coverage have kept them alive.

Inevitably, and rightly, the stations give priority in importance and length of coverage to clubs like St Helens, Wigan, Bradford, Leeds, Hull and Warrington. Listeners and fans of those clubs would expect no less. But when the round-ups and match reports come around, National League games get both their turn and their space, retaining the family feeling which is surely at the heart of our game.

Over the years reporters have covered matches with a variety of equipment, starting with cumbersome tape recorders and even more primitive studio editing equipment, which literally consisted of metal grooves in which the tape was laid, to be manually edited by razor blades. Evening round-ups would see reporters dashing back from matches, rushing into the editing studio heavily laden with boxes and cases, and hastily cutting together interviews before dashing into the studio with a half-written script with just five minutes to go. But they managed it, and the fans at home hung on every word, especially those who had just got back from the match.

At network level rugby league has had to struggle to make inroads. The old North Region did occasional commentaries on top games from the 1950s onwards, and in the past two decades first Radio Two and now Radio Five Live and Five Live Sports Extra have become more prolific and regular in their coverage, though the emphasis, as with television, is on the big battalions of Super League.

The fact remains that only the local stations have shown and kept faith with the game from the grass roots upwards. Mike Latham made this point strongly in an excellent article in *Rugby League World* in which he interviewed many of the pioneer broadcasters. He quoted John Helm in saying: "Local radio broke the mould. It was a massive thing for rugby league. As well as doing commentaries we started feature shows, chat shows and phone-ins in which listeners could speak to coaches, players and club officials".

These 'extras' are now commonplace on local radio, Manchester and Merseyside host popular Thursday night hour-long shows, and on the commercial side Wish, founded in

1996 has, with its sister station Wire, launched regular phone-ins. In London, Harlequins RL receive regular coverage, not just match commentaries on BBC local radio, and there is a strong link between the station and the club.

Again it has to be said that Super League invariably tops the bill, but National League club will be given its proper allotment of air time, depending on the strength of the story. In addition, awareness of news stories among the lower leagues can lead to extensive coverage on the regular all-day news desks. When I covered a play-off game between Workington and Swinton a couple of seasons ago, a Swinton player was allegedly racially abused by an opponent during the game. Radio Manchester led their sports bulletins with the story and its repercussions on Monday morning.

Sadly, rugby league still has to fight for extensive coverage on some stations, but others, as one regional presenter, Jack Dearden, is prone to say: "Keep the faith". By doing so they, unlike the national television networks with their obsession with Super League, are helping to stave off what would surely be an inevitable shrinkage, or even meltdown, among a host of clubs who would otherwise give up the ghost. And any League official who believes that the faithful followers of these clubs would readily switch their allegiances to Super League could be making a huge mistake.

Keith Macklin

Keith Macklin's autobiography will be published by London League Publications Ltd in November 2007.

The Man for All Seasons

The thing that inspired me to start writing was the old saying about being at work "They could write a book about this place. It would be a best seller." This was so true of many of the places that I had worked at and after 30 years, I decided to see if I could do it. I was also keen to write about rugby league and the thought of writing a novel combining work and my favourite sport was quite exciting.

My credentials for attempting it were good. I had been a fan of the game since I had first entered the boys' pen at Knowsley Road in 1947 and was aware of its fascinating history going back to 1895. I had worked in industry for most of my life and had made many friends at work who were rugby league people. I had had much enjoyment both stood on the terraces and talking about it at work and so in 1988, I turned a long held idea into practice and started on what I first called *Tales of a Northern Draughtsman*.

People often say to me "However do you write a book. I wouldn't even know where to start." Well to begin with I didn't know either. It had always been my job to produce drawings that others could easily understand so I had experience of providing information for an interested audience. I had full knowledge and interest in my subject matter, northern working class life and humour and I also had workmates, who on hearing of my new pastime would often say "Here's a story for you, Geoff. Put this in your book." and then tell me something from places where they had once worked.

I expected that 'proper' authors would begin by spending time carefully planning the general theme of the novel, deciding on the main story line and secondary story lines, creating the main characters, where and when it was set and how it would end.

But I didn't do any of that. It all happened rather quickly one evening after I had spent the lunch break listening to a fellow draughtsman talking about a firm called Greenwood & Batley in Leeds. Highly entertained by what I had heard, even inspired by it, by the end of that night I had written the first two pages. Such was the way I started writing and that was how I continued.

The Sixties

I set the novel in the early sixties because I had many memories of those years. I was in the final year of my apprenticeship and about to start work in the Accessories Division of British Insulated Callender's Cables at Prescot, whose initials B.I.C.C. could equally have stood for the Biggest Individual Collection of Comedians.

It was the start of the Beatles era and I had been at school with Stuart Sutcliffe. It included that winter of 1962-63, great to write about later, but terrible to endure at the time. I also remembered the films, *This Sporting Life*, which I enjoyed for obvious reasons and *A Kind of Loving* which was set in a drawing office.

It was obvious that South Lancashire would be the location. This was my home territory although by 1988 I had lived away for over 20 years, first in London, then in Hull and finally in West Yorkshire. As a result I was in a time warp but as I was to discover this is very useful when writing a novel set in the past.

The first thing I did was create a place where many of my characters lived and worked. Two great local landmarks were Bold Power Station and Bold Colliery, still standing then but soon to be demolished. Opposite them had been fields, through which the road from St Helens Junction to Earlestown ran. Those fields seemed an ideal place to put the fictional town of Ashurst.

Doing this solved the rugby league connection. No way did I want to create a team called Ashurst Hornets that played against the likes of Huddlesfax Trinity or Castlestone Rovers and who once almost beat Leeds or Bradford Northern in a semi-final. That was too unreal for me. Ashurst was near to St Helens, Wigan, Leigh and Warrington and so those would be the teams my characters would support. They would also be the towns from where many of those who worked at Wilkinson's Engineering Works would come from, by bus, train, car or bicycle.

The office comedian Charlie Eccleston lived in Thatto Heath, while his sidekick, Mick Henderson was from Platt Bridge. Both were keen rugby league fans who supported two of the most famous clubs in the world and argued about it all day long. Their section leader was Alan Groves who lived in Grappenhall on the far side of Warrington. Well he did until he ran off to Malaga with a woman who worked in the gas showrooms! Most lived in Ashurst including the main character Alan Greenall, and Sam Holroyd, known as Yorky, since he came from Mytholmroyd. His inclusion in the drawing office was no accident because it enabled me to include Lancashire-Yorkshire banter and rivalry as a regular theme throughout the novel.

A Thrum Hall classic

As a child I had a grandfather who loved to talk about his experiences in life, first at school, then working down the pit, serving in the First World War, most of which was spent as a prisoner of war working down a lead mine in Prussia and being employed at Pilkington's in St Helens. I was equally lucky to have a grandmother who also could talk at length about her life and times. It was from them that Alan's Granny and Grandad were created as two strong characters in the novel.

As far as the rugby league was concerned, for years I had been entertained by players on the field and by spectators off it. Hearing all the chat and the banter on the terraces often provided as much entertainment as what was happening on the pitch. "Call yourself a prop, number eight. I wouldn't let you prop clothes in our yard" from an old woman at Thrum Hall to a giant Whitehaven forward was just one of many classic comments that I drew from real life.

I soon realised that if I described real events as fiction, the more realistic the novel would be. That is why the first chapter was called 'The Petition'. It dealt with the campaign to stop Lord Beeching closing Ashurst Station and the branch line to Leigh. The idea for this was based on events linked to the same lord trying to close St Helens Shaw Street Station and the line that ran through it from Wigan North Western to Liverpool Lime Street. That campaign was highly successful as the station is still there although it is now called St Helens Central. Not surprisingly the campaign to keep Ashurst Station open was equally successful.

It was useful to have my family tree going back to 1791. That is why 'Greeno' was born in the same week as I was in 1939. I also used the date of births, marriages and deaths of my relatives to provide the basis for Alan's grandparents to talk about what various members of the Holding/Tabern/Pickavance family had done in the past.

An example of my unplanned approach to writing occurs in Chapter 10 of *One Winter*. It was only here that the idea of including Granny and Grandad first surfaced. That was also when the idea of introducing romance in the shape of the mysterious office girl Thelma arose. She was a young orphan girl from Cardiff who had drifted into Ashurst a few months earlier. Alan had bumped into her on Christmas Eve and on learning that she had nowhere to go the following day had taken her to the traditional family gathering. She fell ill that evening and two months later was still there and virtually adopted by his grandparents.

Why did I choose to make her Welsh? Well it helped me develop a story line about how she was made aware of the existence of another code of rugby and then became hooked on league after just one visit to Knowsley Road.

They now spend Saturday afternoons watching the Saints home and away so it became necessary for me to get the details of every match right. Here I am indebted to Alex Service, the club historian who provided me with all the details of that 1962-63 season, and helped make it easy to combine fact and fiction.

Writing about the past in this way has the effect of making the past come alive, not just about games that I could remember watching but also about games from the distant past. A good example of this occurred after a match at Watersheddings when Alan and Thelma are in a pub, talking to an old Welshman who had once played for Ebbw Vale in 1908.

I also brought real players into the novel at this point. Charlie knew Alex Murphy because both had lived in Sunbury Street in Thatto Heath. At her first match, Thelma picks her favourite player, not him, not Kel Coslett the Welsh full-back or Tom van Vollenhoven who were all playing that night, but the scrum-half Wilf Smith, because he was the smallest man on the field and because she liked to watch him feed the scrum and tackle men twice as big as he was.

By 1996 the novel, now called *One Winter* was finished. Over the next two years, I wrote to every publisher I could find. I even sent it to Mills and Boon and tried to pass it off as a romance set in a twee little Lancashire village, all without success. One publisher wrote back to say that she received 25 submissions a week and published six books a year. That was the size of the problem I faced. Finally Michael Wray, the brains behind *The Final Hooter* fanzine pointed me towards Andy Searle who was just setting up the Parrs Wood Press. He was not too sure about publishing a novel but took a gamble with it, one that paid off for around three thousand copies have since been sold.

By now I was keen to write a sequel. Again there was little planning, I just wrote when I felt like it, usually most evenings after work. I did however make sure that the ending made the reader wonder what happened next because by now I was aiming to write a novel for each of the last four decades of the 20th century.

In writing *One Spring* I took into account advice from a professor of English Literature and a keen Fartown supporter. He suggested that I should introduce slightly different or unusual story lines to the sequel. I thus developed the character Les Earnshaw, a former Wilkinson's draughtsman who had become an author. His novels were set in his fictional town of Garsdale which were based between Ashurst and Wigan. Les becomes famous and even appears on television in a hilarious interview with David Frost. Another slightly bizarre story concerned Peter Starr who worked in the machine shop. His interest in UFO spotting led to him leaving Ashurst and going to California where he becomes involved with a group of weirdoes called the Zartracs and from whom he only escapes with great guile.

On more familiar ground there is a visit to Wembley for the 1978 Cup Final against Leeds and a party in the Manor House pub in Ashurst at which a number of rugby league players turn up. They include Eric Fraser, former Warrington full-back and Great Britain captain and Ken Large who had been Tom van Vollenhoven's centre. Why those two in particular? Well I knew them both as I used to collect their union subs when we all worked at the B.I.

Two years later it was time for *One Summer*. This runs from 1979 to the week before the miners' strike starts in 1984. Romance and rugby league are still there but the rock 'n' roll has gone even though one draughtsman knew John Lennon and played in a band called the Rainmen (so called because one lived at Rainhill and three lived at Rainford). It was the start of the Thatcher years, and so music was replaced by redundancy, now a harsh reality for many people, including me.

I had started doing book signing sessions by this time and came to realise what quickly would attract a passing shopper. The most obvious is the front cover, which is what he or she sees first. In *One Summer* it is Mal Meninga scoring a try against Castleford, a good one if you were a rugby league fan. It wasn't if you weren't, as many people would often wrongly assume the book was just about rugby and walk past.

Equally important is the first line and the rest of page one. In *One Summer* it is 'Quick lads. Hang up some garlic. The vampires are coming'. Also important is the list of chapter titles, which includes 'The double Dutch holiday fund', 'The tea lady from Leigh' and 'Auntie Vera is staying with us for a bit'.

My new book, *One Autumn* will again dwell on humour in life, though humour at work now seems to be on the wane. It will also be full of nostalgia for it will be set in the period just before the emergence of Super League in 1995.

I am faced with a real problem in writing this novel though. Many of my original characters have now turned 65 and no longer working. But because a feature of my writing is to frequently return to the past, usually prefaced with comments like "Do you remember that bloke Tarzan from Widnes who worked in the foundry", tales about people from *One Winter* can still appear, even including ones about those who have now died like Stan the war hero.

Two types of readers

I have had quite a lot of feedback from readers, which is always useful for an author. Some have told me they would have liked more rugby while others thought there was too much. But most have said they found it easy to identify with my characters. From what I have been told, I would like to think that I have brought back many memories for my readers, made many people laugh and in some cases even shed a tear, which is something that rugby league can do for you as well!

Geoff Lee

A new edition of Geoff Lee's first novel, *One Winter*, is available from London League Publications Ltd at £9.95. For information about obtaining *One Spring* and *One Summer*, visit www.geofflee.net . *One Autumn* will be published by London League Publications Ltd in the autumn of 2007.

The case for an 'open' game

Peter Lush questions whether rugby league should still have 'amateurs' and 'professionals'.

Before the momentous events of 1995, it always annoyed me when rugby league was described as the 'professional' code, usually by rugby union writers or supporters. Of course these comments are no longer heard since rugby union went 'open' in 1995, meaning that the top players could be openly financially rewarded for their efforts on the pitch. The reality has always been that the majority of rugby league players have always been amateurs, playing the game for enjoyment and not for financial reward. This was true when the professional clubs were part-time, and is still true today, when less than 20 British clubs employ their players on a full-time basis.

The origins of 'amateurism' are in Victorian sport and the class-ridden basis of sport and society in those days. The ruling class could afford to spend their leisure time playing sport. However, as industrial society developed, the working class also began to have more leisure time. Participation in sport, and watching sport for recreation developed for working people, which previously had been the preserve of the upper class. Particularly in the north, competition developed between clubs. As club facilities developed, they began to charge spectators for admission. Once this had happened, professionalism was inevitable. Clubs would offer incentives to the better players to join them to keep their supporters happy watching a successful team.

Association football managed to accommodate amateurs and professionals under one ruling body, except for a short-term split in the early twentieth century. The FA was founded in 1863, to draw up a common set of rules. Initially based around the public schools, and former public school players in amateur clubs, its leaders were farsighted enough to accept the development of the Football League, an openly professional competition. In the early 1880s association football went through a similar process to that which would afflict rugby a few years later. There were suspensions of players for alleged 'professionalism', but in 1884, the FA recognised that professionalism was inevitable, and it was fully accepted the following year. In 1888 the Football League was launched, and in 1892 the FA Amateur Cup was started, a final recognition that the professional teams would inevitably come to dominate the FA Cup.

This was not the end of football's problems with amateur status. With some 'amateur' clubs able to attract crowds of 5,000 or more, 'shamateurism' developed, with 'expenses' being paid to players to induce them to move clubs. In 1974, despairing of ever controlling the situation, the FA declared that the age of 'amateur' status was finished, and the game became 'open'.

This had benefits for some senior amateur clubs, who could now sign former professional players, and with the development of the 'pyramid' structure outside the Football League, work towards playing at a higher status. The financial side of payments to players became a problem for the Inland Revenue, not the football authorities. However, for the vast majority of real amateur players, who played solely for enjoyment, with no financial reward, and often at some expense, with membership fees and travel costs to be paid, the game continued as before.

In rugby, as is well known, the Victorian era ended in a different outcome. The RFU were determined not to accommodate any element of professionalism. This caused major problems in the north, where the club game had developed through cup competitions and in the early 1890s leagues. There were accusations of inducements to change clubs and of professionalism. Players and teams were suspended. The competitions inevitably brought about a form of professionalism, although the point that brought the dispute to a head was 'broken time' – the right for players to be compensated if they missed work to play. The dispute resulted in the bitter split of 1895, the formation of the Northern Union and ultimately rugby league.

In other sports, the days of amateur status are long gone. Cricket was unusual as amateurs and professionals had played together for many years in county cricket before the game went open in 1963. Some amateurs received considerable expenses, or jobs with their county clubs, and it was not until the 1950s that professionals regularly captained county teams. There were many other distinctions between amateurs and professionals – different changing rooms, entrances onto the pitch, and whether their initials went before or after their name on the scorecard. Tennis went open in 1968 and athletics followed. Golf still has amateur status, but mainly to distinguish different types of tournament. Amateurs and professionals compete in some tournaments.

The birth of BARLA

The creation of BARLA in 1973 was very important for the survival and development of amateur rugby league. It is clear that the RFL was failing to develop and promote the amateur game, which BARLA say was down to 150 amateur teams and around 30 youth teams. The leagues and clubs taking control under the banner of BARLA probably saved the amateur game from further decline.

The existence of BARLA also showed very clearly that rugby league was widely played on an amateur basis. The gradual erosion of the gap between the two codes, following pressure from rugby league, so that amateur players could play both, initially for students, then for amateurs, would have been far more difficult without BARLA.

But why, when rugby union is 'open' does rugby league persist with 'amateur' status? The BARLA rules allow for current professionals to play for BARLA clubs on a 'permit' basis. Each team is allowed two of these permit players, with further restrictions on playing in cup games. There is no limit on the number of former professionals registering with a club, but only three may play in one team. However, if a former professional registers with the last BARLA club he played for, he does not count as a 'permit' player. Also, a professional whose contract has expired and is under 21 does not count as a former professional.

However, there is a further restriction on players playing for international or representative teams within BARLA. Any player who has played rugby league as a 'professional' is not eligible for selection, and only 'bona-fide' amateurs can be selected.

One of rugby league's criticisms of rugby union prior to 1995 was that former professionals of other sports could play rugby union, and only rugby league players were 'banned'. BARLA's current rules continue these problems. A former rugby union full-time professional could play for the BARLA representative teams, and for a club without a permit. But a player who played as a part-time professional in National League 2 for a couple of years in his early 20s would need a permit to play for a club, unless the club was his last BARLA one, and would not be allowed to play for a representative or international team. Similarly, a former association football professional, or American

Football professional could play, with the rugby league player who has never played another sport misses out.

Admittedly it is unlikely that a former rugby union full-time player would be in this position. But with the switching between codes by young players today, it is not impossible. For example, Gavin Gordon played for a few years as a professional with the London Broncos. He didn't quite make it in Super League, and has continued to play for West London in the Rugby League Conference. He has now been selected for the Ireland Wolfhounds team to tour New Zealand in May, but if this tour was under the auspices of BARLA he presumably would be ineligible because of his 'professional' history.

Isn't it time to finally sweep away these Victorian classifications, and make everyone 'players'? For the vast majority it would make no difference. But for former professionals there would be a difference. It would also allow some of the larger BARLA clubs to offer small payments to their players if they so desired, or win bonuses. It would also allow them to sign their players on contracts, and given them so protection if a larger club want to sign them. Clubs who in the past had problems collecting the nominal £50 from professional clubs who signed one of their players would have some protection and would receive transfer fees for players who were under contract to them.

There are three other reasons for making rugby league 'open'. One is the question of 'shamateurism' – i.e. the unofficial payment by clubs to players who claim to be 'amateur'. As far as I am aware, this is not causing problems in our sport at the moment, although in *Rugby League World* (January 2007) Cliff Spracklen from Bramley Buffaloes calls for "A more healthy and honest approach compared to the 'shamateurism' that exists at some so-called amateur clubs."

Cliff Spracklen advocates that "players can be paid where the clubs have the means". The question of 'shamateurism' is inextricably linked to the other reason to make the game 'open' – clubs who want to develop and try to climb the 'pyramid' towards the semi-professional game.

Another advantage of an 'open' structure is that theoretically a club can work their way gradually to the top level. In association football, the original Wimbledon FC went from amateurism in the 1960s to being semi-professional to joining the Football League and ultimately playing at the top level. In rugby league, with the notable exception of the London Skolars, it seems to be almost impossible for a club to progress into semi-professional competition.

Many current BARLA and Rugby League Conference clubs would not want to move from their present status. They do not have a catchment area of support which would allow them to play at a higher level. But as the sport develops, particularly outside the traditional heartlands, a route for this to happen needs to be mapped out. Part of this would be having players on contracts on an open basis. Otherwise, 'shamateurism' can creep in, as supposedly amateur clubs want to compete and play at a higher level.

The Rugby League Conference operates as an 'open' competition. Open competition does not mean that any player can play. It would be inappropriate – say – for a Super League contracted player looking for a couple of competitive matches to test his fitness, for example, to play for an amateur club. This happened in the early years of the Conference, and the rules were changed to make this illegal in the future. But that is a matter of playing standards, not of status. Similarly, it would be appropriate, in my opinion, now that clubs from the game's traditional areas are in the Rugby League Conference, for there to be a restriction that players who have played a certain number of BARLA National Conference games should not play in what should still be recognised as a development league.

National League Three has shown some of the problems with 'amateur' status. Is it realistic to expect players to compete in a national competition without some form of payment? Although NL3, in its new brand as Rugby League Conference National is an 'open' competition, unless the clubs have the resources to pay the players, it is hard to see how it can survive, given the amount of travelling involved. The clubs who have left the competition have returned to more regional based competitions. Yet it is with some of these clubs, outside the heartlands, where there is the potential for future semi-professional clubs. The game does not need another part-time professional club in Yorkshire or Lancashire, but it does in the midlands or the south.

A third reason for 'open' status was raised in an article Phil Hodgson in *League Weekly* (29 January 2007). He is a leading writer on the amateur game, and was expressing sympathy for two clubs who had been docked points in the National Conference League for playing two players who had been registered as contracted professionals by Hunslet. The clubs were not aware of this, and evidently the players either were not aware of the rule, or were keeping quiet and hoping everything would be ok. Apparently Hunslet had lodged the paperwork for these players earlier than expected, ruling them out of BARLA competitions.

Hodgson says that "club secretaries... need the knowledge and wisdom of barristers these days if they are not to fall foul of amateur rugby league's increasingly complex legislations and procedures".

However, he also says that, despite being a strong believer in rules, he has covered Hunslet games when both the Hawks and their opponents "include several players whose names I know very well from the National Conference League." He goes on to say that some players switch between NL2 and the National Conference league "like a cuckoo in a clock".

The press 'blind eyeing' amateurs playing in a professional competition is horribly reminiscent of the days when well-known rugby union players played trial matches in rugby league, and the press loyally reported that "A. Trialist" or "S. O. Else" looked promising. The rugby league reporters knew that in those days, even playing a rugby league trial as an amateur was enough to get a player a ban from rugby union.

One central registration system for all clubs in an open game would solve this problem. A player could legitimately have a trial with a more senior club, or go on loan for a period, and it could all be done openly and above board.

This article is not advocating the abolition of BARLA. There are some problem areas, particularly representative teams, and the number of competitions, which the game outside Super League and the National Leagues need to resolve. But in the twenty first century, the nineteenth century concept of 'amateurism' needs to be put to rest, in favour of an open game.

London and the south east

Reports on some of the clubs in London and the south east, and the state of the game.

London Griffins

In *Our Game* issue 13 I wrote about the first season of the London Griffins who were formed as the official supporters' team of London Broncos. Based in Richmond upon Thames, London Griffins started off playing IMBRL semi-contact tag matches against a mixture of supporters and social teams from around the country.

That first season ended with a first trophy after picking up the plate at the National IMBRL 7s in Hull, and hope for an even better season in 2006.

Encouragingly 2006 was indeed a season of great progress which ended with a further two trophies in the cabinet and even more importantly for the long term, a real, tangible development from that of a social team to a rugby league club.

The year began with the aim of seeing how far we could develop both on and off the pitch. We opened the season by heading up to Sheffield to compete in the second Sheffield IMBRL 7s against a mixture of fellow supporters' sides and local teams. A very strong Griffins side dominated from start to finish and took the scalps of Hull Irregulars, Sheffield Forgers and Halifax on the way to being crowned champions.

A few weeks later the first XIII-a-side game of the season saw Sheffield Forgers travel down to London to play in a curtain raiser to the London Skolars versus Sheffield Eagles National League 2 fixture. As with most Griffins games the kick off coincided with a torrential downpour which made slick handling and skilful rugby difficult. It was with great credit that the team battled to a 38-32 victory.

Our next XIII-a-side fixture was on 1 July against the Wigan Web Warriors at our new home ground in Osterley. This was the team's first full contact fixture. The Web Warriors have been the dominant force in full contact IMBRL and a number of players also play for Shevington Sharks in the North West Counties League. This was the biggest day so far in the club's short history and our performance on and off the pitch would be the catalyst for the club's future direction. A competitive and entertaining game played in extreme heat was won 38-14 by the Web Warriors. The result was almost meaningless for the Griffins as a side that contained only five players with any previous experience of full contact rugby league battled gamely for the full 80 minutes showing an immense amount of effort, determination and no little skill.

As the outcome of the day sunk in, the decision was made that the club's future should also include playing regular full contact fixtures and a successful application was made to the London Amateur Rugby League for the 2007 season.

Before we could start thinking about 2007 there were still a couple of outstanding matters left in 2006. First up were South London Storm, again played in atrocious weather. Last season saw the times meet twice with one win each so this season's fixture was important for both teams. The Storm side was made up of a mixture of first and second team players plus coaching staff. Both fixtures in 2005 were competitive with Storm winning the first 44-22 and Griffins edging the second 26-18 in an absolutely epic game. The 2006 fixture showed just how far the Griffins had come in a year as the team missing several of its best players romped to a 52-8 victory.

There was one last act for 2006 when a strong squad headed up the M1 in October to try and go one better at the National IMBRL 7s in Hull. In a season of highlights the team saved the best until last and went unbeaten through the tournament to be crowned 2006 National IMBRL 7s champions after extra time victories in both the semi-final and final.

A number of fixtures were cancelled which lead to a slightly frustrating time on the pitch but when we did manage to pull the shirt on a team with real promise emerged. In October 2005 we appeared for the first time at an IMBRL event and less than a year later the team dominated the IMBRL tournaments picking up all available trophies. More importantly than that, London Griffins have shown that whatever the level, born-and-bred Londoners can compete and succeed in the game of rugby league.

A new challenge awaits in 2007. There is a desire to stay close to our roots as an IMBRL team and we will continue to play IMBRL matches. Indeed it is planned that some supporters' games will take place at the Twickenham Stoop prior to Quins RL Super league games.

However The London Amateur Rugby League will be the club's bread and butter competition for 2007 and since the summer the whole club have been working overtime to make sure every base is covered both on and off the pitch.

A committee was formed to give some structure to the club and two head coaches, Chris Heading and Adam Hill, were appointed. Both are also part of the core playing squad so are well immersed in the culture of the club.

The next stage was to try and find some sponsorship to cover costs for insurance, ground hire, equipment and new playing kit. It's well known that sports at grass roots level often struggle for funds and it is to the credit of all at the club that we've so far managed to secure nearly £2,000 for 2007. £500 of this has come through a player sponsorship scheme where individuals have to try and find their own personal sponsor for a cost of £25.

The balance has come through our new team sponsors for 2007-08: Richmond Housing Partnership, through its Urban Academy scheme; SAR Consultants; London League Publications Ltd; sendintheclowns.org.uk; code13consulting.co.uk; forty-twenty.co.uk and Sheen Sports and fitness centre.

We were also able to successfully apply for a lottery grant via the 'Awards for all' scheme. While team and player sponsorship funds will go towards developing the first team through new kit, insurance and equipment, the lottery grant is part of a concerted aim to become an integral part of the community in Richmond.

One of the key early tasks here before we obtained the grant was to begin to get some exposure in the local press. The *Richmond and Twickenham Times* and *Richmond Comet* have begun to regularly feature Griffins stories and we plan to further develop this in 2007.

Thanks to Awards for all, the London Griffins Development programme will launch early in 2007 and aims in partnership with Quins RL and Urban Academy to really begin to develop the sport in Richmond. Four players will be attending a Level 1 coaching course in January 2007 with more to follow later on. A number of players will also attend refereeing courses in February.

London Griffins attracted most of the current squad through offering new players and those who had drifted away from the game the opportunity to play rugby league at a competitive yet social level. Even though 2007 will see us move some what away from the social aspect with regards to the first team, we still see maintaining and developing social players as one of the best ways to attract new players. Initial plans are in place to develop a London Tag Rugby League competition to run through the summer months. This will enable new coaches to cut their teeth in a less pressurised environment and allow players new to the game to develop skills without the pressure of full contact while offering them, if they wish, the opportunity to move up to the Griffins first team squad.

The RFL though Caro Wild and Harlequins RL via community development manager Kurt Pittman have been hugely supportive and there are a number of future irons in the fire with regards working in partnership with Quins RL.

London Skolars have also been quick to offer their support and in an exciting opening for 2007 we played a curtain raiser to the Skolars versus Quins friendly on 3 February against Southgate College Eagles. Other plans for 2007 include defending our two IMBRL titles and a trip to Ireland in May to take part in the annual Kilkenny 9s. Late in the summer there is also the possibility of a game against a German side.

As a club we are very aware that we need to walk before we can run and ensure that all the right boxes are ticked before we progress to the next stage of our development. However we don't apologise for being ambitious, the last two years have shown what can be done on and off the pitch with hard work, dedication and some talent. We have only just begun to touch the surface of what London Griffins are capable of achieving.

Giovanni Cinque

Storming around South London

Richard Pitchfork reports on the progress of one of London's longest-established amateur clubs.

South London Storm go into their 10th year in 2007 after being formed by passionate Rugby league fans living in and around London in 1997 as the South London Saints. Storm based themselves at Streatham & Croydon Rugby Union Club in Thornton Heath where they are still based now after building up a good strong relationship with the rugby union club.

The name was changed from the Saints to the Storm on entry to the RL Conference in 2000, which South London entered.

The RLC was a baptism of fire for Storm as they only managed a couple of wins in their first two seasons but they helped to raise the profile of the sport in a small corner of the capital as they focused on a chance to get rugby league into schools and colleges.

2002 can be seen as a turning point for the club as many 'League centric' players became involved with their knowledge and passion for League rubbing off on many union converts and on the club as a whole. The club reached the 2002 Shield final beating Bedford Swifts 54-2 and also winning the RLC 'club of the year' award.

2003 saw the inception of the National League 3 and Storm stepped forward to carry the capital's mantle into the competition as the second team stepped up to take their place in the Rugby League Conference. The team beat northern sides such as Huddersfield Underbank and Sheffield Hillsborough Hawks and finished the season just outside the play-offs.

Continuing in the NL3 in 2004 the club continued to show its strengths beating notable northern clubs and just missing out on the play offs once more.

The NL3 teams were also given the opportunity to play in the Challenge Cup, which the Storm took up and enjoyed two appearances in. In the 2003-4 cup run they were beaten in the First round by West Bowling 36-4. In the 2004-5 cup run they beat West London Sharks 24-20 in the first round before bowing out away to Castleford Lock Lane in the second round 52-24.

Due to the problems of large travelling distances on the inception of the RLC Premier Division in 2005 Storm entered the division which was spread on four regional lines before a four-way national play off for the national title.

This allowed for two major leaps forward, the second team was able to play against the fellow second teams of the premier division sides and more emphasis could be placed on the junior set up. The juniors became a main focal point for Storm's energy as four clubs picked up the mantle of developing the youth talent. The long standing Croydon Hurricanes continued their growth; the Thornton Heath Tornadoes took on the task of helping take up the ever-increasing numbers at the Hurricanes. The Brixton Bulls expanded the Storm's reach further north into an area crying out for sport. And the Addington Lightening helped Storm expand to the south.

These junior teams have been helped by notable volunteers from the playing staff of the South London Storm and have been helped off the field by the network of off field staff of the Storm. This has helped the junior clubs form their own off field connections and on field coaching staff with the added fall back of the Storm's set up helping them grow from strength to strength.

All the added growth brought success to the on field team at South London with the Southern Premier Division title being won by the Storm's first team and narrowly missing out on the national final after loosing to the Welsh Champions. Storm added the Club of the Year title once more for 2005 in recognition of the strides forward made with the Youth teams.

The second team made the play-offs of the RLC division with six of the team for the last match of the season coming through from the Hurricanes under-16 side of the year before. Along with this the Southern Premier Grand Final winning first team also included four players who had come through the ranks of the Storm two years before. Showing the strength that Storm is producing through the ranks and emphasis put on the junior set up.

2006 could be seen as the year the Storm came of age. With the emphasis on the junior set up the club became much more a community club and the spirit of this shone through the club. More players from the junior set up were playing with the seniors and this atmosphere produced a strong club ethos and mentality. Many of the young senior players also continued their links with the juniors helping to coach, which will continue this breeding process on.

The junior sides field teams from under-7s through to under-16s at the Croydon Hurricanes and under-9s through to under-12s at the Thornton Heath Tornadoes, Brixton Bulls and Addington Lightening.

Tournaments for these teams also including the teams of other senior clubs at Storm's level are played every other week throughout the summer giving them much needed competition and interaction within the clubs.

This spirit carried through the club as the first team retained their Southern Division Title in 2006 and went on to win the National title. Also in the final six of this team had come through the junior set up. The second team made up of mostly those coming through the junior set up won the London Amateur Rugby League title.

Off the field due to the immense junior activity, which Storm is rightfully proud of, they also won the 2006 BBC London Non Professional Sports Team of the Year award and the 2006 Rugby League Conference Team of the Year award.

Storm will continue into 2007 with the juniors at the forefront of their thoughts and with new age groups being introduced to the clubs, with more junior players coming through the ranks the club looks healthy in its 10 year.

Kent Ravens

When looking down the fixture list for 2007 many may be surprised to come across the name of Kent Ravens. Some will say that didn't release that they played rugby league down this county while others will wonder how the Kent Ravens have made it to the Conference Premier in only their fourth year of existence.

These heights seemed miles away when the club, formed in 2004, played in the London Amateur League. Ravens struggled, losing all seven matches and even getting outshone by the only other Ravens team: the under-11s who won every tournament and competition they entered that year under the guidance of Vicki Bacon. The Ravens first team may have struggled with player numbers and results at that point but they never forfeited a match or walked away. This 'stick with it' attitude paid dividend in 2005 when by August the club had massed ten titles and an extra three teams including women, under-15s and under 13s.

The reason why the Ravens started in the first place is a question that has been asked to chairperson Alan Bacon thousands of times and he explains that "My wife and I were involved with another local club but became disheartened by the lack of help or publicity their junior sides got" he continued "so we thought why not run a club the way each player and coach wants their club run and this is what we did" with that the Ravens were born on 12 June 2004, the fact the club had an easy to use web site, merchandise and a level playing field for all at the club to get credit helped with recruiting from all walks of life and all areas of the south, many a distance from the clubs' ground including Harrow, Ashford, Tunbridge Wells and so on.

The 2006 season was planned as settling season for the Ravens, the first team had moved up into the conference and the club had started a new under-9s team. But again the club were lucky to get on board many new volunteers such as Shane Rossi (under-11s coach), Kenny Bell (women's coach), Alex Osborne (under-9s coach) and many more and the season snowballed as every team went from strength to strength as the season went on. The first team recorded great wins over local rivals Greenwich Admirals, Hemel Hempstead 'A', St Albans 'A' and Haringey to help them qualify for the play-offs.

Other than the promotion the big news regarding the Ravens for 2007 is their new ground: Princes Park Stadium is the new home of the Kent side. Though due problems with the turf the grand opening for the Rugby League side has been delayed until Friday 3 August, with no competition from other League matches scheduled that day, a massive crowd and a grand opening is expected.

Playing across the road at Acacia Hall, The Ravens' training ground for the majority of 2007, the season started in March when the first team take on the improving London Griffins in a friendly under guidance of Lionhearts coach Glenn Tyreman.

London Griffins versus Wigan Web Warriors in 2006 (Courtesy London Griffins)

Kent Ravens versus Greenwich Admirals in 2006 (Courtesy Kent Ravens RLFC)

South London Storm versus Australian Legends
touring team at Blackheath RFC in 2003 (Photo: Peter Lush)

and the Junior Ravens play their first matches in the RFL southern youth leagues, while the women start their campaign in a stronger Women's London League a few weeks later.

In summary the 2007 season is looking to be the biggest and most competitive season for the Kent Ravens with a new home, new competition and new coaches, though the club is proud of its history, with the excitement of 2007 everyone is looking forward to the future.

Alan Bacon

Youth rugby league in London: The state of play

Gavin Willacy reports.

Statistics do not tell the whole story. The RFL claim London to be a thriving metropolis of rugby league. There can be no argument that more kids are playing rugby league in London than ever before. But how long they are playing for, in how many games and at what standard is harder to fathom.

The game is flourishing at secondary school age, to a degree. The Champion Schools tournament is going from strength-to-strength in most regions, with more schools playing at more age groups. The North London Year 10 tournament in November was a pleasure to behold. Amid a whirlwind of chaotic activity were a series of entertaining matches between the likes of Highgate Wood, St Thomas More and White Hart Lane schools. But far more startling was the sight of several superb players: from a 'catch me if you can' winger to a now-you-see-it-now you-don't half-back, hilariously rotund props who kept trundling with four or five kids hanging off their giant thighs to tackling-machines who never stopped hitting the ball-carrier all over the pitch despite the rest of his team opening up like Tower Bridge to let the opposition in time and again.

It was clear to anyone there that in two years time there should be some quality Academy players in the capital. In five years we could have several professionals from that day. Interestingly, nearly all the most exciting talent on display was black or mixed race. Rugby league in London is as multi-cultural as life comes.

With London Youth League divisions at under-12, under-14 and under-16 level, there is competition for anyone wanting to play. A variety of teams enter these competitions, with London Skolars, South London and West London responsible for most of them.

All is not rosy though. As with all development competitions, not all fixtures take place and some teams fall apart through lack of numbers or staff as the summer progresses. North London could not stage a Year 11 tournament – St Thomas More progressed directly into a play-off with Hemel's champions – while the Haringey Hornets under-16s last year played several games with only nine or ten players before collapsing. Fortunately, most of those players have been playing the game all winter as part of Southgate College Eagles.

Matt Harrall and John Constantinou represented London & the South at the Regional Festival in Manchester in October, while Harrall – an inspirational captain and loose-forward who learned the game at Highgate Wood – and Essex-based hooker Doug Hann went to the England colleges trials in late January. When Essex Eels hit the wall last year, the Hann clan (the whole family are league addicts) committed to Southgate and even joined the college sports trip to Manchester in December 2006 when they trained with Salford City Reds development officer Tom Wild.

The 16 to 19 age bracket is a major issue in the capital at the moment. RFL officer Caro Wild has overseen a huge increase in playing numbers and matches up to under-16 level and open age rugby, but there is a major gap for many of players at 16 unless they are good enough to be signed up by Harlequins Academy.

Southgate are now in their third season. At the end of the first one, I wrote in *Our Game* that I was 'determined Southgate will play on the national stage' in 2005. We did just that, shocking many in the student game by going to Leeds and turning over Park Lane College at Leeds Rugby Academy. We were taught a lesson by Warrington side Priestly in the next round, but kept pride intact.

I said we would become Southgate Rugby United in 2005-06 and play both union and league. That didn't happen. With both seasons in the student world running concurrently and several of our players new to rugby entirely or union players learning how to play league, we felt it was unfeasible to alternate between the two. Instead, we have dedicated ourselves to league and only compete in occasional union sevens tournaments. That has enabled the greenhorns to learn the basics of league with minds uncluttered by rucks, mauls and line-outs. After all, rugby union schools and academies abound: we are the only FE college with a rugby league team south of Doncaster!

And there's the problem – or the challenge. Finding someone to play is a huge part of my job. This season I have spent hours and hours trying to arrange fixtures. Even when you do, it is not until the opposition appear on the pitch that I know I have succeeded. We have had teams pull out the night before, abandon the league or refuse to travel to London to play us in National Cup!

In 2005-06 we played six full-sided matches and in two small-sided tournaments. Getting Portsmouth University and the College of Law up to play in the SESSA (Southern England Students) Nines at New River in April 2006 was an achievement but one that has not been built on. We hope they will return this spring.

The London Youth League has now had two campaigns: the first saw Hemel and South London compete in the final with Southgate and St Mary's in the consolation places in 2005-06. In autumn 2006, six teams entered the competition only for Hemel and Essex University to withdraw, leaving the remaining four teams to play just six fixtures. Sadly, several of those went unfulfilled, leaving Southgate to squeeze past 11-man South London in a magnificent final, 42-36 after extra-time, following a 24-all draw in the league meeting. Farnborough   played a couple of games, re-establishing league in that area.

Clearly, three games is not much use to anyone, let alone a whole scheme. It was clear we needed to play more games and against players our own age. We couldn't play anyone under-16 for insurance reasons and adults provide another safety and care issue. Our fixture list resembles a hotchpotch of sporadic matches against a variety of opponents, from Feltham Young Offenders Institute to London Griffins.

We are countering that next season by joining the Student RL Colleges Premier Division, guaranteeing a dozen games against colleges who take the sport seriously. But it means four-hour journeys up the motorway every other week to find reliable opponents. With Tane Taitoko being assisted by his Skolars' coach Latham Tawhai, we are launching the 'Skolarship' when, from September 2007, players will come to Southgate full-time to play rugby league while completing their educational commitments. With the two national cups, the London Youth League and the 9s and 7s, that will fill our midweek calendar through next winter.

When late spring arrives, our players should be well prepared to progress into Skolars' open age teams, if they are not signed by Harlequins. This summer, the lads will play in the Southgate Skolars – a joint-venture team in the London League Merit comp – as they gradually increase their experiences.

Southgate and Skolars are working together to fill the gap between 16 and open age rugby, a gap that stretches from the south coast to South Yorkshire. If we can do it, anyone can.

If you would like more information on the 'Skolarship', please contact Gavin on gavin.willacy@southgate.ac.uk *or 020 8886-6521 x6394. Any players aged 16 to 19 are welcome to training with Tane – contact him for more details at* tane.taitoko@southgate.ac.uk

Obsession – rugby league

David Roberts reflects on his new addiction to rugby league.

It started innocently enough with a work mate who's originally from Merseyside and a Widnes follower coming to a union final at Twickenham with me and during the course of the game talk coming around to a role reversal and me attending a league match with said friend. Little did the aforementioned mate know what he was letting himself in for. Since attending my first game in July 2006 at Harlequins my thoughts have not wandered very far from the game.

Since the beginning of this season I've driven everybody mad talking about rugby league. Luckily there are a few people where I work just outside Southampton who do have some idea about the game but no matter. Fan or not they have heard about it from me. With the above mentioned work colleague, I even spent part of one lunch hour trying to explain to a very confused Polish guy whom on seeing my copy of *Our Game* started asking numerous questions and was probably even more mixed up after we tried explaining the game.

I've spent many hours trawling though web-sites searching for every bit of information that can be found.

Being a supporter of clubs in various other sports- football, baseball, college American Football - my reason for following teams are never the most obvious. In association football it's because the teams local or where I'm from. In other sports it's because I like the place or the fans. As for rugby league it's because of the shirt.

Having looked through different places I came to the obvious answer that St Helens had the best shirt, most history and a historic stadium. Reading Saints web-sites though, most red and white fans seem to think Knowsley Road is a dump. I shall find out in August when I travel north for the first time to see them play at home to Hull. Not before seeing them at The Stoop though in April.

Being a life-long football fan and regular every Saturday at a game somewhere the last thing I would have thought of doing until last year was giving up my cherished 90 minutes for a game of rugby league. This has already happened as Harlequins is the nearest team to me this is where my weekend afternoons during the summer are going to be spent.

It's just a shame the excellent Sportspages in London shut down last year. For 15 years I went into the shop walking past the rugby league items with giving them a second glance.

Now if the shop were still around I'd sweep everything up connected with the game. Why support a team from the north when you have a Super League club within a train journey's distance? Having sat with the Salford fans at the Stoop during the first-half of their recent televised Sky game then changed sides and sat with Quins fans during the second 40 minutes the difference was chalk and cheese. The 100 or so City Reds supporters were noisy and passionate. As for Harlequins supporters, they were more like a cricket crowd. Just polite applause apart from when they scored.

Originally being from the north myself might, of course have had something to do with it as well!

Editors' note: The East Stand at The Stoop is now used for away and 'casual' fans. The hard-core Harlequins fans are now in the Lexus Stand, and as the editors can confirm, are as noisy as any group of fans in rugby league. However, we hope David enjoys his trips to The Stoop in future.

Rugby League Ireland – busy times

Manus Lappin reports on developments in Ireland

On the international front it has been a busy year for Rugby League Ireland. Inspirational Great Britain props and Irish stalwarts Barrie McDermott and Terry O'Connor both retired from the game, however their decision to stay involved in a coaching and managerial capacity with the Wolfhounds was a major boost to the squad. Although both men are clearly still capable of gracing the international stage, in their new roles as assistant coach and assistant manager respectively, mean their influence is ever-present, and with their combined enthusiasm and appetite for their new positions neither Barrie or Terry will consider taking a backward step!

After four years as head coach of the Irish Wolfhounds, former Great Britain and Leeds star Daryl Powell has stepped down as Irish Wolfhounds head coach. Daryl ably led the Wolfhounds to many memorable successes, but due to work commitments with Leeds, Daryl has handed over the reigns to former assistant coach Andy Kelly. He is no stranger to the Irish setup having been assistant coach for the last five years. Speaking on his appointment Kelly said: "I have been involved with Ireland since the 2000 World Cup and I've always had a tremendous depth of belonging and affinity with Ireland. I was happy to be involved as assistant coach, but when the opportunity presented itself for me to take the head coaches role, I didn't think twice." Kelly also took the opportunity to thank former coach Powell for his efforts and commitment over the last four years, sentiments that everyone involved with RLI would like to echo.

Kelly's first game in charge was a trip to Moscow where Ireland played Russia in the first of its Rugby League World Cup qualifier back in October. On the day Ireland thrashed Russia 50-12 with Widnes full-back Gavin Dodd scoring a hat-trick of tries while Warrington stand-off Chris Bridge bagged 22 points from two tries and seven conversions. Ireland's win against Russia set a new record beating their 43-10 victory over Scotland at Navan two years ago.

On the back of a great victory on the road, Kelly knew he would face stiff opposition from Lebanon when the two sides met in Dublin in November 2006. The game was played at Shelbourne Rovers FC on the North Side of Dublin city, and Lebanon boasted no less than 14 NRL players in their starting line-up.

Despite having home advantage, Ireland found it difficult to break down a well drilled Lebanon defence and as the first half drew to a close, Ireland trailed 10-0 despite being camped on the Lebanon line for the closing 10 minutes.

Whatever Kelly said to the players at the interval seemed to spark Ireland into action. Three minutes after the restart Ireland's Scott Grix had opened the home sides account with a fine 40 metre dash to touch down. The final 40 minutes was a titanic battle with both sides playing like their lives depended on it, few could argue that 18-18 was a fair reflection of the final score setting up a massive winner takes all game between the two sides when they meet in Lebanon in 2007.

While the senior Wolfhounds continue to go from strength to strength, the Wolfhounds 'A' squad will make history in May 2007 when they embark on their tour to New Zealand. This is the first Irish representative rugby league side ever to tour the Land of the Long White Cloud and head coach Damien Welland is keen to put on show the wealth of indigenous talent that exists on these isles.

Speaking of the tour, Welland said "This will be a fantastic experience for our young players to play rugby league in New Zealand, and make Irish Rugby League history in the process. With the Rugby League World Cup scheduled for 2008 in Australia, this tour will provide a great opportunity for 'A' players to get themselves noticed."

2006 also saw the first ever development squad compete in an international game. The squad travelled with the 'A' team to Wales to play their Welsh counterparts. The addition of this team to RLI means that competition for the 'A' team will intensify and standards across the competition will improve and standardise.

The 2006 season also saw the Student RLI team continue its development with inter provincial games between Munster and Leinster Students and an SRLI team took on the Irish Exiles in Dublin. The continued improvements of the student network bode well for the future and game time against the exile students will give the players chance to gain valuable experience ahead of competing in international competitions.

On the domestic front the season format went to an All Ireland league to give teams the chance to play each other. New clubs joined in Carlow and Athlone. Carlow are a senior rugby union team and they made a big impact reaching the final and hosting the game as well. The coming season may even see a second Carlow team join the fray in the new league structure. Athlone had looked like competing the previous year but it didn't materialise and last season saw them take the Kilkenny 9s by storm and show what potential there is in Westmeath. RLI stalwart Patrick Harkins continues to spread to word to his home town and next season will see the team cementing their place in the competition.

The all Ireland league format was a trial to help teams across Ireland take each other on and a lot was learnt from this. The 2007 season ahead has taken these lessons on board to give a three-tier league with the top performers competing against each other and then two geographical leagues for newer teams to develop and seek promotion. The All Ireland league saw the 2005 champions, Treaty City Titans, come out on top for the second year in a row beating new boys Carlow in a great final. The Dublin Blues and Kildare again proved to be great teams throughout the season. All other clubs took strides to improve their standing too with some classic games. This rivalry will only improve in the new league format. The 2007 season will see the introduction of a National Cup Competition, adding to the Silverware that will be up for grabs. This tournament will be open to all competing side as well as perspective new clubs who wish to experience the game, further details at www.rli.ie

Away from the domestic game the inter-provincial game between Munster and Leinster took place as a double-header with the students in Tullamore. Munster won both fixtures with the senior side retaining the title between the provinces.

Manus Lappin is the PR and media director of Rugby League Ireland.

From Wigan to Wales: The 1970s and beyond

Phil Melling reflects on launching rugby league in Swansea in the 1970s.

The sponsorship of the Challenge Cup and the World Club Challenge by Leeds Metropolitan University is an important development for Rugby League. Leeds Met has undoubtedly secured some wonderful publicity at a bargain price while the Rugby Football League has gained an enthusiastic sponsor for two of its most prestigious events. In so doing it has demonstrated the importance it attaches to an area of our game where we have long appeared second best and struggled to compete with our primary competitor, rugby union.

What astonished me when I first came to Swansea in 1978 was the extent to which the senior and middle management of the University was in the hands of people who were leading members of two elite social institutions: the Dining Club and the Rugby Club. In effect, these clubs ran the University – its politics, its policies, its short and long term strategies. Most of the senior professional appointments were held by men who ate well and spent their Wednesday afternoons watching the rugby union 1st XV at Sketty Park. As one might expect Swansea University - always known and referred to as 'College' – had a well-established rugby union tradition going back over 50 years and in the 1970s and 1980s college students like Paul Thorburn, Mark Wyatt, Mark Bennett and Adebayo Adeybayo went on to play top class union for club and country. Although the College owned it, the pitch at Sketty was regarded by rugby union folk as sacred space and if we in the rugby league club had the temerity to train or play on it we were sent a letter or called in and warned against our future conduct. I was a lecturer at the time and this put me on a collision course over a number of years with a highly influential member of the University, the director of sports education and first team rugby union coach, Stan Addicote. Stan liked to keep his eye on things – I suppose that's one way of putting it – and it was his decree that the Sketty Park pitch was to be used solely by the rugby union first XV. The argument relayed to the ground staff was that the pitch simply wouldn't stand up to the wear and tear inflicted by other sports, including rugby league. Sometimes, in bad weather, we had to use it. Our matches were played on a Sunday afternoon and if the pitches at Fairwood – pneumonia park on the edge of Gower – were waterlogged or frozen or badly rutted – and if teams had travelled long distances we had no alternative but to sneak our way down to Sketty. Occasionally we were given special dispensations. Between 1979 and, lets say, 1990 we probably played a dozen matches on the Sketty pitch. Contrast that with the visiting tourist sides – the Australians, the Springboks, the All Blacks – who, whenever they came to West Wales, set up camp in Swansea and were allowed to train, sometimes for a whole week, until the Sketty pitch was a ploughed-up paddock and virtually unplayable.

In those days anything was do-able if you were given the green light by the College authorities. That's not to say that Stan Addicote didn't ease up. Eventually he did and in a way he learned to accept things. But if my memory serves me correctly he never actually came to watch us play, which is disappointing given that he was head of physical education and technically interested in the progress made by all sports. I'm sure he would have learned a lot, if not from us then from other teams. We played to a standard. As a tiny outpost of rugby league we reached the UAU final on two occasions, won numerous domestic and regional trophies and provided a solid nucleus of players for the Welsh national student team. During the period from 1988 to 1993 when Clive Griffiths and I were looking after the side we were European student champions for three years and in 1992 we reached the semi-finals of the Student World Cup in Australia. Given its size Swansea should never have been able to do what it did, but between 1978 and 2003 there was always a conveyor belt of quality players available to us. One thinks of Rob Appleyard who played for Wales at rugby union to the loose-forward Chris Atkinson (see *Open Rugby* 1981 for Phil Larder's comments), Janis Alksnis from Latvia or the stranger than fiction Matt Vale, a star in Australia in 1992, but whose peculiarities could never be underestimated, especially the way he used to train in his best shoes and his fathers overcoat.

Without doubt we had access to talent – the oddballs and mavericks who didn't fit in with the serial drinkers in other sports – and the players who were attracted from rugby union like Mark Bennett, Dinyl (Dinky) Francis and Graham Price. Sometimes the players were warned. Phrases like: "I might not be able to stop you from playing rugby league but I can certainly prevent you from playing union: you won't get picked" – were common place. Clive Griffiths became well aware of this in his preparations for the 1992 Student World Cup when Huw Daniels, Nicky Lloyd and Alan Hardman at Cardiff Institute were told that if they chose to go to Australia they could forget a future in college rugby union. To their eternal credit, they all chose us.

The educational authorities were complicit at all levels in the systems of punishment that the rugby union insisted on; indeed, secondary and higher education institutions were themselves the agents of control. A close and cloistered relationship existed between the world to which we belonged and the WRU in Cardiff. Many of our players who reached a high standard in rugby union would receive letters from the WRU warning them that they risked jeopardising their so-called amateur status if they continued to dabble with rugby league. And the WRU could only know this if someone was keeping them informed.

Systems of control extended at all levels of education. In the primary school that my son went to in Brynmill the games master was interested only in rugby union; association football wasn't an option for the kids – astonishing when you think of the fantastic football traditions that Swansea has and that Brynmill School is no more than two miles from the Vetch Field. Had my son wanted to go to Swansea University and had he been any good at rugby union a place would have been found for him – as it often was – via the back door. In the days before rugby scholarships it was well known which were the soft departments where a nod and a wink would get you in. And later on if you did have union ability and a modicum of academic ability the same nod and a wink would – apparently - get you onto a postgraduate course at Jesus College, Oxford. These were the days of grants and no fees. Financial support was all taken care of. No questions were asked, no answers were given.

If you might have expected something like this in Wales you would certainly not have expected it in a place like Wigan, where I grew up in the 1950s and 1960s. But the truth is, it wasn't much different. Even in Wigan rugby union operated a vertical monopoly of control throughout the educational system making sure that from primary school to public school, via grammar school, no one was able to play rugby league. A policy of sporting apartheid was rigidly enforced in Wigan Grammar School in which rugby league was enemy number one, not football or cricket or fives or fencing – sports we are all encouraged to play, alongside rugby union. Rugby league was officially ignored, even though we were only a couple of miles from Central Park and opposite the school gates, in Parsons Walk, lived one of the great full-backs of rugby league, Martin Ryan. Our sports masters were rugby union guys – Murphy, Balmer, Taylor – and our best players, like Des Seabrook who looked after me when I was a first former in Banks House, went on to play for Lancashire.

What is remarkable about this, as Tony Collins has recently pointed out, is the unwillingness of the Rugby Football League, during the period Bill Fallowfield was at the helm, to at least question the rigidity and bias within the grammar school system. Even in a rugby league heartland rugby union was able to equate its game with a certain level of academic intelligence – and the occupations, skills and social positions associated with it – and to limit rugby league to the secondary modern system, where the game was played by (so-called) academic failures from the wrong side of the tracks. Bill Fallowfield to my knowledge never challenged this system. He allowed rugby league players to be associated in the popular mind with hewers of wood and drawers of water; those who would spend their lives in manual jobs. One suspects that, in Fallowfield's view, those who played rugby union got ahead in the world. This being the case, grammar schools would never tolerate rugby league officials undermining the social networks and class identities which rugby union had put in place.

When we played rugby at Wigan Grammar School we played rugby union from beginning to end. Our opponents were Arnold School at Blackpool, King George V Grammars School at Southport, Thornleigh at Bolton and West Park at St Helens. But rugby league was off the agenda. On school visits and speech days we got lectures from old boys like Johnny Bradburn (who took over JJ Broughtons sports shop in Wigan and later sold out to Dave Whelan and JJB sports). Johnny had played up at Wigan Rugby Union Old Boys (the Grammar School Old Boys club) and when he talked to us about what was special and distinctive about Wigan I never once remember him mentioning Ken Gee or Ces Mountford or what Billy was doing down the road. That was special to us, as were Dave Bolton and Fred Griffiths; as special to us as Danny Hurcombe, Jim Sullivan and Tommy Howley had been to my own father. Unless you were signed by Wigan, as my best friend Alan Curliss was, you only watched rugby league; you did not go inside of it. On Wednesday, you took the bus up to Prospect from the school gates or outside Lowes shop and later on when you left school you went to the Old Boys in Douglas Valley. You were kept, without knowing it, well away from the amateur game because that's where the secondary moderns ended up. The physical locations made the point. Those who made it went up to Douglas Valley, a rural parkland sat on the edge of Wigan Plantations. Those who played amateur rugby league were Irish Catholics. They went to St Patricks and played in Scholes on an ex-corporation rubbish dump next to the canal. That St Pats produced players of genius – tougher, hungrier, more intelligent – and the Old Boys didn't, was irrelevant. By that stage you'd been given your lesson.

There were sports teachers at Wigan Grammar, like Frank Balmer, who had played a few games of rugby league and got caught. Frank had been banned from playing rugby union but he kept his head down at school and Ashley Smith, the headmaster, let him carry on. Deep down we all knew why Frank kept quiet. In a way, we had been taught the same lesson. You'd passed the eleven plus and a door had been opened. It was all down to Reece Edwards, the director of education, who lived in a phenomenally fancy house on Wigan Lane. Reece drove a Rover but was never a happy man. I played with his son, a lad who caused Reece a lot of trouble. Like Frank, I learned to keep my head down, especially when Reece got involved and came outside. I believed that only an idiot would turn their back on the opportunity the Grammar School offered. You were entering another world. At Wigan Grammar the godfather was Dickie Nutt and his Senate was the upper VI. If your Latin and Greek were up to scratch and you made it to the crypt on a Wednesday with Dickie, there was always a chance you would move on up to Keble or Wadham. Dickie had connections.

I have a friend at Swansea, John Leytham, who comes from Wigan. John taught history at the university here and is a big Wigan rugby league fan. He also has a different take on the game. Unlike myself or Tony Collins, John believes that class did not play a fundamental part in the making of rugby league in Wigan – not at the highest level. He argues that people who supported the professional club were essentially class-less, because that is exactly what the club itself was. John has a point. The bigger clubs, certainly the more successful ones, transcended class barriers and undermined the class perceptions of what rugby league was. Johnny Bradburn might forget to mention Central Park but everyone knew that Central Park was larger than life. It was a club with a transnational and multicultural identity in which race was more important than class and, in this way, it overwhelmed class structures and class perceptions. At the flick of a wrist Wigan could go anywhere in the world and pick up world class talent, as it had done throughout its history: Charlie Seeling from the All Blacks, Tiny van Rooyen from South Africa, Billy Boston who came to the club via Cardiff, Cork and Sierra Leone. In other words, what made the club special was the racial outwardness that lay behind its vision of the world.

When I grew up in Wigan in the 1950s the town was almost uniformly white, except for the occasional trainee engineer from India or Pakistan who attended the Mining & Technical College in Library Street. Wigan Rugby League Club was not a party to this. It seemed, in a sense, unhappy with what had happened to the town, as if it disputed and rejected the white identity which the class system rigidly enforced, a system in which those who lived in Wigan and stayed in Wigan knew their place. Wigan Rugby League Club blew away all that was associated with the idea of Wigan as a whites-only world. The club opened the town up and made us see what lay beyond it. This was a point I tried to make in a play I wrote, *The Day of the African*, which we first performed at the George Orwell Heritage Centre in 1985.

Wherever I went I took with me certain ideas that Wigan Rugby League had taught me and when I came to Swansea in the 1970s I wanted to try these ideas out. Few others seemed to be doing this – although Mark Newbrook at Reading University was in a similar mould and taking more stick than most from rugby union. There were some difficult times for us. Now and again I was taken to one side by lecturers and union aficionados in the University – Phil King and Roger Elias come to mind in Geology – and told to watch my step. None of this had any effect on us. We attracted lots of attention in the press, local as well as national (if anyone is interested I have dozens of articles on file) and Maurice Oldroyd and Tom Keaveney weighed in with support from Huddersfield.

In those days BARLA was never found wanting. Maurice came down to Wales regularly and arranged for us to be kitted-out in the 1974 Great Britain jerseys. This was important and made us feel very distinctive. I remember we couldn't afford logos and labels, so we did our own: crazy motifs of swans with balls that looked like eggs. Our confidence was high because of the support we received and the visits that were made. Two characters stand out from the rest: Albert Fearnley and Laurie Gant.

Albert and Laurie operated as a double act and for our first training session in January 1979 we ended up in the dining room at Fairwood Playing Fields on Gower. Snow had fallen and the pitches were lakes of ice and we put the tables and chairs outside. Thirty of us ran round the refectory while Laurie puffed away at his pipe and Albert swore and called us all pufters. Albert was one of the great gurus of rugby league: lovely, generous and hard as nails. His one-liners were always worth turning out for. As a motivator, he was miles ahead of his time. Tragically, he was unable to fulfil his potential and his larger-than-life talents as a coach appeared too late to take advantage of the new opportunities that rugby league was beginning to offer. Of all the people who came to Swansea from 1978 to 1995 to help us out – Frank Wilson, Phil Larder, Tommy Dawes, Arthur Beetson, Maurice Lindsay – Albert Fearnley stands apart. He had a unique talent for encouragement and his good humour was legendary. Only occasionally did he let things slip and only then when he decided to hit the Carlsberg Special Brew. There were some conversations you didn't follow up, such as the time he stayed in The Dragon Hotel on the Kingsway. We were going for a drink and Albert phoned his wife from the lobby. "No love," he said, "Carlisle's a wonderful place. I'm on the Florida Orange".

I suppose we were a bit of a novelty for BARLA and we got showered with publicity. Our results used to get announced on Radio Manchester at six o'clock, usually from places like Oxford or Reading or Birmingham – and sometimes Cheltenham – if we played away. In the early days Lionel Hurst was another great rugby league pioneer but other than him and Bob Fleay there was no-one within a hundred miles who gave us that much support. After a while we got visits from David Watkins but the Cardiff Blue Dragons didn't have much of a missionary approach to rugby league. Danny Sheehy and Clive Millman became influential, especially Danny. When he and Kerry Sheehy started the club at Aberavon the response from the local community was fantastic. What Danny and Kerry achieved at Aberavon was nothing short of miraculous and, without doubt, it's they who sowed some of the earliest seeds for everything that has happened in the later years.

In the years before Aberavon we had regular visits from Wigan St Patricks and Dewsbury Celtic. I can never speak highly enough of these clubs and the way they supported us. Their behaviour was exemplary, although St Pats did have one unfortunate incident which involved a few of the boats in Mumbles harbour and the police rescue helicopter, but Cliff Fleming sorted it out. BARLA was also exceptionally good at providing us with referees and we were never left short. Referees travelled down on a Saturday, stayed over, and went back Sunday evening after the game. The most intriguing was a guy who was a member of the Sealed Knot, the English Civil War Society. He came from Yorkshire and drove a Robin Reliant. He once came straight from the battle of Naseby dressed in his uniform – I think he was a Roundhead – and proceeded to do his warming up exercises on the side of the pitch. I remember him as a very large man who gave up his weekends and regularly drove the 500 to 600 miles to help us out. What a gem. He refereed a game against Oulton, a club Tony Fisher coached and sometimes played for. This was the game where the Oulton captain took us to one side and told us about Tony: "You can hit him over the head with an iron bar", he said. "We do it in training. He doesn't feel a thing."

Life in those days was great fun but everything got much more professional when I teamed up with Clive Griffiths as Welsh student team manager in the late 1980s. Clive, like Shaun Edwards, is one of the great lost talents in rugby league. If Albert Fearnley was the most charismatic person I met, Clive was, without doubt, the most talented. He ended up winning a Grand Slam for Wales although David Waite never rated him as a rugby league coach. How pitiful is that, given what Clive achieved in two World Cups? Iestyn Harris says he is the best coach he ever played under and there are dozens of quality union players – like Rob Appleyard – who would say the same. Clive's background as a player with Llanelli meant that he knew where the bodies were buried in Wales. He was also a student at Cardiff Institute and played for Wales and because of this he was enormously important in the development of the game and no-one ought to forget that. Clive had connections, people respected him and he could open doors. In the early 1990s he and I produced between us a fantastic student team – I doubt there has ever been a better one – the first to beat the French at home in 1989 and European champions for the next three years. I am sure these were among the happiest years of Clive's life, as they were of mine. We had at last begun to make real inroads into Welsh sporting life, our methods were experimental – way ahead of anything that rugby union was doing, especially the use of videos – and new teams were beginning to take shape and put down roots.

Phil Melling is the author of *The Glory of Their Times* (2005 – with Tony Collins) and *Man of Amman* (1994).

Scottish rugby league's early days

Gavin Willacy reports on new information on the history of rugby league in Scotland.

It has always been assumed that rugby league in Scotland developed through the student game in the late 1980s, taken on by open-age amateurs until the international teams and national competition launched in the mid-1990s. When I wrote my history of Scottish rugby league - *Rugby League Bravehearts* (London League Publications, 2002) — I did mention that some schoolboy league had been played in the 1970s thanks to Henry Callaghan, but no details were in the public domain.

Harry Edgar, creator of *Open Rugby* magazine and currently editor of *Rugby League Journal*, gave me more details last year and, out of the blue, Henry got in touch recently. It turns out that he developed a vibrant and passionate League community 30 years ago that should have a place in the annals of the games history and be fully lauded by Scotland Rugby League. Here Henry tells the full, extraordinary story of his adventure.

"My first memory of rugby league was in 1946, when at the age of five, I went with my dad and my grandad to the willows to watch Salford's first game after the war and I've been hooked ever since. We played league and union at school but after school I played union until I was about 35 simply because there wasn't much league about. All the time though I was passionate about Salford, especially during the glory years in the 1970s.

It was a great wrench to come up to Scotland in 1974 but in those days rugby league was on BBC every Saturday and I never missed a game.

My son went to St Mary's school in Hamilton and I was at a parents' meeting one evening where they were decrying the lack of a football team at the school. They asked for volunteers to run one but nobody came forward so I offered to run a rugby league team. They all looked at me as if I was daft but agreed that rugby league was better than nothing.

They had a shale football pitch at the school so we started off with touch rugby and they loved it. Then, of course, they wanted to tackle and to play against other teams so we booked a pitch at the new Strathclyde Park and went round the other schools in Hamilton, Chatelherault and St John's.

Suddenly one Saturday morning I had about 80 primary school kids on the park all wanting to play rugby league. Fortunately one parent had turned up who offered to help: Doug Welsh, a staunch union man who became a great friend and colleague.

We trained on a Saturday and played touch on the shale under floodlights on a Wednesday. We had a mini-league between the schools and introduced other schools. It's all in the dim-and -distant past but I remember St Blane's in Burnbank and I think St Ninian's and, eventually, I think St Johns RC College in Uddingston.

Very quickly we decided to form Hamilton Lions and wrote to BARLA to find the nearest schoolboy teams and eventually we were put in touch with Mick Docherty from Egremont Rangers.

They came up and slaughtered us and we went down to play them at Derwent Park as a curtain-raiser and amazingly we only lost 3-0. [Among the Hamilton Lions team was the son of John 'Yogi' Young, the former Celtic star and Lisbon Lion, now manager of Falkirk.] That was the occasion when Paul Charlton gave me his Great Britain shirt.

We then developed a pattern whereby we trained or played schools games, every second week, then played against English teams on alternate weeks.

The guys from Cumbria were very helpful. They had pre-season sevens and nines competitions to which we were always invited. As a club I remember playing against Askham and Dalton. We also played in Leeds at Belle Island, and at Gildersome and Warrington. Fred Lindop, the referee, brought up a team of amazingly mature looking under-15s from Wakefield. I remember we took about 50 kids to Gildersome (Morley) all of whom stayed with different families. They all had Sunday lunch ('Sunday dinner' down in Yorkshire) and every single one had roast beef and Yorkshire pudding!

We also took about 50 kids to London to play a tournament against Gildersome and a London team run by a guy whose name I think was Dave Part and then we watched the Challenge Cup Final at Wembley.

Looking back I find it hard to believe that we came so far in such a short time because the under-11s – who were part of the original lot from St Mary's etc - went a whole season playing against English clubs and lost only one game, the last of the season to Leigh Miners.

Privately we were told that we would get the curtain-raiser to the next Cup Final at Wembley, but there was a bit of an outcry from the homelands who had been doing their bit for years so it didn't happen. We did however get the curtain-raiser to the England versus Wales game at Knowsley Road against Mick Naughton's famous Widnes Tigers and won 9-3. At one time we were running teams at under-11, under-13 and under-15/16.

One day I got a letter from a guy called Steve Strang who had just returned to Edinburgh from Australia and had written to BARLA to see if there was any rugby league in Scotland. They gave him my name. Originally I think he just wanted to play, but I told him what I was doing and asked him to think about doing the same in Edinburgh. He not only thought about it, but he did it. He was a fantastic guy. He was not married, he had no children, but he went into some of the toughest schools in Edinburgh, got them playing rugby league and eventually formed Liberton lions.

He put quite a bit of his own money into the club for strip etc because the kids parents were either not interested or didn't have the money. We had many an inter-school and inter-club competition and independently he took teams down to England and brought teams up to Scotland to play.

He persuaded the groundsman at the Royal High Rugby Union club in Edinburgh to allow a game of rugby league between Hamilton Lions and Liberton Lions while the first XV were playing union on the adjoining pitch. I will never forget the expressions on the faces of the members as they warmed to the fact that kids were playing rugby and then they realised that they were playing rugby league!

He also persuaded the Liberton RU club to let him use their ground and on one occasion he arranged a game between a youth team from Leigh and his team and also an adult game between the Leigh lot and players from Liberton RU, which I had the misfortune to referee. The Leigh team included a couple of Dowlings who were England amateur league players and the Liberton guys were not quite prepared for the physicality of amateur rugby league

Over the whole piece we had frequent visits from Albert Fearnley and Laurie Gant, the official rugby league directors of coaching, and we put many guys through official coaching schemes. I took my Grade 3 coaching qualification at Crystal Palace along with Stan Wall who at that time was a Grade 1 referee and who is the wee guy you see standing beside Sean Long whenever he takes a goalkick. I took my Grade 2 at Lilleshall at the same time as Phil Larder who, believe it or not, was a bundle of fun. Steve Strang and I both got Grade 1s in Edinburgh. Between the two clubs we had at least 10 guys with coaching qualifications.

Sadly I had marriage problems, my boys moved back down south with their mother and I moved to Edinburgh. I soldiered on for a while, but problems developed within the committee, then I got a job which involved working weekends. At the same time Steve was really fed up with the lack of parental involvement in Edinburgh so we decided to call it a day.

Our last game was a combined Scottish team at under-16 (some of the same guys who at under-11 had played in the England versus Wales curtain-raiser at St Helens) as a curtain-raiser to Carlisle's first home game in rugby league. We were playing against the auld enemy - Egremont Rangers - who at that time were one of the top youth teams in the country. By that time we had outgrown our kit, so we asked Egremont if they could lend us a set. They agreed.

I remember we got to Carlisle and parked in a car park close to the ground. We assembled the squad of bitter rivals and gave them their positions. Some of the Edinburgh guys were quite difficult to handle, but I told them that they were about to meet the biggest, oldest-looking, most fearsome under-16s they had ever imagined, but that if they forgot their differences and stuck to the game plan they were good enough to win. I also told them that Mick Docherty, great coach as he was, would do everything he could to put us at a disadvantage.

Egremont duly arrive: big, strong, powerful, awesome. Fortunately, we were prepared. They gave us a bag of jerseys, with apologies for the fact that they were soaking wet – good old Mick!

We won 6-3 and after the game Bill Oxley, who the previous year had managed the Ashes tour to Australia, came down from the stand, sought me out and said: "Henry, that was great, they didn't just win, they played great rugby league".

It was so sad that that was our last game.

However it was said that what we did in Scotland, while it didn't last, did provide an inspiration for development in England. When we had at least eight schools playing in Scotland, there was not one school playing rugby league in Warrington.

My mate Brian Chambers immediately got off his backside and addressed that problem, got his badges, coached BARLA in Australia and coached the Army. Many others did the same.

So maybe we helped to achieve something lasting after all."

Henry Callaghan now lives in Aberfeldy, along with Gareth Morton's parents, who travel to England each week to watch their son play for Hull KR. He is keen to become more involved again with Scotland Rugby League and would be pleased to hear from any old friends: Grandtullylogos@aol.com

A new era at The Halliwell Jones Stadium

Neil Dowson and **Andrew Topham** reflect on Warrington's new home and the campaign to make the move, three years after moving there.

Warrington Wolves had been seeking a move to a new stadium for some time in order to secure the club's finances and it's long term future in the top flight of rugby league. The advent of Super League and full-time summer rugby changed the game forever and it became essential for clubs' to provide better spectator and corporate facilities. Wilderspool Stadium had served the club well for over 100 years, but it was in a poor state of repair, lacked spectator and corporate facilities, land locked and further development would have proved very costly.

This latest search for a new stadium started in 1997 and went all around the Borough of Warrington before settling in 2000 on the northern edge of the town centre. This ideal location was sited at the former Carlsberg Tetley brewery on the A49.

On 20 October 2003, 1,238 days after the initial planning application was submitted the club took ownership of The Halliwell Jones Stadium. During this time many events took place that shaped the look and outcome of the proposed development:

31 May 2000

Tesco Stores Ltd submitted outline planning proposals for a 12,449 square metre foodstore, plus car parking, together with a 12,000 capacity stadium on Winwick Road, in a multi-million pound deal with Carlsberg-Tetley Brewing Ltd and Warrington Sports Holdings (the owners of Warrington Wolves). The joint application provided an alternative plan to the foodstore and mixed housing development originally proposed for the redundant brownfield site, formerly the Carlsberg-Tetley Brewery in June 1998. Lord Hoyle, Chairman of Warrington Wolves said, "I believe not only the fans, but the whole of Warrington will welcome the opportunity this presents for the Town to have an all purpose Community Stadium."

17 July 2000

A great turn out by the Wolves faithful for a rally meeting at the Parr Hall boosted the push for the local Council to accept the plans and grant planning permission for the proposed new stadium.

A rousing speech by Lord Hoyle set the stage for an interesting evening, "There must be no room at all for any complacency, we mustn't think that we have got that approval. What we've all got to do from tonight onwards is work together to make sure that we bring that about. We've got to say to the planning committee that this project carries the overwhelming support of all of you.

It's absolutely vital to the club's future. We need to develop a stadium that not only that we can be proud, not only that Warrington can be proud of, not only the Rugby League can be proud of but anyone who comes here from anywhere in the country can be proud of as well."

24 July 2000

Letters of support for the People's Stadium were handed over to the Mayor. Over a thousand letters came from local businesses, schools, community groups, amateur sports clubs and local residents supporting the planning application for the stadium and the Tesco store.

23 August 2000

The Town Planning Committee voted 7-4 in favour of joint planning application between the Wolves and supermarket giants Tesco, the proviso being that the decision will be referred to the Secretary of State.

Letters of support and petitions signed by the clubs fans helped sway the decision of the Planning Committee, as did the impassioned plea of Wolves fan Mark Fearnley. Wolves chief executive Peter Deakin addressed the massed fans on the Town Hall lawn:

"That was the first major hurdle and I'd just like to thank the councillors that voted for us, it wasn't as tight as I thought it would be with a 7-4 vote. It's a great vote for us and there is a resolution there that it will go through to the Secretary of State for him to review. He has 21 days to make a decision whether it goes to a public inquiry or not. We hope he sees that this has value added community that will support the development of this new stadium."

11 January 2001

The club received news from the Government Office for the North West, regarding the Secretary of State's decision on the new stadium. "The Secretary of State is of the opinion that a public inquiry should be held with regard to the new stadium application. The public inquiry starts today and it will be made by the Planning Inspectorate from Bristol."

The club commented: "Whilst we are initially devastated to receive this news, this is not an insurmountable obstacle. The Warrington community has already illustrated its passion for a new stadium in the town."

21 April 2001

Warrington Wolves fans in a happy mood from the previous night's 56-22 victory over St Helens packed a pre-inquiry rally at the Parr Hall. The fans heard about the Wolves's plans to tackle the dissenters with their community development programme schemes and need for a state-of-the-art stadium for the town. Lord Hoyle also urged supporters to "celebrate the past and look forward to a stadium of the future!", and finished by saying, "You're the best supporters in rugby league, so let's have a stadium worthy of your support. Let's go and get it!"

MP for Warrington South, Helen Southworth also took to the podium to tell how one theme is constant throughout her visits and work around the town, the Warrington Wolves Community programmes. Mrs Southworth called for a new state of the art stadium that the town and the club's supporters deserved and could be proud of: "We've got to get out there and get it!"

15 to 24 April 2001

Public Inquiry at the Parr Hall took place. The club through Lord Hoyle, Neil Dowson and Adam Jude put the case for the new stadium. Speakers from all over the Borough attended including the then Whitehaven coach Paul Cullen, representatives from Super League and members of the local Council and local residents had their say on the proposed development. There was an evening dedicated specifically for the fans in which many speeches were given in favour of the new stadium and Tesco store.

19 December 2001

An early Christmas present was delivered when planning permission was granted for the development of the new stadium. The estimated cost being in the region £8 million, with the opportunity to expand if the need arose. Chief executive, Andy Gatcliffe commented, "It has been a very long and tortuous process

for all of us at the Club, not just for employees of the Club but also for the supporters, the sponsors and the people of Warrington. We are absolutely elated with the news and it is right and fitting that Warrington Wolves being the premier sport in Warrington will now have this new stadium.

23 May 2002

Following almost six months of negotiations Warrington Wolves and Tesco announced the final site layout for the new stadium and Tesco Extra store. Agreement has been reached on a site layout that utilises the old Tetley Walker brewery site to its best potential. Lengthy negotiations took place and finally plan 89B has been agreed. The stadium is to the south of the site bordered by Dallam Lane, Buckley Street and Winwick Road and will run east/west with the main stand to the north. The Tesco Extra store will be located to the north of the site; between the two will be parking primarily for use by the Tesco Extra Store shoppers. Draft designs for the stadium were produced that give a capacity of 14,000.

6 December 2002

The Council's Development Control Committee gave a unanimous "Yes" to the joint stadium and Tesco store development project at a meeting on Thursday evening. The drawn out saga of the Stadium campaign was finally given the go-ahead with detailed planning permission being heard and passed by the eight members of the committee.

16 December 2002

First ground was broken in the 'Cutting of the first sod'. The Contractors Barr Construction officially moved on to site to begin work on the ground, with an expected 45 weeks to construct the stadium.

22 February 2002

Foundations marked out and the first steel construction were erected, beginning with the main North Stand development. Media and PR officer Gina Coldrick commented: "The progress on the new stadium since the breaking of the ground in December has been phenomenal. The steel construction will go up very quickly over the next couple of weeks and brings a visual reality to all the hard work of planning and petitioning of the last couple of years. It is very exciting times for the club and fans."

21 September 2003

A full-house crowd of 9,261 witnessed the final Super League match at Wilderspool Stadium. The sun broke through the clouds, the girls danced, the opera singer performed, the crowd chanted and the team, in their commemorative strip, delivered a stunning performance and made the play-offs for the first time in the Super League era. The visitors Wakefield Trinity Wildcats were demolished 52-12, with Graham Appo scoring three tries and kicking 10 goals, while Sid Domic had the honour of scoring the final try. Paul Cullen later decribed the game as being "A performance that did justice to the great players who have honoured this club throughout its entire history."

24 September 2003

The stadium name is announced as being The Halliwell Jones Stadium. Chief Executive Andy Gatcliffe announced, "The board of directors of the club is extremely pleased to have 'captured' such a prestigious and quality partner, namely, north west motor group Halliwell Jones as our new stadium naming rights sponsor."

20 October 2003

The stadium construction is now completed and the keys to the Stadium are officially handed over to Warrington Wolves from Barr Construction. The fit-out of the stadium and the development of the stadium management plans continue at a pace to be ready for the first match.

15 February 2004

The club held an open day to allow the fans get their first view from inside the stadium. Over 3,600 supporters turned up for it. The Safety Committee with the Police, Fire Service, Warrington Borough Council Building Control and the club in attendance carried out a full review of the club's stewarding procedures and their Management Plan and unanimously agreed to issue a Safety Certificate with a capacity of 14,206.

21 February 2004

The first match at the The Halliwell Jones Stadium, was the opening round of Super League IX, against Wakefield Trinity Wildcats, live on Sky Sports TV. The Wildcats provided the opposition in Wolves' last ever Super League appearance at Wilderspool Stadium

The match an all-ticket sell-out had a few teething problems with some spectators turned away at the turnstiles as the crowd reached capacity. Those that were there witnessed the dawn of a new era with a Warrington victory by 34-20. Australian half-back Nathan Wood became the first player to score a try at The Halliwell Jones Stadium. Other try scorers were Paul Wood with two, Lee Briers and Dean Gaskell, with Briers kicking seven goals, as Warrington christened the new stadium in style.

The first three years

As the club now embarks upon its fourth season at The Halliwell Jones Stadium it seems an age since the move from Wilderspool Stadium. Warrington Wolves have been able to use the stadium to develop its income streams to secure the future of the club and to become a top six side in Super League.

Two months into its first season, The Halliwell Jones Stadium held the Challenge Cup semi-final between St Helens and Huddersfield Giants. It was a great occasion with an almost capacity crowd basking in the sunshine watching St Helens at their exhilarating best.

Negotiations with Warrington Primary Care Trust were completed to develop the void area under the Martin Dawes stand to create a health centre. Health Services@Wolves was opened in April 2005 with over 20 healthcare services. The centre has been a great success bringing quality healthcare with easy access to the people of Warrington.

The North West Development Agency helped to finance the fit-out of another void area in the stadium. The first floor of the north stand has been developed into the Community Learning Floor, which opened in August 2005. The floor was purpose-built to the requirements of the community partners to bring them together to deliver participation and learning opportunities. The partners include Warrington Borough Council, Warrington Collegiate, Warrington LEA and the Warrington Wolves Foundation.

These two additions created a unique situation as The Halliwell Jones Stadium became the first stadium in Britain to have its own Health and Education services.

In June 2005 the stadium hosted four matches of the 6th UEFA European Women's Championship. UEFA were so impressed that they awarded The Halliwell Jones Stadium the 'stadium of the tournament' award.

The RFL has also staged a number of 'big games' at the stadium. In November 2004 the final of the European Nations Tournament took place between England and Ireland. The following year the New Zealand tourists played England and in 2006 the National Leagues' Grand Final triple header was hosted. A full house and an electric atmosphere saw Hull Kingston Rovers win through to Super League.

The stadium and Tesco store development has proved to be a catalyst for the re-development of the northern part of Warrington town centre. The A49 gateway into town had been derelict and a real eyesore for many years. New units have now been built in Buckley Street next to the stadium. Derelict and empty buildings in Winwick Street have been demolished and the redevelopment around Central Station has now commenced with work scheduled for the remainder of the street over the next few years. It was the new stadium that kick-started these developments.

The club has further developed facilities within the stadium, with an IT training suite and a physiotherapy centre, which are leased out to generate income.

The winter of 2006 saw new drainage and an irrigation system installed and the whole playing surface was re-turfed. The stadium is ready for the new season to host more dramatic and exciting rugby league matches.

A new stadium development

The Halliwell Jones Stadium was the first new stadium built since the Taylor Report that has incorporated a mix of seating and standing areas for supporters. The stadium has been visited by many clubs from various sports such as association football, rugby league and union and even Aussie Rules, who are looking at their own new stadium development. While we would have liked to get everything right about the development we did not. This is a quick 20 point guide to help any rugby league club with their new stadium plan:

1. Keep the design simple as money will be at a premium.
2. Maximise the pitch size, as a minimum ensure that the grassed area is at least 120m x 74m and get experts in to draw up a pitch specification.
3. Ensure that there are covered stands on all four sides of the ground.
4. Ensure that there is adequate floodlighting, a minimum 1,000 lux is required by Sky TV, and will need to be adequate for high-digital television.
5. Have hospitality facilities in at least one stand and with a kitchen that is big enough to cater for all potential guests.
6. Ensure that there are sufficient toilets and kiosks; spectators want good clean facilities and do not want to queue.
7. Maximise the changing space area and have four team and one referees changing rooms.
8. Don't forget the press facilities, you will want good publicity.
9. Provide space for the grounds-staff and their equipment.
10. Provide plenty of storage space.
11. If cash is tight, allow for void areas in the build process that can be developed at later stages when funds are available, a future fit-out is cheaper than a new build.
12. Develop partnerships with the local council, education, health services, community and other sports in the area and do not forget to involve your supporters and sponsors.
13. Sub-lets can develop non-rugby related income streams that will help keep the bank manager happy.
14. Grant applications tend to be minimal these days, but check with the RFL, Sport England and your local authority.
15. Consider fans requirements, i.e. ask them, standing is what they often want and it is cheaper than seating.
16. Consider how fans will get to the stadium, a bad location with no public transport will severely affect attendances and club finances.
17. Consider parking and traffic implications, you will need to be party to a travel plan and aware of the environmental impact. Think green!

18. A new stadium will be a big change for the club, look to franchise out those operations that the club does not have expertise, requires capital outlay and could be costly to run, e.g. catering.
19. At the development stage, work hand in glove with the Safety Committee, involve SKY TV and consider the views of the local disability groups.
20. Be aware that the bigger the scheme the higher the running costs, so chose a stadium size that you feel that is financially manageable.

Neil Dowson is the finance manager of Warrington Wolves. Starting his 10th year at Warrington Wolves, he was the 'driving force' behind the new stadium project. Andy Topham has been the Webmaster of the Warrington Wolves website for 10 years. He is a lifelong Warrington Wolves supporter and played for Woolston Rovers. They wrote the book *End of an Era – Wilderspool 1898 to 2003* and are heavily involved in heritage projects at the club.

Photos and illustrations courtesy Warrington Wolves RLFC

Rugby League Benevolent Fund

When Warrington Wolves supporters received their 2007 season ticket renewal forms they noticed all the adult prices had increased by £1. Not that anyone complained as the Club were donating the extra £1 per ticket to the Rugby League Benevolent Fund. The charitable trust was established by the RFL in 2005 and has raised over £60,000. The money goes towards supporting players whose lives have been affected by serious injuries sustained while playing the game.

Andrew Whitlam, the RFL media manager, recognises that all clubs have given their support to the fund involved in various initiatives to raise money. Commenting on Warrington, the first club to donate from season ticket sales, he said: "It is tremendous what Warrington Wolves are doing. Any funds generated are extremely valuable and important. Serious injury in rugby league is very rare but when it does happen it is important that the players involved get the correct support."

The RL Benevolent Fund is administered by a committee of trustees, which meets regularly and offers support to seriously injured players via the RFL's welfare officer David Phillips. Chaired by former Huddersfield Giants director Tim Adams, the other committee members are Phil Clarke, David Hinchliffe, Gary Hetherington, RFL chief operating officer Nigel Wood and Nick Shaw, a partner with Addleshaw Goddard.

Phil Clarke, whose own playing career was ended by a broken neck sustained while playing in Australia, acts as spokesman for the fund and at the launch at the 2005 RFL Presidents Ball said: "Although serious life changing injuries are rare in rugby league, it is critically important that any players are affected receive the best support possible. The creation of the fund will begin the process of delivering this. The family and community spirit which exists within rugby league will greatly assist the growth and development of the fund over the coming seasons and supporters attending the sport's major events can take satisfaction from the fact that they are contributing directly to this important initiative."

The fund will receive £1 from each ticket sold for all future Challenge Cup Finals and Super League Grand Finals, as well as the profits from future RFL President's Balls. Other fundraising ideas have included dinners and sponsored walks. Last year a "Three Peaks Challenge" was organised with people attempting to c1imb the highest peaks in Britain. Up to the end of the 2006 season, nine players had benefited from the fund, receiving wheelchairs and gym equipment.

Donations to the fund can be made by cheque payable to the Rugby League Benevolent Fund sent to the headquarters at Red Hall, Leeds, LS17 8NB. You can further help by using a Gift Aid application form which means that for every pound donated the fund gets an extra 28 pence from the Inland Revenue. The RFL Benevolent Fund registered charity number is 1109858.

Garry Clarke

Mike Gregory

Garry Clarke reflects on Mike Gregory's time at Warrington, while **Huw Richards** reviews his hard-hitting new autobiography.

At Warrington Wolves last home game of the 2006 season the Warrington Past Players Association inducted Mike Gregory into their Hall of Fame. Aged 42, the youngest member of the club's Hall of Fame, Mike watched from the stands as his two young sons, Sam and Ben, accepted the award for their father on the Halliwell Jones pitch.

Signed from Wigan St Pats during the summer of 1982, Mike made his first team debut against Huyton in a Lancashire Cup tie at Wilderspool Stadium on 5 September 1982. Playing 246 times for Warrington, scoring 45 tries, his last game for Warrington was against Leeds at Headingley on 2 February 1994 in the Challenge Cup. These are just the bare facts of the playing career of one of the best, and most influential, players to wear the famous Primrose and Blue colours.

Starting his playing career in the days when top flight rugby league was still a part-time sport in which the top players also had full-time jobs to pay their way, Mike, always trying to improve his game and his fitness was a founder member of the Wire Wide Awake Club. This was a group of young players who undertook voluntary morning training sessions, before going to their day jobs, in addition to their official twice a week club sessions.

After a brief summer stint down under with Cronulla Sutherland under the coaching of the legendary Jack Gibson, Mike returned to Warrington without a day job and became one of the first of the new breed of full-time professional rugby league player, years before the introduction of Super League. This was a competition which his high tempo all action style would have been ideal for, but which he never played in, as his playing career ended in 1995, one year before the start of Super League.

Never giving less than 100 percent in any game in which he played, Mike turned in many outstanding performances for both Warrington and Great Britain, but two in particular will remain in the memory forever.

His best performance in the primrose and blue was his Herculean effort in the 1990 Challenge Cup final which to most neutral observers should have won him the Lance Todd Trophy. At times he seemed to be taking on the Wigan pack single-handed. He scored a try just before half-time to drag his side back into contention and set up a late consolation try for Dave Lyon. But it was one 70-yard run late in the game, which showed his commitment to the Wire cause. With the game already lost he chased back forcing one Wigan player after another to hand the ball on until finally the numbers game beat him as Mark Preston touched down in the corner, albeit after a brilliant last ditch tackle on Shaun Edwards.

Making his Great Britain debut in 1987, he will be best remembered on the world stage for the try he scored late in the second half of the third test against Australia at the Sydney Football Stadium in July 1998. Racing 70 yards, with legs pumping like pistons and head thrust back, he left Australian superstars such as Wally Lewis and Wayne Pearce trailing in his wake to score a never to be forgotten try. Ignoring the supporting Martin Offiah, the run typified his determination to succeed even when the odds seemed to be stacked against him, a determination he still has today.

Playing 20 times for Great Britain, he is Warrington's most capped test player and when in 1990 he led Great Britain on their tour of the Southern Hemisphere he became only the second Warrington player, after Eric Fraser, to captain the national side.

A player whose career had always been hampered by injuries, Mike returned from the tour carrying a number of injuries. He then suffered a serious knee injury in a Lancashire Cup tie against Runcorn Highfield in 1990. He admits he was never the same player after that injury, but as one would expect he tried several times to his wav back, but after only sporadic appearances on the next four years he finally left Wilderspool during the summer of 1994, linking up with his former Great Britain team mate Andy Gregory, by now coach of Salford.

Mike only played a handful of games for the Reds as his injuries took their toil on his battered body and he hung his boots up, embarking on a successful coaching career.

A Wiganer adopted by Warringtonians as one of their own, Mike's relationship with the Wire fans was summed up by his comment to the press after the aforementioned Challenge Cup Final defeat by his hometown team. Slumped in the dressing rooms, with tears in his eyes, after one of the finest games he had ever played all he could say was "what about all those fans we have let down". A relationship which continues to the present day as demonstrated by the thousands of Warrington supporters who turned up to support Mike at his benefit on a freezing cold day in January 2005 and saluted not only a great rugby league player, but also a great person.

Biting Back
The Mike Gregory Story
Mike Gregory with Erica Gregory, Steve Manning and Dave Hadfield

But for the bite of an Australian insect, British league fans might well now be discussing Mike Gregory's prospects as Great Britain coach in succession to Brian Noble. So the story told here is not merely one of an exceptional individual, but of a man whose most significant league achievements possibly still lay ahead of him. And those achievements were already pretty considerable – a top player for a decade who both played for and captained his country, scored perhaps the most memorable try (Sydney 1988) – as well as producing undoubtedly the finest attempt (Wembley 1990) to prevent one – of those times, and coached teams to the Grand and Challenge Cup finals.

Not least of his talents, evident as both captain and coach, has been bringing people together for a common purpose. That gift applies to books as well. The risk with such a long list of collaborators is that of a bland or garbled narrative and it says much for Gregory and his three co-writers (plus Andy Wilson, acknowledged in Dave Hadfield's typically warm introduction) that a clear, consistent voice emerges.

The tale of his early and playing years is amiably told, that of a Wigan lad with a propensity for getting into physical scrapes – had the prognosis following a broken jaw at the age of four been fulfilled, league fans would never have heard of him – that evidently followed him through life.

Fastidious readers may wish for fewer incidents concluding with 'blood and snot everywhere', while the tale of his courtship of Erica can expect a second career as a staple in anthologies devoted to the Northern male. All of this, though, is part of Gregory's charm. Nothing is less appealing than the autobiography whose narrator is the impeccable hero of every scene. Here, more often than not, the fall guy is Gregory himself. The much admired model pro of the late 1980s and early 1990s is quite willing

Mike Gregory in action for Warrington (Photo: David Williams, rlphotos.com)

to remind us of, and castigate himself for, stupidities such as breaking his hand showboating just before a cup final and still playing or the misfiring humour of his 'tough shit' comment to New Zealand after winning a test match.

As England Academy coach, he points out he was "Probably the only person in the history of the game not to select Stuart Fielden". There is an awareness of himself and others evident in his choice of anecdotes and his observation of characters like Warrington's extraordinary kitman 'Ocker' Aspinall – whose many idiosyncrasies included, in effect, selling players their own shirts – and a succession of eminent coaches.

Those accounts make it clear that, aside from his other achievements, Gregory's playing career was also the ideal preparation for his subsequent incarnation as a coach. He was able to take in the varying philosophies and styles of figures as varied as Maurice Bamford, Jack Gibson, Mal Reilly and Phil Larder – to analyse, interpret and distil those lessons, along with those of his own knowledge, outlook and experience, into a philosophy of coaching that emphasised managing players by understanding and responding to individual needs and temperament.

All of this would be interesting in itself. Inevitably though, it will be overshadowed (at least for everyone not from Warrington) by Gregory's account of his time as coach of Wigan and the illness that led to its curtailment.

There are insights here that go beyond his own harrowing experiences to say something about the reasons for Wigan's decline in recent years. Gregory was long aware of a tendency to neglect local talent – he was a victim himself as a teenager of no interest to his home-town club until he signed elsewhere – but underlines quite how much it has cost in recent years as youngsters of proven talent have been discarded only to prosper elsewhere – this review is being written 48 hours after watching Luke Robinson and David Hodgson perform brilliantly for Salford against Harlequins – while expensive buy-ins have stumbled. This failing is laid firmly at the door of an arguably over-interventionist management, incarnated by Maurice Lindsay, taking rugby decisions that should be left to coaches.

This failing pales, though, alongside Lindsay and club owner David Whelan's handling of Gregory's illness. Wigan, it is worth remembering, have a history of fallouts with key figures, at different times estranging local heroes as iconic as Jim Sullivan and Billy Boston, almost as long as their honours board.

Nothing, though, quite like this. Gregory tells the story of the diagnosis – a long drawn-out process in itself – and development of his illness with clarity, frankness and an absence of self-pity. He leaves little doubt that if his illness were curable by ability to look harrowing misfortune in the face and simple determination to overcome it, he would get better.

In the telling we see rugby league at its best. Gregory talks of the support he has received from Warrington, from the players union and other players – there is that authentic league rarity, a heart-warming anecdote about Ellery Hanley – from doctors and the indomitable Erica.

The exception to this is his employer. Lindsay promised in the early stages that Wigan would look after Gregory. Their support has fallen short even of that outlined in Churchill's famous order 'send all help short of actual assistance'. Gregory had to pay the travel and medical costs involved in treatment in the United States. Energy that could have been devoted to fighting the illness had instead to go on an employment tribunal. It was Warrington who staged a testimonial match. Lindsay is depicted as a figure of feline slipperiness, Whelan one of monumental insensitivity. The moment in which Whelan, drawing on experience in his own family, effectively tells Gregory that there is no hope for him, chills but does not necessarily surprise – as Gregory implies, it is all too typical of a certain type of businessman who feels that his skill at making money conveys infallible judgment on any and every other subject.

Whelan's praise for Erica as 'a real fighter' for her husband was entirely justified, but conveyed at a comparatively early stage in the proceedings the club's view that they were in a fight – that a disabled employee was not someone to be supported and who, given the right assistance, could have continued to coach, but a problem to be eliminated. Gregory's battle from then will also, one suspects, acquire a second literary incarnation as a classic case history of a disabled employee forced to fight for his rights.

Many readers of this book may end regretting that Wigan's relegation battle of 2006 had not ended so happily. It is characteristic of Gregory that he would not agree. He makes it clear that he still wishes the club and Brian Noble well, and reserves his bitterness specifically for Whelan and Lindsay.

Where all will agree is in wishing one of the outstanding figures of the last two decades of British rugby league – a magnificent player turned fine coach, both talents underpinned by his being a decent, courageous and self-aware human being – well in his battle against the depredations of illness.

Biting Back: The Mike Gregory Story
Mike Gregory with Erica Gregory, Steve Manning and Dave Hadfield, Vertical Editions £17.99
(hardback 287 pages, ISBN 1- 094091-18-0, 978-1-904091-18-9, published 2006 in hardback)

The Mike Gregory Trust Fund

The Mike Gregory Trust Fund was set up by friends and family to help raise funds for Mike's treatment. Mike has been overwhelmed by the support he has received since his illness was made public. Flanked by his family and backed by an army of friends and former teammates, the depth of concern shown for him has been a reflection of his standing in the game. The same goes for the legions of people who only knew him vantage point of the stands and terraces.

Mike holds a special place in the public's affections, which have raised thousands for his Trust Fund and underlined the warmth of the human spirit.

The first event was Hike for Mike, when fans, legends and rugby league stars marched from Haigh Hall to the JJB Stadium. That was followed by a string of other money raising events including Warrington's benefit match, a triathlon by Hindley-based athlete Adele Oliver, various dinners and events at functions hosted by the Great Britain Lions Association. There was a 150-mile bike ride from Whitehaven to Sunderland, which was led by Mike's friend Chris Hurst, a sponsored walk by Swinton and Widnes fans from their respective home grounds to the Halliwell Jones Stadium on National League Finals day. Thousands of fans from many clubs turned out for the Mike Gregory Challenge Match organised by his old amateur club Wigan St Patricks.

Mike said "Right from the beginning when people found out I was ill, they have been amazing." To make a donation to the Trust fund send a cheque, made payable to "The Mike Gregory Trust Fund" to: The Mike Gregory Trust Fund, 12 Lord Street, Wigan WN1 2BN, or visit www.mikegregorytrust.co.uk

Garry Clarke

20 years at Wigan St Patrick's

Simon Lowe talks to Wigan St Patrick's coach Dave Ruddy.

A Carnegie Challenge Cup tie at home against Leeds Met University on Saturday 3 February 2007 was quite simply a game that the vast majority of 'Pat's folk' expected us to win at a canter. One should never pre-judge an event however, and the 38-24 winning score line in favour of the students surely testifies to the 'you never know what can happen' philosophy. The team from Leeds, representing the competition's sponsors, were the best team that Wigan St Patrick's had faced all season so far.

St Patricks coach Dave Ruddy has 20 years experience at *The mighty Wigan Saint Pat's* (a song oft-sung by the players as they approach base on the team coach) and he was 'tingling' with pride that his team had come back from being 24-6 down at half-time. With the score at 24-18, the students were visibly wilting and Pats, who were gaining more confidence by the minute, sent the ball wide. It was intercepted by the Met right-winger who raced 70 yards to place the ball behind the sticks. He seemed to be as quick as Martin Offiah had been in his hey-day. To me that try was the turning point in the game, and St Pat's had to accept defeat gracefully.

Dave Ruddy did just that as he smiled at me outside the ground with a bottle of Grolsch in his hand. Last season we very narrowly missed out on a place in the Grand Final, having lost in extra time. It was also my first introduction to this ruddily-complexioned and altogether hugely, genuinely, affable and jovial man. This season was different but Ruddy's pride in his team had not altered one iota.

"Happy New Year Simon!" he said as he firmly shook my hand outside the dressing rooms just before I sounded him out about my penning this article which he at once acceded to participation in without barely a moment's thought.

"I nearly told the silly old bastard to f... off!"

Oh good heavens I thought... but he was not talking about me. He was talking to a groundsman and me simultaneously. The subject of his derision was a well-known Pat's supporter who is never one to be found short of an opinion.

This fan had, before my brief chat with Dave Ruddy expressed his opinion that St Pat's had hit an all time low. I suppose that this incident clearly highlights that there are always two or more sides to the same story, and that supporters at the same game can see a totally different game. Dave Ruddy continued: "They're the best team we've played... I'm tingling with pride. I'm so proud of how we played!"

The emotion was written all over his face: "We would have done it except for the interception. They (the Mets) were wilting." This was both my and the groundsman's take on the matter.

When the try was scored, I had been some yards away, but within earshot of Pat's chairman William Atherton. His posse always stand behind the sticks and Atherton sends his long-suffering St Patrick's ARLFC 'widow' Janet regular text messages of the score. He is a near neighbour of mine and a completely level-headed as well as rational man albeit not when the first team are in action, together with his son Anthony 'Athi' Atherton.

It was the best game of rugby that I had seen for some time. The Challenge Cup was there in the pavilion and I have never been so close to it; my dad and I enjoyed a picnic that I had prepared earlier. We watched the game; my best mate and my dad loved it.

Derek 'Mr B' Birchall, Wigan rugby league schoolboys coaching wizard and recently retired teacher, and also the man who wetted my appetite for Pat's in summer 2005, said at half time: 'I'm all for spreading the gospel, but not at Pat's' expense.'

In the previous so-near-to Grand Final season I had regularly stood with both Ruddy and Derek post match and it was not uncommon for both to be very forthright with each other. Ruddy simply refers to 'Mr B' as a great person as they both "Don't suffer fools".

We were genuinely stunned at the half-time interval score line, were reflecting on the fact that the television cameras would not be following us in the next round, and also admiring our new advertising hoardings, that the sponsors of the cup and Leeds Met were leaving for us after the afternoon's cup tie.

A Leeds Met official informed me, immediately after the final whistle, and he was clearly delighted, that: 'It was a disciplined game." A passionate Gary Hetherington of Leeds RLFC, and part of the Mets' party looked delighted post match.

I then met St Patrick's ARLFC Open Age coach Dave Ruddy in the club bar on a late February evening. The first open age team have just trained well in awful slushy conditions; the second team are struggling for numbers for the forthcoming Saturday as some of their players are needed by Ruddy. Both teams are away which costs a lot of money in terms of hiring coaches. Indeed the seconds have themselves even sounded out Wigan RUFC, one of Ruddy's old clubs as a player, for player availability. After Ruddy has left to return to work, a club life member says that he is: 'Fully committed and on the ball.'

Ruddy admitted to me that his coaching philosophy is simple. He needs to be at the club as often as he can be, especially on training nights as his presence affects his players. They need to see him there; they all put their bodies on the line for nothing. An equal dislike is that of fickle supporters who pat you on the back and turn their back depending upon whether there has been a victory or a defeat. He himself is a non-salaried coach who does the job for love. His salaried job is that of a BT technician and he works after 9pm so as to not disrupt his commitments to his coaching duties.

Dave Ruddy's coaching career began in 1987 after he was forced to stop playing the game that he passionately loves. His playing career began at under-11 level for St Joseph's RC Primary School near to the centre of Wigan, where he captained the side; he later attended grammar school playing both rugby league and union, to the extent that at under-18 and Colts level he played the XV-a-side code on Saturdays followed by the XIII-a-side code the following day. He had offers to play professionally for Wigan and Widnes, but furthered his career in union. He played for Lancashire Colts; the North of England and attended an England under-19 trial in Birmingham.

For two years he played at Douglas Valley, the home of Wigan RUFC but being one of the team's better players he was to join Orrell RUFC, a move which left him with the tag of traitor, he believes even to this day. Career honours included winning the Lancashire Cup and being runners up in the Northern Merit.

His rugby league career was resurrected between 1983 and 1987 when he played for Salford RLFC. I must have seen him play at this time and his career finally ended with a back injury, uncannily against Wigan. This on the pitch injury however was not the real reason for his enforced retirement from the professional code: an injury at work suffered while mining in a nearby pit was the cause of severe complications.

Ruddy took the Rugby Football League coaching courses, and was phenomenally successful passing with 100%. We reminisced about names of the period such as Jack Melling, who was in charge of the coaching courses and Dennis McHugh.

Thus Dave Ruddy, having stopped playing and been successful with his coaching badges, was offered a chance to become involved in the coaching at Clarington Park, the home of the mighty Wigan St Patrick's ARLFC. He quickly became assistant coach to current president, then first team coach Jimmy Taylor. The club went on to win lots of trophies and Ruddy believes that the first five years of his coaching career were the best. The unexpected BNFL National Cup Final win of 1988 against Elland, in front of record 5,500 crowd at Central Park is still oft-spoken about at the club.

Ruddy recalls that David 'Davie Boy' Jones scored two tries on the day; prior to him playing for Wakefield, Oldham, Leigh, Rochdale, Chorley as well as Burdingkin in North Queensland. Jones still plays for the second team at St Pat's now and again.

In 1992-93 St Pat's were National League Champions and played Hull Dockers in a Charity Shield type game at Blackpool's Stanley Park inside the athletics track at the seaside resort's stadium. Ruddy's men triumphed 14-10.

In 1997 the first team was struggling desperately. The side that had been so successful during the early part of the decade had now disbanded. Ruddy explains that scenario by stating that it is a common phenomenon in the amateur game that players have mortgages, marriages and just drift away from the game in general. However the 1997 season saw a new chairman in Atherton, and the arrival of a 'new kid on the block' as it were with the arrival at the club of Australian Deon Duell.

Deon is currently in his second season at Blackpool Panthers having left Pat's at the end of 2005-06, his last game being the semi-final eliminator against Dewsbury's Thornhill Trojans which had resulted in a 19-14 defeat for Pat's after extra time. At the time I remember Deon as a very confident centre, with a strutting arrogance and disdain for the opposition and injected life into a flagging Pat's team. The team won nine out of 10 games to stay in the Premier Division. It certainly was a nerve-jangling time for all involved, and for Ruddy and Atherton in particular.

Ruddy will not be drawn on who his best three players of his coaching career are (he did inform me, but swore me to secrecy) but he says of Deon Duell: 'He is in my top three of players whom I have coached. Deon is also a lovely man.'

Another recently finished player for the Pat's, but this time due to retirement at the end of last season, is Darren Fletcher. 'Fletch' was a stand-off; former pupil of Derek Birchall and is now Ruddy's assistant coach. Ruddy describes him as: "An awesome player who we badly missed in the Grand Final Eliminator. As my assistant he organizes drills in training sessions and is well respected by the lads."

Ruddy also refers to current captain and loose forward Mel Alker, brother of current Salford City Reds hooker Malcolm Alker, as an awesome presence at the club. Steve Simm is a very effective and classy full-back or centre in the current team and it is evident that Ruddy takes a great deal of pride in coaching both him and Mel Alker. Deon Duell and Darren Fletcher are the players whom Ruddy misses greatly in the current campaign as they were the old heads that he could turn to and rely on in moments of crisis on the pitch.

One burning issue for the club, and for Ruddy, is its ground. In the last 12 months I have paid a handful of visits to the nearby, but a division lower, Ince Rose Bridge ARLFC. Its ground is fairly new; has a superb new indoor training facility and more importantly it is secure, being surrounded by strong perimeter fencing. This is regrettably not the case at Pat's.

This situation clearly matters to Ruddy as he quickly points out to me that one of his ambitions for Pat's is for 'better fencing.' He is appalled that local residents have complained to local councillors that the club should not erect fencing around the ground as they would be left with nowhere to exercise their dogs! Ruddy's players must contend with dog excrement as they attempt to train and play.

One recent horrific story in the local press was that of an open bladed knife being planted into the first team pitch. This was thankfully discovered by one of the groundsmen before anyone was injured. A stunning and starling response from a local resident was allegedly that the club had planted it themselves, in order to prove the need for perimeter fencing.

It is pointed out to me by Ruddy that events are set in place to erect fencing so that the club will be secure in the near future, as well as a club ban on dogs because he has recently received a letter from the juniors club secretary that one of the under-9 players was bitten by a spectator's dog while playing. Ruddy described this recent incident as "A total and utter disgrace."

Ruddy told me that improvements to the ground will also entail a new roof on the club house at a cost of £7,500. The club would also benefit from an indoor facility like the one at near neighbours Rose Bridge.

International coaching is a field of recent experience for Ruddy. President Jimmy Taylor is head coach of the Great Britain Rugby League Community Lions. Ruddy was appointed as assistant coach for a recent four day trip to Perpignan in south west France. This was a trip included four Pat's players. Ruddy described the trip as: "Four great days of back-to-back rugby. We took flights to and from Barcelona and there were twice daily training sessions."

Once again his enthusiasm is written across his face as he tells me how enjoyable and informative the international experience was for him. Indeed his enthusiasm for rugby league is second to none. I tentatively ask him whether he receives any financial remuneration for his coaching duties. "You must be joking! I do it for love," he replies with one of his beaming smiles.

Academies are a topic that we briefly discuss. Not Tony Blair's educational institutions but those at professional clubs. Quite simply they have cost amateur clubs like Pat's a number of players. I believe that some players are reluctant to return to the amateur game if they are unsuccessful at professional level with a club's academy.

Former Pat's old boy and captain Tim Sharkey is a player whom Ruddy wants to mention. He played from full-back to prop and is: "Like a son to me, a special person. I have attended his birthdays, marriage, child's christening... you name it."

He is clearly proud and delighted by the bond which exists between him and his past and present players. Deon Duell stayed at Ruddy's house during his early days at the club. Craig White is another former player whom Ruddy speaks of with genuine pride. White has been involved with Leicester RU and has been a rugby union British Lions conditioner.

Ruddy loves the 'friendships for life' that he has made and will continue to make via his involvement in the game. This may just involve a pint after a game in Hull or even better: "To be dressed in St Pat's colours after a game in Yorkshire or Cumbria; where if you have won then you know that you are a decent side; and to look at the spectacular views of the scenery that is God's own country; and to know after a win that it does not get any better."

He concludes: "Amateur rugby league is the best sport in the world." And with that he leaves to return to work. The time is just approaching 9.30pm ... it has been a training evening when all is said and done.

The decline of English rugby union

Glyn Robbins reflects on problems in the 'other' code.

The recent problems of the England rugby union team have, I'm sure, causing wry smiles and quiet pleasure for many rugby league fans, as well as the entire population of Wales. I can share this Schadenfreude. Nobody likes a clever dick, particularly if he's dressed in a Barbour coat and drives a Range Rover. That said, I was pleased when they won the World Cup in 2003. Despite my name, I am English and like my fellow east Londoner Billy Bragg, I have some sympathy for the idea that English people should be able to express their national pride, without invading someone else's country. But the road for English rugby union has been steadily downhill since and I think there are some interesting aspects to this for both codes.

I have come to see the post-World Cup period as an allegory for New Labour. Of course, both teams wear the red rose, but it goes deeper than that. Like New Labour in 1997, in 2003 English rugby achieved an historic victory that defied history and natural talent. For both teams it was, above all, an effort of will and an almost messianic belief that led to victory. Success was not founded on passion or invention, but on dour managerialism. While New Labour played to Middle England, New England played the percentages – safety-first rugby that left as little as possible to chance, while relying on the sheer bloody-mindedness of some of the older players. Even now, the likes of Martin Johnson and Jason Leonard seem to belong to a bygone era: players who remembered

the amateur days and knew the value of unglamorous sweat and toil. The same could be said for an older generation of Labour politicians, who know what a hard day's work is like, but are now surrounded by 'career' politicians.

The similarities between the two victorious head coaches are also quite striking. They were born within three years of each other and are both hallmarked products of the upper middle class. I'd be surprised if Clive Woodward doesn't support New Labour and of course, after they won, Tony Blair was very keen to support England! While his professed interest in football is, in my opinion, just one of his smaller and less serious lies, it's no surprise that Blair did like rugby at school. Both men enjoy a reputation as smooth media operators and both have prioritised cultivation of the media to a point where the message overwhelms the reality. Listen to Woodward analysing a game and it's quite possible to imagine Blair talking about a war! It's the language of 'tough choices' and 'judgement calls' – the whole lexicon of managerial-speak mixed with psycho-babble that has become so familiar in British society since 1997. Finally, both Blair and Woodward are absolutely rooted in their allegiance, loyalty and deference to the Establishment. Sir Clive would see his knighthood as his just deserts, just as Tony will when he becomes Lord Blair.

When New Labour won they sang 'Things can only get better', but just like the England rugby team, they just keep getting worse! Pride comes before a fall of course, but both are also being exposed by their fundamental lack of substance. New Labour has little or no life outside of Westminster and even after the Word Cup, English rugby union has not been able to escape the limitations of its cultural traditions. For a brief moment, the country got interested in rugby union, but the truth is that it will only ever be a minority sport. The suggestion that it could become a truly 'national' game was an illusion created by marketing men, out for a quick buck, who didn't know what they were talking about – New Labour again! Three years on, the bubble has burst and rugby union has shrunk back to its core support. The loss of morale is apparent in the performance of the England team.

If the Iraq war was Blair's nemesis, the 2004 Lions tour to New Zealand was Woodward's. It went spectacularly wrong from start to finish, but in a distinctly New Labour style. First there was the hype, fuelled by Sir Clive's reputation as a World Cup winner. Then came the bulls..t – the dreadful song and the mission statement. Next, there was the extravagance, waste and complete detachment from everyday life. The team had to have five-star hotels, or they wouldn't play well and in a classic example of New Labour culture, there was a vast retinue of hangers-on, consultants and 'experts' – more chiefs than Indians. Finally, there was the pathetic attempt to massage the news stories. When there was a reported rift between head-coach Woodward and over-rated centre Henson, the Lions management manufactured a photo, engineered by none other than the New Labour spin-master himself, Alastair Campbell. But as with the New Labour government, the fine words were never matched by deeds and the Lions got stuffed.

The final comparison – and perhaps a lesson for New Labour – is the succession. When Woodward went off in a huff, complaining to the end that nobody appreciated him, he was inevitably replaced by his Chancellor, Andy Robinson. Like Gordon Brown, Robinson was portrayed as a more down-to-earth, principled version of his former boss. But he continued the same policy of (neo) conservative rugby and uber-managerialism, with four 'captains' on the pitch, but no clear policy. He didn't last long and with the appointment of Brian Ashton, English rugby seems to have made a return to its more traditional roots. Time will tell if a similar fate awaits Prime Minister Brown and New Labour.

Beyond the individuals, the wider malaise of English rugby union lies in the destructive effects of professionalism and its ugly sister, commercialism. Union has entered a period of wanton consumerism, like private art collectors paying a fortune for a painting no-one will ever see, most recently exemplified by the sad case of Andy Farrell. They've bought the painting, but they don't know where to put it.

The logic of sports history suggests that the England rugby union team will rise again, but probably not in time to defend the World Cup in 2007. The question remains if the Labour Party will ever recover.

Photo: Jason Robinson – international star in both rugby codes. (Peter Lush)

The club they couldn't kill

Glen Dwyer reports from Australia on the Newtown Jets.

The Newtown RLFC, the first club formed in Australian rugby league, last appeared in the NSW Rugby League first grade competition in 1983, now nearly 25 years ago. While the Jets (formerly the Bluebags) have plenty of stories worth telling from the 1980s and 1990s, this article primarily focuses on Newtown's fortunes since 2000 and the old club's prospects for the future. The club celebrated their 99th birthday in January 2007.

Looking into the abyss

Newtown was suspended from the NSW Rugby League's competitions in October 1983 due to spiralling debt levels, falling support in the club's confined inner-city catchment area and the breakdown of negotiations involving a move to the satellite city of Campbelltown in the far south-western rim of the greater Sydney metropolitan region. No doubt Newtown had also been the target of a long-term plan to rationalise the number of Sydney-based clubs in the NSW Rugby League premiership competition.

 The Jets somehow survived as an organisation the next seven years despite not fielding a senior team, due mostly to the tenacity of the club's board members and their stoic determination to get the club back into an acceptable level of senior rugby league activity. Two of those Directors, Barry Vining and Terry Rowney, are still senior figures within the club and are unarguably two of the most significant figures in Newtown's 99-year history. Rowney in particular has ploughed literally millions of dollars from his own pockets and from his string of business enterprises into keeping the club alive, and is regarded as a very much larger-than-life figure in NSW rugby league circles.

The return of those boys in the royal blue jerseys

Newtown's emotional return to senior Rugby League came in 1991 when the Jets joined the NSWRL Metropolitan Cup competition, a third-tier competition that was a direct descendant of the NSWRL Second Division of the 1960s and early 1970s. Former Leeds and Great Britain legend Lewis Jones ended his stellar career in this competition as captain-coach of the Wentworthville club in outer western Sydney. Cronulla-Sutherland and Penrith were promoted into the NSWRL first grade competition from the Second Division ranks back in 1967, but there is no longer any possibility whatsoever of other clubs ever rising from this relatively humble level of rugby league into what is now the National Rugby League (NRL) competition.

 The Jets came into the Metropolitan Cup debt-free, but they certainly weren't one of the wealthier clubs in the competition. In fact, they would have been out-spent several times over by some of their oppositions such as Wentworthville, Ryde-Eastwood, St Mary's and Guildford who were all securely funded by successful licensed clubs (or in NSW street parlance leagues clubs). It remains one of the somewhat bewildering practices at this lower level of rugby league in Sydney that some of these smaller leagues clubs are happy to hurl huge pay packets at very ordinary footballers who in turn play in front of crowds of less than a hundred people, and yet those same clubs' administrators can be complete tightwads when it comes to funding junior and schools development programs in their own area.

Newtown somehow managed to attract a better class of player and the club was administered more professionally, enabling the Jets to dominate the Metropolitan Cup in the nine years, 1991 to 1999, that they participated in this third-tier competition. The Jets won first grade premierships in 1992 and from 1995 to 1997 in succession, as well as being preliminary finalists in 1994 and 1998.

Surviving the Super League war

The Jets had entered into a partnership with South Sydney in late 1994 with the intention of eventually becoming the Rabbitohs' reserve grade team. However, the Super League war burst upon the scene in April 1995 seriously disrupting and weakening every level of the game in Australia for the next three years. To South Sydney's immense credit, they stood by their deal with Newtown for the entire five years until they themselves were culled from the NRL in October 1999. It was a measure of the personal honour and integrity of men like George Piggins who refused to renege on the partnership with Newtown, even though the Rabbitohs had plenty of financial incentive to do so. Souths largely funded Newtown between the years 1995 and 1999 and it was no coincidence that the Jets enjoyed the greatest success (relatively speaking) of their entire club history during this alliance period with South Sydney.

Once were Warriors

Following South Sydney's eviction from the NRL in late 1999, the Newtown club stood alone and impecunious, once again looking at the grim prospect of total oblivion. However, the business nous and strategic thinking of Terry Rowney and Barry Vining, along with another long-time benefactor in business entrepreneur John Singleton, came to the club's rescue. The Jets negotiated an eleventh hour deal with the NRL's Auckland Warriors club, whereby the Newtown Jets would become the Warriors' Sydney-based feeder club. The rationale for the Warriors was that the agreement would place their reserve players into a higher standard of football and a tougher proving ground than the New Zealand domestic competition. Newtown would be playing in the NSWRL First Division competition, soon to be relabelled as the NSWRL Premier League. This was a much higher standard of Rugby League than the lowly Metropolitan Cup, with the Jets own playing resources to be reinforced by up to 15 of the Auckland Warriors own contracted players. This partnership deal was only given the go-ahead barely two weeks before the competition commenced, with the Newtown players in the opening competition round against the St George Dragons meeting each other for the first time in the dressing rooms prior to the game. In typically flamboyant style, the Jets club patron John Singleton hosted a superbly-catered 2000 season launch function at the Sydney Cricket Ground, where Singo's Jets team of 1981 had narrowly lost to Parramatta in the Grand Final that year.

The 2000 season proved to be relatively successful for the Jets, although they failed to draw the larger crowds that had been budgeted for by playing in a higher standard competition than the decidedly downmarket Metropolitan Cup. Still, a crowd of more than 2,000 turned out to see the Jets make their return to Henson Park, the club's home ground since 1936, for the first time that season. The Jets didn't return to using Henson Park for all of their home games until the 2001 season.

Players familiar to English readers who turned out with Newtown in 2000 included identities such as Mark Tookey, Clinton Toopi, Wairangi Koopu, Jerry Seu Seu, Awen Guttenbeil, Cliff Beverley, Joe Galuvao Shontayne Hape, David Myles and Terry Hermannson. The Jets certainly had their moments in that season but ultimately missed the play-offs on a points for-and-against count-back. This partnership was destined to be short-lived as the cash-strapped Auckland Warriors went into liquidation while the new consortium, fielding a team to be known as the New Zealand Warriors, chose not to retain the effective, but expensive, Sydney-based feeder club arrangement. Six of the Auckland Warriors players who had played with Newtown in 2000 went on to be key members of the New Zealand Warriors NRL Grand Final team in 2002. One thing that the whole 2000 season experience proved was that the battered old club in the royal blue colours could still 'cut the mustard' against high-standard opposition playing at major rugby league venues.

Nobody loves you when you're down and out

The Jets once again stood on their own and competed in the NSWRL Premier League for four tough seasons from 2001 to 2004, during which the club's operating and administrative costs were largely underwritten by the deep pockets of Terry Rowney. 2001 proved to be particularly tough going, with the Jets claiming last place by a proverbial country mile and clocking up 18 losses in a row. Knowledgeable fans wisecracked that Newtown was out to overtake Doncaster's infamous run of losses as portrayed in the classic 1981 Yorkshire Television documentary *Another Bloody Sunday*.

There was distinct improvement in the on-field performances and in club morale in the subsequent seasons of 2002 to 2004 where the combination of Terry Rowney's continued financial backing, the blood-and-guts coaching style of the redoubtable Colin Murphy and the recruitment of several more than useful players saw the Jets draw well clear of the wooden-spoon danger zone. Indeed, Newtown challenged for a place in the finals series right up until the final competition rounds in both 2003 and 2004.

Henson Park hosted a senior level international Rugby League game for the first time in February 2003 when Newtown played the touring USA Tomahawks. More than 2,500 supporters turned out in appallingly humid conditions to see the Jets win easily but more importantly, impress the NSWRL hierarchy that the club was capable of hosting a major occasion and that the Jets were back in business for the long run. Tomahawks players Bob Balachandran and Jeff 'Sergeant Slaughter' Preston impressed keen judges as to what class rugby league players they could have been if they had taken the game up at a younger age.

The Wild Bunch

Some of the better known players who appeared with the Jets in between 2002 and 2004 included an eclectic parade of NRL discards, young hopefuls, rogues and more than a few 'Jack the lads' whose NRL careers had been terminated for reasons of misbehaviour. Classy half-back Craig Field joined the club in mid-2003 after a controversial past, but he surprised everybody by turning in two superb seasons with the

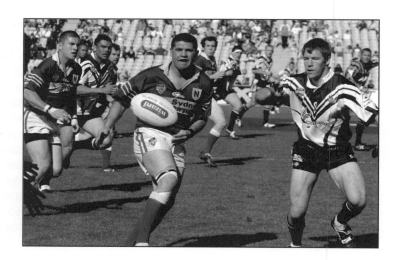

Top: Alf Duncan.

Left: Glen Dwyer, John Raper and Colin Murphy at Newtown jets season launch at the Sydney Cricket Ground, March 2000.

Bottom: Micky Paea in action in the 2006 Grand Final

(All photos: Gary Sutherland Photography, Sydney.)

club. Newtown's innate quirkiness and knockabout ambience seemed to appeal to the street-wise Field, who had previously played with South Sydney, Manly-Warringah, Balmain and Wests-Tigers. The wildcard Darrell Trindall, well known to St Helens supporters for all the wrong reasons, had a short stint with the Henson Park club before the parties agreed to part company.

That tearaway Aboriginal duo of Wes Patten (formerly with Balmain and Gold Coast) and Robbie Simpson (formerly with the London Broncos) laid on some spectacular entertainment at Henson Park, especially during one madcap season when both of these rascals served midweek periodic-detention sentences so that they would be available to play with the Jets on the weekends. Another superbly gifted Koori footballer was the former Manly-Warringah and Cronulla-Sutherland winger Alf Duncan who became a genuine cult figure with the growing Henson Park crowd base. Duncan scored some breathtaking tries, including one 90 metres effort against Parramatta at Henson Park where he sidestepped, outpaced and palmed off no less than seven Eels defenders.

The former Australian test centre Russell Richardson (formerly of Cronulla and Souths) had a guest spell with the Jets in 2003 during which he scored 10 tries in five games while redeeming his self-esteem, his reputation and his professional playing career in the process. Terry Rowney and the colourful players' manager Gavin Orr (himself a former Easts and Newtown player) imported several Kiwi players from the New Zealand Bartercard Cup competition to Henson Park for the 2004 season. From this group James Stosic, Phil Leuluai and the enigmatic Clifford Manua all won themselves contracts with NRL clubs for 2005 and beyond.

Has anybody here seen Murphy

Newtown coach Colin Murphy, who had held the coaching reins from 1994 to 1997 and then again from 2000 to 2005 would be a worthy subject of any future no-holds-barred biography. An irascible, emotion-fuelled figure, Murphy had played with the Jets from 1974 to 1983 and for many Newtown fans he was the living embodiment of the Newtown Jets fabled 'never say die' club ethos. He coached the Jets to a hat-trick of Metropolitan Cup first grade premierships from 1995 to 1997, and on that basis alone has to be a contender for the title of being the most successful coach in the history of the club. In my view, Murphy's greatest coaching achievements were in the years 2001 to 2004 when armed with a peppercorn budget, a motley crew of other clubs' cast-offs from which to choose his squad along with the near-Third World playing and training conditions at Henson Park, Murphy managed to keep the Jets more than competitive against clubs whose operating budgets dwarfed Newtown's many times over. Murphy was not retained as coach beyond the 2005 season and is so often the case in these difficult circumstances the parting was acrimonious. One thing is for sure – when the club's centenary year is celebrated in 2008, Colin Murphy will be justifiably hailed as one of the real giants of the club's history.

Swimming with the Sharks

Yet again through the aegis of those capable directors Terry Rowney and Barry Vining, Newtown entered into a new joint venture with the Cronulla-Sutherland Sharks club for the 2005 season, whereby the Jets would act as the Sharks reserve grade squad. The improvement in the quality of available playing resources was apparent from round one of the 2005 Premier League competition, with the Jets looking like semi-final aspirants from the outset. Newtown had a sensational run of thrilling home ground victories at Henson Park, playing in front of several crowds of more than 2,000 and attracting unprecedented levels of media interest for a Premier League club.

Full-back and winger Nathan Merritt had an extraordinary season, breaking the club's full season points-scoring record and setting a new record for the number of points scored by an individual player in a competition match. Merritt racked up an amazing 40 points in a game against Penrith, including five tries and 10 goals. The Jets reached the Premier League semi-finals series for the first time, bowing out with a narrow loss to the eventual premiers Parramatta in the preliminary final played at Telstra Stadium.

The partnership with Cronulla-Sutherland came to a mutually amicable dissolution at the end of the 2005 season. Although the partnership was an unqualified success on the field, there were issues of logistics, geography and club culture that were difficult to reconcile.

A feather duster one day, a Rooster the next

As one partnership ended, a new one was about to begin. That indefatigable pairing of Rowney and Vining had been busy sounding out potential business partners, pointing to Newtown's improved infrastructure (the Marrickville local government authority had recently weighed in with an $800,000 refurbishment of the Henson Park dressing rooms) and the club's proven track record of being able to run a professional rugby league team efficiently and effectively.

The Jets managed to strike a new agreement with one of the NRL powerhouses, the mighty Sydney Roosters (the former Eastern Suburbs). This was a joint venture that had genuine long-term prospects – both clubs were NSWRL 1908 foundation clubs, both had shared the tenancy of Henson Park in recent years, there was a perceived synchronicity between the two clubs and there had been previous overtures about a joint venture between the two organisations. Sydney Roosters legend Arthur Beetson openly declared his support for a partnership with the Jets, stating that such a deal "should have been stitched together 15 years earlier!"

This type of joint venture between rugby league clubs might seem mystifying to British readers but there is a compelling financial rationale from the NRL club's perspective. Significant savings can be made by out-sourcing an NRL club's Premier League or reserve grade team, with the non-NRL partner being able to cover a wide of operational costs on behalf of the NRL club, freeing up scarce funds for other uses. However, the NRL club has to be certain that their own full-time contracted players will be properly looked after in terms of training and match preparation requirements by the partnership club.

The new Roosters-Jets partnership began somewhat shakily with some early season reverses, but after about five 2006 competition rounds the new look Jets hit full stride and rarely travelled in lower than second place on the premiership table for the remainder of the season. Once again big crowds turned out at Henson Park to see the team in the time-honoured Newtown colours serving it up to traditional 1908 opponents like South Sydney, North Sydney, Western Suburbs and Balmain.

So near and yet so far

The Jets strode authoritatively into another finals series and after thrilling wins over Penrith and St George-Illawarra faced up to those old foes Parramatta in the 2006 NSWRL VB Premier League Grand Final at Telstra Stadium, shown on live TV across eastern Australia before an estimated audience of more than 750,000 viewers, as well as 80,000 people in attendance at the Olympic Stadium.

As has so often been the case in Newtown's chequered history, there was to be no fairy-tale ending. The teams finished deadlocked at 19-all at fulltime, with Parramatta winning 20-19 by kicking a field-goal in golden point extra time. Despite the terrible disappointment of losing by the narrowest of margins, Jets Director Terry Rowney had this to say: "After everything that this old club has survived and after everything we've been through in the past 25 years, who are we to be disappointed with getting the chance to play on Grand Final day at Telstra Stadium and to appear on live national television? 23 years ago we were lying in the grave with the dirt being shovelled into our faces!"

The oldest club in Australian rugby league mightn't have won the 2006 NSWRL Premier League Grand Final but they surely won the admiration of rugby league fans everywhere with their fierce determination to survive and their ability to bounce back as a going concern.

Reading the tea leaves

What does the future hold for the Newtown Jets? Obviously consolidating the existing partnership with the Sydney Roosters has to be a priority. It is for an initial five year deal with an option for a further five years. There's no doubting that the club would find it difficult to compete in the Premier League competition as a stand-alone entity and there's little doubt that current sponsorship support and crowd support would dwindle away if the team was in the wilderness for an extended period. Likewise it is difficult to see the Newtown Jets prospering in a lower echelon competition with no-name opponents as in the Metropolitan Cup days of the 1990s.

The Jets have a small licensed club of their own - the Jets Sports Club in Tempe, several kilometres away from Henson Park. This is a small enterprise unable to provide the hundreds of thousands of dollars necessary to sustain a team effectively in the Premier League competition.

Rugby league in Australia has certainly stabilised itself since the ravages of the Super League war of the mid-1990s, but the game faces fierce competition for crowds and sponsorship dollars from the other football codes and other sports in Australia. The state governments in NSW and Queensland have imposed tough legislative regimens on licensed clubs, meaning that the flow of poker machine dollars into rugby league's coffers will be more restricted in the future.

While the Newtown club has shown it can ride the waves of Dame Fortune's adversity by having survived against all the odds for so long, one gets the distinct feeling that the times are never going to get any easier for the perennially-battling Newtown Jets.

Glen Dwyer is a Director and the media officer at Newtown Jets. For more information about the club, visit www.newtownjets.com

The curious case of the Universal Football League

Tony Collins recalls the Australian rules and rugby league merger idea of 1933

In the winter of 1933 the Australian sports scene was presented with perhaps its most dramatic proposal ever: that Australian rules football and rugby league football should merge together to form what was to be known as the Universal Football League. Revealed on the front page of the Sydney sports weekly, the *Referee*, the goal of the merger would be to develop 'one common code of football for Australia', that would be to the Australian winter what cricket was to its summer. Coming just months after the Bodyline tour of Douglas Jardine's English cricket team had seemingly driven a wedge between the two leading sporting nations of the British Empire, the merger seemed to point the way to a football code that was in origin and in geography wholly Australian.

The idea had been mooted in early July 1933 by Horrie Miller, secretary of the New South Wales Rugby League (NSWRL). He had been in Melbourne to see the departure of the Kangaroos to Britain and had travelled back to Sydney with Con Hickey, secretary of both the Australian National Football Council (ANFC) and the Victorian Football League (VFL, the forerunner of today's Australian Football League). Hickey was going north for the eighth Australian National Football Carnival, which was being held for only the second time in Sydney in August, and on the journey north Miller had apparently suggested that they explore the possibilities for a merged game.

As announced to the press, the road to the new merged game was simple. A conference was to be held between the NSWRL and the ANFC during August 1933 to coincide with the Sydney Australian rules carnival. Featuring representative sides from all Australian states, the carnival was seen by the ANFC as a major evangelical event in the previously unpropitious territory of league-dominated Sydney. But now it appeared that the carnival could be a harbinger of much more important events. The NSWRL/ANFC conference would, it was envisaged, be the start of a process whereby rule changes would be gradually adopted by each sport to bring them into line with each other. The immediate aim of the meeting would be to formulate, in the words of Hickey: "a proposal of devising ways and means of an amalgamation ... by adoption of a common code of laws of the game to operate throughout Australia, and eventually the world, incorporating the best features of the rugby league code and the Australian."

To emphasise the joint nature of the initiative, Miller underlined Hickey's sentiments and went on to state that the ultimate goal of the conference would be to establish a code of football rules that would:

1. be just as common to the whole of Australia as the laws of cricket;
2. provide the requisite recreation to the players; and
3. provide football with greater box office appeal to the public.

Initially, the proposal generated much enthusiasm among the administrators of the two sports. "Just imagine it," said James Joynton-Smith, the patron of the NSWRL, "the game featuring that outstanding high-marking and cultivated drop-kicking of the Australian rules, and those brilliant passing movements, sizzling wing runs, and the side-stepping and dodging of rugby." Shortly after his return to Sydney in late July Miller published a draft set of rules which aimed to do just that. It envisaged a game of 15 players per side on an oval pitch. Tries were to be worth three points and goals two points. Rugby league tackle and play-the-ball rules would be used, but the scrum would be replaced by the referee bouncing the ball.

Offside, in rugby league terminology, would be allowed for players attempting to catch the ball from a punt. Standard rugby posts would be used but the Australian rules' point posts would be removed. Running with the ball was to be encouraged, and the knock-on and forward pass rules of rugby would be retained, which meant that bouncing the ball during a run and the hand-pass would be abolished. Full rugby tackling would be allowed, but only from the waist down, and shepherding and tackling airborne players would be outlawed. On paper, it seemed to some to be a workable plan.

It was at this point that the cold light of reality began to shine through. Harold 'Jersey' Flegg, chairman of the NSWRL and Miller's great rival, declared that he had no interest in a merged game and would not even attend the conference with the ANFC. "It involves matters much greater than drafting the new rules … the original and existing games have their own powerful appeal to their players and public, and [have] the sentiments which history inspires," he told the press.

The Queensland Rugby League followed Flegg's lead and also refused to participate. Rumours circulated that the idea was merely a publicity stunt to promote the Sydney Carnival, so much so that the ANFC's Mr Stokes felt compelled to deny them. The question of how the proposals would affect rugby league relations with Britain was also raised. And Con Hickey backtracked somewhat by stating that he was more interested in promoting inter-state contests between NSW and Victoria than a completely new sport. The programme for the Carnival itself contained an article that seemed to discount completely the idea of international competition for the new code; it would be 'a code that would prove popular in every state and be purely national'.

At a practical level, the proposed rules raised more questions than they answered. The most obvious was that Australian rules did not have an offside rule whereas rugby league had very tightly defined laws on offside. Hickey told the press in a somewhat blasé fashion that the offside problem "is rather complicated. Still we could look at it from every angle and I have no doubt arrive at a satisfactory conclusion." Miller's reply was even more unconvincing as he waved aside the potential difficulties with the claim that the NSWRL "possess a certain amount of administrative and inventive genius".

The proposal collapsed at the very point at which it should have taken off. On Friday 11 August the first, and only, experimental match was played at Sydney's Agricultural Grounds. It was played XIV-a-side under slightly different rules to the ones proposed by Miller. Effectively Australian football rules applied in the middle two quarters of the pitch and rugby league rules in each of the end quarters. The two teams were made up of junior Queensland rules players, many of whom allegedly carried sheets of paper with the new rules written on them. Whether this was true or not, the match was clearly a farce and its seriousness for the future of the two sports was demonstrated by the ANFC president, Norwood's E. H. Tassie, who told his companions to expect him back from the match no later than 9pm.

At the NSWRL's general committee meeting the following week, S.G. Ball proposed that the fusion discussions be abandoned and that Miller's report on the discussions should not even be circulated to the NSW clubs. A furious row allegedly broke out between Miller and Jersey Flegg, who accused Miller of disloyalty to the game. Not a single delegate spoke in favour of the fusion discussions and by a margin of 15 votes to

10 it was decided not to circulate the report. The ill-feeling between Miller and Flegg was smoothed over somewhat with the unanimous passing of a motion 'repudiating' suggestions of disloyalty on the part of any members of the committee, although the bad blood between the two continued to flow over the next two decades. Hearing the result of the NSWRL meeting the ANFC council decided to 'take no further action in the matter'.

The fusion proposal died as quickly as it was born and was never raised again.

New rules for hard times?

But this was not the first time such discussions had been held. Most of the protagonists, not to mention the press, were well aware of two previous meetings that had been held between the two codes to discuss the possibility of fusion, the first in 1908 and the second in 1914.

The first meeting had taken place when the first Australian rugby league touring team departed for Britain from Melbourne in August 1908. Their arrival in Victoria coincided with the Golden Jubilee carnival of Australian rules, which, like the 1933 Carnival, included rules teams from every state and also one from New Zealand. Tour managers J. J. Giltinan, Bill Cann and Jack Fihelly met briefly with representatives of the VFL to discuss the possibility of a merged game. There was undoubtedly a political and possibly entrepreneurial element to this and to the subsequent meetings. The leaders of both the NSWRL and the VFL were skilled in the arts of organisational politics, having decisively defeated their respective incumbent governing bodies, the NSW rugby union and the Victorian Football Association (VFA). The arrival of their distant competitors in the cities they dominated would have alerted both their curiosity and their defensive instincts. Attempts, sincere or otherwise, to co-opt the arriviste threat was an astute tactical move.

The 1908 and 1914 meetings must also be seen in the context of the revolution which was taking place in world rugby in the first decade of the new century. Rugby league's abandonment of the line-out and introduction of the play-the-ball, the reduction in the number of players to XIII, and the overturning of the amateur shibboleths had put rugby in a state of flux. The idea that those developments could be taken further to incorporate Australian rules football would not have been perceived as too far-fetched to the men who had led the overthrow of the rugby union authorities in NSW and Queensland.

This self-confidence was clearly apparent in the 1914 meeting. In July of that year a rugby league match had been held in Melbourne between the British touring side and NSW to promote the game in Victoria. The match had been preceded by a rules game between Beverley and Carlton and on 4 August (a momentous day in history for far more important reasons than mere football) the ANFC voted to organise a conference with the NSWRL to discuss a common set of rules. Although that has generally been thought to be the end of the matter, the two sides actually met on 2 November 1914 and a copy of the minutes of their discussions survives in the J. C. Davis Papers at Sydney's Mitchell Library.

Reading the minutes it is clear that many of the 1933 proposals, and particularly the rules under which the exhibition match was staged, were simply a rehash of these earlier discussions. For example, the idea of the middle half of the pitch being Australian rules and the two end quarters being rugby league rules comes from this meeting. The pitch

78

itself would measure 170 yards long by 100 yards wide. In first 45 yards of each half 'modified rugby league rules' would be played but in the middle 70 yards Australian rules would be played. Goals were to be 18 feet wide with a crossbar 10 feet high. Tries would be worth three points and goals one point, with a 'flying goal', a goal kicked while running would score two points. Teams would be XV players per side, the scrum would replaced with a bounced ball, and the rugby league tackle rule introduced. The aim of these proposals was summed up in the remark of the NSWRL's Ted Mead: "undoubtedly the foot passing in the Australian game is brilliant, and the hand passing in the Rugby game is brilliant. Would it not be possible to put these features into one game?"

As in 1933, it is also quite clear that neither side had much idea about the other game. The NSWRL's Johnny Quinlan sought to persuade the VFL of the efficacy of scrums: "The scrum is not dangerous; really very few accidents result. Tackling was regarded as one of the most spectacular features of rugby." At one point, rugby league's Bill Cann implies that he hasn't even seen a game of Australian rules: "he and his co-delegates did not have a grip of the Australian game. He did not think they could get it in a room," recorded the minutes. The discussion on what rules to retain or discard sounds suspiciously like horse trading: "if we abolish the scrum, you allow the tackle and abolish hand passing forward", says one of the NSW representatives. The conference lasted two days and ended with the somewhat contradictory recommendation that exhibition matches should be organised but that "it would be inadvisable at the present juncture to publish the result of their deliberations". Unsurprisingly, given that the country had flung itself behind Britain's war effort, nothing more was heard about the discussions.

But by 1933 the world had moved on. Rugby league had consolidated and deepened its position as the dominant football code in NSW and Queensland while Australian rules stood unchallenged as the football code of the southern states. Given the obvious problems with the idea of a fusion, one must ask why it was mooted again. The fact that it was only being raised at the time of the Sydney carnival - and the proposal had only ever been raised when either a big rugby league match was held in Melbourne or a major Australian rules event was held in Sydney - suggests that there was an element of public relations and political manoeuvring to it.

Economic factors also perhaps played a role. In 1914 the NSWRL was dissatisfied with the poor returns it was making on both outgoing and incoming tours; the 1908 tour to England had made a huge loss, for example. The depression of the early 1930s had reduced spectator numbers at club matches in Sydney to some extent, but for finals and internationals crowds remained robustly healthy. The first test match of the 1932 Ashes series brought 70,204 people to the Sydney Cricket Ground, then the biggest crowd ever at a football match in Australia and one which would not be exceeded at a VFL Grand Final until 1938. The prospect of a game that could offer regular inter-state matches would have been attractive to the NSWRL, especially if the matches could replicate the success of cricket clashes between NSW and Victoria.

Despite this, none of the discussions appear to have sparked even the curiosity of football supporters in Melbourne or Sydney. Indeed, it is difficult to find any report of the proposals or discussions in the Melbourne press. The 1933 discussion ended almost as soon as the Sydney carnival was over without a single public voice being raised in favour of the proposal, lending weight to the idea that 'merger' was merely a public relations exercise. As Charles Brownlow noted during the 1914 discussions, 'the supreme test must necessarily be public approval'. But the sporting public of NSW and Victoria did not show any interest in, much less approved of, an artificial attempt by administrators to suck a new sport out of their thumbs.

Evolution of the football codes

On the evolutionary tree of football, Australian rules emerged from the same branch as the other handling codes, albeit slightly earlier. Although it is often claimed that the Australian game is unique, this is a geographic rather than a technical judgement. Indeed, there is a much stronger argument that association football, despite its ubiquity, is the unique code of football because of its prohibition on handling the ball and tightly prescribed tackling laws. The origins of the sport can be traced directly back to the football played at Rugby school. The use of the rugby-derived ball, the mark and even behinds - variants of which were used in rugby in the 1880s - demonstrate the survival of rugby DNA in the AFL's bloodstream even today. As late as the 1940s it was common for English visitors to Australia to refer to the sport as 'Australian rugby'.

Although regional and cultural differences have played significant roles in the evolution of the handling codes, much of the development of the laws of the games of league, Australian, American, Canadian and, more recently, rugby union football was and is based on developing solutions to the problems posed by the original rules of Rugby football. The two key problems with which the codes have always grappled are those of the importance of offside and what to do when a player is tackled in possession of the ball.

The offside issue was one of the first to be settled in Australian rules through the simple expedient of not having an offside rule. For the other codes, their more direct links with rugby rules meant that offside was more problematic. The American and Canadian games overcame the shortcomings of the complexities of rugby's offside by sanctioning the forward pass and allowing receivers to run downfield. In 1933 there was significant tension between league's offside rule and the way the game was played. Looking at footage of the 1932 rugby league Ashes test series in Australia, one can see that a major feature of the game was the kicking duel, in which each side's full-back would kick the ball far down field, hoping to catch the opposite full-back out of position or force a mistake. The British captain, Jim Sullivan, was a master of this tactic. But the offside rule meant that players could not advance on the opposing full-back unless he moved, and two good full-backs could keep a kicking duel going for many minutes, effectively bringing the game to a halt.

The idea that the offside rule should be suspended so that the full-back could be challenged when catching the ball may have had some appeal, especially if it led to the introduction of the flying mark. The rule discussions could therefore have been seen as a way of revivifying the mark in rugby league, which had practically died out, although it did not finally disappear from the rule book until the 1960s. It is interesting that in 1914 Charles Brownlow noted that John Clifford, the manager of the English league touring side, had commented how much he liked features of the Australian game, such as the long kicking and each player taking his own shot at goal, both of which had been features of rugby when he had played in the 1880s.

For the Australian rules side, the discussions were a way of engaging with the second and most intractable problem that bedevils all handling forms of football: what to do with the ball when the player with the ball is tackled? American and Canadian football had solved the question with the development of the snap at the line of scrimmage and rugby league had done so by allowing the tackled player to rise and play the ball behind him. But in this respect Australian rules had remained somewhat closer to its Rugby School roots. Its insistence that once a player was held by a tackler the ball had to be disposed of, by either dropping, kicking or hand-passing it, was closely related to the rugby union principle that a tackled player on the ground had to release the ball to allow to be played by the feet. However, the reality of playing football meant that players were unwilling to release the ball when it was not to their advantage. Furthermore, the uncertain mechanics of retrieving the released ball meant that ugly loose scrummaging in rugby union or scrambling for the ball on the ground in Australian rules would quite often be the result.

As much was conceded by Charles Brownlow in the 1914 discussions: "one very fine point was when a man was caught or when he was only touched, it was not a satisfactory point in the Australian game, and the players here might be able to adopt the rugby tackle in a modified form." Con Hickey was also critical of his sport's tackling rules in the 1933 discussions and told the *Referee* that the league rule would "wipe out a tremendous lot of the free kicks now given in our game". It may well have been the case at the time that, from a Australian rules perspective, the rugby league play-the-ball rule - an evolutionary mid-point between the uncontrolled rugby union release of the ball and the totally controlled North American snap - would have appeared to be one solution to the scramble on the ground following the surrender of the ball during a tackle.

Perhaps paradoxically, the discussions on how to merge the rules of the two games underlined the extent to which Australian rules was historically a form of rugby. Leaving aside the practicalities of changing the culture of the two sports, the fundamental problem of the merged rules that were drawn up in 1914 and 1933 was that they would lead to the league-derived rules being quickly abandoned. For if there was no offside rule, why should players bother passing the ball or even scoring tries? The most effective tactic would be to kick the ball as far as possible downfield with the aim of scoring goals. Hickey himself anticipated that this would be a problem during the 1914 discussion, arguing the rules players would not 'attack in the sense understood by the Rugby players. They would be more likely to shoot the ball from one point to another, and secure a goal before an attack could be developed.' Indeed, league dealt was to deal with a similar problem in the early 1970s when, with tries then worth three points and drop-goals two points, a number of teams used the tactic of simply advancing downfield with the aim of scoring a drop-goal rather than expending extra effort in attempting to score tries. The solution was to reduce the value of a drop-goal to one point in 1974.

But the offside rule was the glue that held the passing game together. Without it, the game would become primarily a kicking game, demonstrating that Australian rules was, in effect, rugby without offside.

Learning the lessons

To a large extent the 1933 episode is deservedly a footnote in football history. However, its very oddness makes it interesting. The evolution of the football codes as a whole has too often been overlooked or downplayed. In fact, as the 1933 merger discussions revealed, all the handling codes of football, and even association football to a much more limited extent, have had to deal with similar problems in the development of their rules of playing the game. And, as the unanimous apathy toward the 1933 proposals suggests, the cultural and emotional hold of a sport over its supporters is not just confined to a shared sense of time, place and tradition. It is also embedded in a sport's rules, which offer a distinctiveness that underpins the identity of supporters with not only their clubs but also with the sport itself.

Perhaps Horrie Miller and Con Hickey did believe that the 'Universal Football League' would be greater than the sum of its parts. However, abstract logic and so-called business sense have little to do with supporters' affiliation to his or her football code or club. Whatever logic was behind the 1933 merger discussions, it appealed to no-one but a handful of administrators. Perhaps the final word on the matter should be left to an anonymous leader writer in the *Sydney Morning Herald*. "Each game is too well-rooted in its own sphere to be shaken and any attempt thereat would almost surely bring nothing but *disappointment* and *disaster*." This is a lesson that football administrators, of whatever code, and media moguls should heed.

War cries and Hakas galore

Sean Fagan looks back at Australian rugby league's war cry.

"Walla Mullare Choomooroo Tingal - Nah! nah! nah! nah!" shouted the first Kangaroos, as they began their war cry.

Upon their arrival in Britain, in October 1908, Dally Messenger put about with the newspaper scribes a dramatic story of the origins of the war cry – most of which, if not all of it, was a piece of fiction.

At the opening of the tour a reporter in a major Welsh newspaper wrote: "It has been adopted, Mr Messenger tells me, from the battle chorus of the once dreaded Stradbroke blacks, the most fierce of the Aboriginals."

While the famous "Ka Mate" haka of the 1905 New Zealand All Blacks and Baskerville's 1907 "All Golds" has an undeniable cultural foundation, the source of war cry voiced by the Australians is more certainly in the collective creative and entrepreneurial wits of rugby league's founder, James Giltinan, and the first Kangaroos.

Since the 1880s, New Zealand teams touring Australia had performed a haka. They didn't invent the concept of a war chant though, with its origins lying in Rugby School in England. Across the world, from the colleges of North America to the football clubs of Melbourne, team war cries evolved into the crowd chants that we all use today.

According to a feature on "Football War Cries" in Sydney's *The Sunday Times* in 1913 and other reports, in the 1890s Queensland rugby union teams emitted a war cry using place names, that began with "Woolloongabba!, Woolloongabba!".

Some wag in a NSW team suggested at the time that the Blues should respond in kind with "Wagga Wagga, Murrumbidgee, Yass, Yass, Yass!" – he didn't get much support. However, when the Australian rugby union team toured New Zealand in 1905, with their limp "best of British" "Hip, hip hoo-ray!" letters began rolling in to newspapers demanding an Australian war cry.

Suggested lyrics and chants were published in the press – all composed from what little each writer knew of, or made up, from Aboriginal words. Some were as simple as having the crowd chant "Kangaroo-roo-roo!" in response, while others followed in a style similar to the Ka Mate haka.

What is uncanny is that the war cry adopted by the 1908 Kangaroos, (and that too of the 1908 Wallabies), is its remarkably similar design to the earlier newspaper versions. More amazingly, this lyrical-style supposedly fitted perfectly with the war dance of the Stradbroke Islanders!

To be fair, while Aboriginal culture does not possess a pre-battle war cry in the manner of a Maori haka, the movements performed by the Kangaroos may have had some link to the Aboriginals of Stradbroke Island. Members of the island's local community today readily recognise some of the words used to compose the war cry.

Before the team had sailed for England, one of the Kangaroos, Queensland's Jack Fihelly, met with the promoter of an Aboriginal troupe who were in Sydney at the time. According to reports in Sydney newspapers, the group originated in Queensland and one of the six tribes amongst its members were men from Stradbroke Island. Almost certainly, Fihelly and the troupe's manager, Archie Meston, co-authored the Kangaroos war cry, with some of the words and phrases coming from the indigenous languages.

83

All of which mattered little to spectators at Kangaroos matches in England and Wales in 1908. In the historic city of York, the local reporter recorded the display as "a weirdly interesting bit of ritual, this battle-cry of the Kangaroos." Continuing, he wrote: "'Blooming nonsense!' exclaimed one unimaginative cynic as the performance was gone through before the game opened. And a performance it certainly is. First the Wasps gave their guests a lusty British cheer. Then, drawn up in two rows, with one of their members as a kind of leader of the orchestra in a slightly advanced position, the Australians, in their blue and maroon jerseys, went through the whole queer display, patting the ground at certain moments and at others waving their arms with Sousa-like, vehement actions – actions very significant if one could only understand them. Certainly the performance amused the spectators, and put them in a happy frame of mind to watch play."

At The Boulevard in Hull, the Australians emerged from the grandstand and onto the field accompanied by their mascot – a live kangaroo. The 'roo had been taken to England by Newcastle's Pat 'Nimmo' Walsh. He had the idea that he could train the marsupial to carry the ball out onto the field in front of the Kangaroos. One writer observed that "the Kangaroos, amongst whom was a genuine specimen, gave their fearsome war cry. The kangaroo, however, did not appear to relish the performance."

Newspaper reviews of the war cry during the tour were mixed, some flattering, some less so. A Welsh newspaper offering, "their war cry was the most weird thing imaginable." One reporter in Bradford recorded that "the crowd cheered vociferously" for the war cry, and forecasted that it "is destined to be a famous shout before the tour is finished." Another wrote "that of the New Zealanders was bloodcurdling enough, but this was more so; it was a yell of defiance, with less tunefulness and more staccato notes."

At Central Park in Wigan, the local team entered the field under the captaincy of New Zealand's Lance Todd. The Australians, and the supporters of the famous Cherry and Whites, got an unexpected shock in the form of the Wigan team performing the Ka Mate haka!

The Kangaroos' war cry was not preserved solely for football grounds. Its first performance in England was at a mayoral reception held in the team's honour at the Bradford Town Hall. Here "the Kangaroos gave their rousing, Aboriginal war cry, which rang tremendously in the narrow chamber."

Whenever the Kangaroos, and the New Zealanders the winter before, were at public functions, such as at the theatre or music halls, they would be prevailed upon to present their war cry. By the end of their tours they had become impromptu stage performers in most of the major cities across the North of England.

Invited to attend a live theatre presentation at the St Helens Hippodrome in November 1907, "the crowded audience" called for the New Zealanders to give "their famous war whoop." On the same stage where barely a year earlier Charlie Chaplin had performed - before he had left for the United States and immortality – Dally Messenger and his New Zealand team mates gave their rendition of the haka. Presenting a haka was so ingrained to New Zealand footballers, and so looked-for by the people of the places they visited, that they could (and mostly would) perform it on demand.

While the Kangaroo war cry did not ultimately become as famous as the Maori haka, it was used until 1967, and many Australian players had fond memories of it.

"Before the game began the Kangaroos thrilled the English crowd with their war cry," recalled Clive Churchill of the 1948-49 tour. "Johnny Graves (Australia's winger), who would have made a fortune in the show business, stood out from the line-up and led us. We sang our war cry on both sides of the field, much to the delight of the crowd."

Ian Walsh, vice-captain on the 1963-64 tour, remarked that, "The English people loved to hear the war cry." Walsh also spoke of a secondary benefit: "It was handy, too, for releasing tension and warming up the players because it involved a lot of stamping and arm-waving!"

"We used to practice it in the lounge (bar) or at the back of the Troutbeck Hotel and whenever we attended a function someone would be sure to ask us to do the war cry." Walsh revealed that the Kangaroos used the war cry for other purposes too: "We said the proper words in England, but sometimes in France we would use the opportunity to roar abuse at the crowd and the referee!"

The Kangaroos' war cry was used for the last time in December 1967 in France. It went out with a whimper as Australia lost a three-test series by 2-0 (one game drawn). By that time the war cry had come to be seen as an anachronism, a reminder of a time when Australia's Aboriginal past was trivialised.

Its demise left Dally Messenger alone as the only Australian to have performed the Kangaroos war cry and the New Zealand haka. A most unique, though obscure, double.

Kangaroos' War Cry

Walla Mullare Choomooroo Tingal
Nah! nah! nah! nah!
Cunal, barrang, warrang, warrang,
Yallah, yallah, yallah, Yallah.
Ah! Jaleeba booga booroolong
Yarrnah meei, meei, meei
Neeyarra, Wlyarra, Jaleeba, Cowoon
Cooewah, Cooewah
Warr! wooh!

We are a race of fighters, descended from War Gods.
Beware! Beware! Beware! Beware!
Where we fight there will be bloodshed.
Go! Go! Go! Go!
We are powerful, but merciful; are you friends?
Good! Good!
The Kangaroo is dangerous when at bay.
Come on, Come on, to Death!

Note: The Kangaroos' War Cry was not performed in English.

A Skyrocket team

Sean Fagan of www.RL1908.com recalls a great team from Toowoomba

They revolutionised how the game was played. This team was the mighty Toowoomba Clydesdales, The Light Blues of 1924 and 1925. They were from the Darling Downs, west of Brisbane, in Australia's northern state of Queensland. Toowoomba is an inland city, with 30,000 inhabitants at the time, 'where they breed them big'.

It was a 'skyrocket' team, including Tom Gorman, Herb Steinohrt, Duncan Thompson, Vic Armbruster, Dan Dempsey, Mick Madsen, Edwin Brown, Bill Spencer and Jim Bennett. They all were, or soon would be, Australian Kangaroos.

Their dynasty began with a match against Jonty Parkin's English tourists - Wednesday 18 June 1924: "The cream of English footballers will cross swords with Toowoomba today." The Lions arrived by train from Brisbane. Never in its history had the railway station presented such a busy appearance. Stepping onto the platform, the newspaper scribes surrounded Parkin. "How will your team perform today?", "What do you know of our men?", "Will you yourself be playing Mr Parkin?"

The Wakefield Trinity half-back preferred to 'boost' his opponents off the field, and bring them crashing down on it. "Yes, we have heard something of Toowoomba," he said. "We are told that your boys are cracks of the 13-man game. We realise that we will have to put our best foot forward when we meet them."

The Englishmen retired to the city's main hotel, to rest up before the big game. The streets of the city were crowded from 11.30am onwards, and from that hour there was a continuous stream of people up to Athletic Oval. The special trains kept arriving. There were 450 passengers on the Wallangarra train, 500 on the Killarney, 500 on the Chinchilla and the two specials from Pittsworth and Clifton were packed. They came from below the Range, as well as from all the intervening centres. The 'sweeper' train from Brisbane was overflowing when it arrived, it left practically empty. Hundreds also came by motor cars, sulkies (small horse-drawn carriages), and motor cycles.

Admission tickets were sold at the railway station, and at former North Sydney half-back Duncan Thompson's sports store. But even sellers with large quantities were quickly sold out. Cars lined the streets for hundreds of yards and many were simply left in the city park.

The two local policemen kept everyone in check: "Their expert supervision of the ground and the lines of traffic was splendid," said one report. It was the biggest crowd ever yet seen at a Toowoomba sports fixture. The stand was full to overflowing hours before the contest was to start. Crowded masses of spectators stand along the touchlines and the space at both ends of the ground. There were more than 10,000. Boys with football programmes were literally rushed, and did a roaring business. The late arrivals could obtain only a very poor view of the game.

A strong westerly wind was blowing, the belt of trees on the Mary Street side broke the force of the wind. In most respects, the day was ideal for football. The sun shone. Those on the western side tilted their heads, lowering their hats to cut the path of the late afternoon winter light from their eyes.

Jonty did not feel well. He stood down from the game. The teams were:
England (colour, white): J. Sullivan; C. Carr, C. Pollard, S. Evans, T. Howley; S. Whitty; W. Mooney; F. Gallagher, J. Thompson, W. Cunliffe, H. Bowman, R. Sloman, D. Rees.

Toowoomba (colour, light blue): M. Ryan; W. Spencer, T. Gorman, J. Cuneen, J. Lindsay; C. Thompson; D. F. Thompson; C. Broadfoot, V. Armbruster, H. Leibke, J. Bennett, J. Dempsey, H. Steinohrt.

Toowoomba's Tommy Gorman won the toss. The Queensland Governor, Sir Matthew Nathan, set the ball rolling at 3.33pm. He didn't send it 'far enough'.

A scrum was set at half-way. Dempsey heeled to Australia's wizard half, Duncan Thompson, away he went at his top. He sent it to Colin Thompson who cut in nicely, before giving it to Gorman. Tom sidled past two opponents, he could have scored. Unselfishly, he gave to Bill Spencer, who went over. Duncan Thompson goaled. Toowoomba 5-0.

England's Cunliffe looked like scoring, but he knocked on. Howley brought off a fine intercept, and went far before he was brought down. Toowoomba were on the defensive, but the English could not hold the ball. "Poor 'John Bull'!" laughed the unsympathetic crowd.

The second try to the local side came just as suddenly as the first. Spencer, receiving near half, brushed off Carr, Cunliffe and Sullivan, and touched down under the posts. Toowoomba were ahead 10-0. Ten points in eight minutes was some going, but the Englishmen never lost heart.

Twenty years old, Wigan's bright star Jim Sullivan sent in a fine line kick, gaining 40 yards for his side. The visitors kept pegging away, and eventually the ball came again to Sullivan, who in-passed to Evans, to Pollard, who went over. Sullivan, for once, muffed the goal attempt. Toowoomba 10-3.

Duncan Thompson, receiving from a scrum close to the England line, sent to his brother Colin, to Gorman, who could have scored again, but sent to Spencer who went over a third time. Duncan Thompson raised the flags - Toowoomba 15-3.

The open, fast play of the Toowoomba backs had the tremendous crowd upon their feet time after time with their flashes of brilliance. From a penalty, Sullivan fired in a beauty between the uprights. Toowoomba 15-5.

England kept pressing, and eventually a movement between Carr, who burst through nicely, to Cunliffe, to Howley, resulted in a good try. Sullivan again goaled; Toowoomba 15-10.

A penalty to England and Sullivan's line kick was worth 50 yards. Another penalty to England, Sullivan landed the goal. Toowoomba 15-12. Jonty watches "a titanic struggle" from the press table. Maybe he should have played.

First scrum in the second half. It happened again! Duncan Thompson receiving from the pack, sent to Colin Thompson, to Gorman, Cuneen and Lindsay, the latter crossing for a brilliant try. Toowoomba 18-12.

The Englishmen dribbled the leather, 'old school' football style. Whitty kicked through, followed quickly, regained, but was smothered by Steinohrt on the line. Mart Ryan retired from the game, having injured his knee. Broadfoot left the scrum and filled the position. No replacements allowed against the English. It was "Their rules, you know."

On resuming Duncan Thompson worked the blind, and gave to Lindsay, who ran over half the length of the field to touch down behind the posts. Duncan Thompson goaled to make it Toowoomba 23-12.

England hit back immediately, for Mooney sent an inside pass to his team mate, Thompson, who went over. Sullivan failed with the conversion - Toowoomba 23-15.

Toowoomba again went on the attack but were brought down close to the line. Sullivan then sent in the best line kick of the match, gaining over 80 yards. What a boot he had.

England tried hard to score in the final five minutes. Nearing time, the Lions' Bowman dribbled finely on his own all the way to the line, Rees fell on it for the score. Sullivan secured the goal. Toowoomba 23-20. There's still time.

Great excitement marked the last few minutes of play. Toowoomba did all they knew to stop England scoring again. A few more onslaughts from the visiting vanguard might have carried victory to the white-jerseyed men of England.

The referee, James Ollier, put the whistle to his mouth, and blew for full-time. The shadows had crossed the field; it was now almost 5.10pm.

Toowoomba had won a memorable game, 23-20. The crowd were in delightful joy at the conclusion. They carried the leading Toowoomba men shoulder high from the field back to the sheds.

There was a fearful crush at the so-called gates as the crowd departed, and the wonder is that no one was seriously hurt. Many of the ladies had a bad time and several were on the verge of collapse when they finally got through. It took a very long time for the crowd to make its way out.

Standing in the centre of town it was a fine sight to see the cars coming from the grounds down Margaret Street. As far as the eye could see in an easterly direction there was one continuous line of motor cars returning from the match. For 15 minutes the cars passed by. The footpaths for over 20 minutes were thronged with people returning from the match.

All the special trains returned at night, and needless to say all were filled with jubilant supporters of the Toowoomba team. One enthusiast from Chinchilla stated, "They are marvellous, and showed us how the league game should be played."

"Of the English, the nuggetty and weighty Mooney was perhaps the best," wrote *The Toowoomba Chronicle*. "Sullivan should go very far in the rugby league football world."

"This great encounter will linger long in the memory of those many thousands who witnessed it, and it has had the effect of putting Toowoomba 'on the map' in a football sense as it never was before."

"The match will probably be talked about when the smallest boy who saw it will be white with the snows of time. Toowoomba deserved its great victory, but the vanquished men of England deserve every credit for the way they stuck to their guns throughout and fought back with true British determination."

"The men played like galloping Clydesdales," said Mayor Annand. The name stuck. Toowoomba were unbeaten for the rest of the 1924 season, and all of the next as well. In 12 games, over those two winters, they scored 323 points for, to 136 against. After England, "the Clydesdales" conquered the representative teams of New South Wales, New Zealand, Brisbane, Ipswich, and Victoria (yes, they had a team then!). They even set up South Sydney, "the pride of the League"; they too went home defeated.

This magnificent team of hard, skilled and entertaining footballers rebuked every attempt to claim their crown. Toowoomba achieved what not only looked to be impossible, it was impossible. It will never be repeated.

Some corner of a foreign field

Ian Jackson reflects on the experience of rugby league in the First World War.

"If I should die, think only this of me;
That there's some corner of foreign field
That is for ever England."

The Solider written by Rupert Brooke (1915)

Introduction

The First World War, or the Great War, appears like a 'black hole' in the history of rugby league, known at the time as Northern Union. The euphoria of the split from rugby union in the late Victorian period was closely followed by international expansion of the game in the Edwardian period principally to Australia and New Zealand. Then the Great War intervenes. The First World War actually began in the summer of 1914 and hostilities ended with the Armistice in November 1918. The conflict was a hugely devastating and profoundly bitter episode in military history, which also affected many aspects of civilian life. In particular, during almost four and half years of conflict over 100 players from Northern Union clubs were killed in action from approximately 1,000 men who enlisted. The clubs also suffered through a fall in attendances in part caused by the cancellation of meaningful fixtures after the fateful 1914-15 season which coincided with the outbreak of war. The experience of rugby league in the First World War tends to be overlooked. However, certain aspects of the game can be examined through the service records of the players who fought for King and country. Also, the experience of the players who enlisted can be set in the context of the Northern Union clubs many of which only just managed to survive until the end of the war.

Northern Union clubs during the Great War

At the start of the Great War there were 25 Northern Union professional clubs. This number was rather disappointing given the many attempts to expand the game in the early part of the twentieth century, which had failed most noticeably in South Wales but also in other industrial areas such as Coventry, Liverpool and Newcastle. Remarkably, by the end of the war only one club did not re-appear, namely Runcorn who were a founder member of the Northern Union in 1895. Runcorn were replaced by St Helens Recreation who were the first and only works team in the history of the game to gain first class club status. Ironically, they did not re-appear after the Second War World, but a separate Runcorn club emerged many years later in 1989 formed from the defunct Huyton RLFC, playing at the same Canal Street ground as the original Runcorn Northern Union club.

Prior to the start of the war, Huddersfield were the premier team in the Northern Union. The club was so successful that it became known as the "Empire team of all talents" as it contained some of the best players from the North of England, South Wales, Australia and New Zealand. Huddersfield had reached the Championship final in each of the three seasons before 1914 and won it twice in 1911-12 and 1912-13. Huddersfield included two outstanding players of any generation, local Harold Wagstaff and Australian Albert Rosenfeld, both members of the Rugby League Hall of Fame. Huddersfield were champions again in 1914-15 but then competitive matches were suspended for three seasons from 1915-16 to 1917-18.

During the war friendly games were arranged instead of competitive fixtures. However, there were so many teams who could not compete that three more clubs were recruited, Brighouse Rangers, Featherstone Rovers and St. Helens Recreation. In effect, between 1915 and 1918 most teams reverted to the amateur ranks and players were generally paid expenses and tea-money. It is possible that the greatest loss of clubs appears to have been in the amateur game. In 1914-15, official rugby league data shows there were 210 amateur clubs but this had reduced to 42 by 1919-20. A similar picture is shown with attendances at professional games which halved by 1914 from the pre-war level of 1913. This was caused in part by many spectators enlisting in the so-called Pals Regiments as part of Lord Kitchener's new army where family members, work colleagues and neighbours joined together in the same units.

Players and spectators enlisting was only one aspect of the war effort. Swinton and Broughton Rangers offered their grounds to the military. Also, the mills and factories back home had to sustain the service men and women in munitions, military equipment, clothing, food and other supplies. Barrow RLFC played through the war mainly because many people in the town had reserved occupations in the shipyards and munitions. Dewsbury, in the heavy woollen district of West Riding supplied military uniforms. Also, there were many coal miners across Lancashire and Yorkshire in reserved occupations.

Rugby League Table: 1914-1915

Place	Team	P	W	D	L	F	A	Pts	%
1	Huddersfield	34	28	4	2	888	235	60	88.24
2	Wigan	32	25	1	6	679	203	51	79.69
3	Leeds	34	24	3	7	486	207	51	75.02
4	Rochdale H	34	24	2	8	306	194	50	73.53
5	Hull	36	24	1	11	705	301	49	68.06
6	Broughton R	30	18	1	11	308	289	37	61.66
7	St Helens	32	19	0	13	368	342	38	59.37
8	Halifax	34	18	3	13	342	268	39	57.36
9	Oldham	34	17	4	13	375	301	38	55.89
10	Wakefield T	32	17	1	14	309	340	35	54.69
11	Hull KR	34	17	2	15	374	324	36	52.94
12	Widnes	32	14	3	15	291	292	31	48.44
13	Warrington	32	14	3	15	242	323	31	48.44
14	Batley	34	15	1	18	229	288	31	45.59
15	Leigh	31	14	0	17	252	185	28	45.16
16	Swinton	30	13	1	16	171	240	27	45.00
17	Dewsbury	32	12	2	18	310	353	26	40.62
18	Hunslet	32	12	0	20	298	356	24	37.50
19	Bradford N	32	11	1	20	249	464	23	35.93
20	Bramley	32	11	1	20	143	474	23	35.93
21	Salford	30	8	4	18	134	313	20	33.33
22	Barrow	32	10	1	21	288	363	21	32.81
23	York	32	9	2	21	261	422	20	31.25
24	Keighley	30	6	2	22	120	542	14	29.37
25	Runcorn	27	0	1	26	84	590	1	1.85

Huddersfield's Douglas Clark – awarded the Military Medal (Photo: Courtesy Robert Gate)

The war effort consumed a huge amount of resources and left little time for recreation and play. There was precious little appetite anyway for entertainment in general and professional football in particular. Football was not really encouraged (whether Association Football or Northern Union) and in some circles football was seen as unpatriotic. With hundreds of men being killed on a daily basis, football did seem at best trivial and at worse a major distraction from the perils facing the country. As a result, the decision by the rugby league authorities to play the 1914-15 season as planned was heavily criticized, especially since rugby union had called a halt to games.

So, the 1914-15 season was the last competitive season to be played during the war. Huddersfield finished top of the league and also won the championship final sweeping all other teams before them.

The players' experience of the Great War

In the initial eight months of the war as many as 1,418 Northern Union players, both professional and amateur enlisted. By the end of the war, it was estimated from 15 of the 25 professional clubs that 760 professional players had joined the armed forces. It is impossible to estimate how many Northern Union spectators enlisted and died during the war but it is likely to be measured in the thousands.

Players from the 1914 tour to Australia which included the famous Rorke's Drift test (named after an episode in the Zulu War in 1879) returned on 24 September 1914 to a country at war. There were players such as Fred Longstaff, Billy Jarman and Walter Roman had gone to Australia in the summer of 1914. Two years later, all three men had been killed. Fred Longstaff was a private in the 1st and 6th Battalion of the West

Yorkshire Regiment (Prince of Wales' Own). He died on 21 July 1916 three weeks after the start of the Battle of the Somme, which was the first such attack to be led by the British. Billy Jarman was a private in the second Battalion of the Scots Guards. He also died in the Battle of the Somme on 15 August and is remembered at the Thiepval Memorial, which is a town at the centre of the offensive. Walter Roman was a private in the 1st Battalion of the Somerset Light Infantry. Roman was a reservist before the war having served already in the South African Campaign (The Boar War). He had risen to the rank of Sergeant, although he was subsequently demoted. He died back home in his native Somerset and is buried at Bridgwater Cemetery. In a cruel twist of fate, Richard Twigg, Roman's second row partner at Rochdale Hornets, died three days after Roman lost his battle for life. Twigg was a Sergeant in the Manchester Regiment and also at the Battle of the Somme. It is likely they were only a mile apart from each other in the initial days of the battle. The disastrous Battle of the Somme was one of the most expensive in terms of casualties in the war and indeed the entire history of the British Army. It claimed the lives of claimed 19,000 British Empire soldiers on the first day alone.

In total, the 1914 England touring side to Australia included three army reservists, namely Billy Jarman (Leeds), Walter Roman (Rochdale Hornets) and Alf Wood (Oldham). Only Alf Wood survived the conflict. When war broke out in Europe all three players had to report to the British High Commission in Australia and joined their regiments as soon as they returned back to England. The final test match in Australia in 1914 included one Australian player and one official who also died in the Great War.

The international nature of the conflict is also shown by the case of H. S. Turtill who was a Sergeant in the 422nd Field Company of the Royal Engineers. He was originally from Christchurch, New Zealand and played for the touring All Golds in 1907 which contained the legendary Australian player Dally Messenger whom many credit with establishing Rugby League in the Sydney area in 1908. Jum Turtill lost his life on 9 April 1918 leaving his wife and family back in England having played previously for St Helens before the outbreak of war. Other British rugby league internationals to die in the Great War are included in the following list:

International rugby honours

1. Jarman, Samuel William (Oldham) Great Britain international tourist, 1914
2. Longstaff, Fred (Huddersfield) Great Britain international tourist, 1914
3. Nanson, William (Oldham) England rugby union international, 1907
4. Roman, Walter (Rochdale Hornets) Great Britain international tourist, 1914
5. Turtill, H S (St. Helens) New Zealand international tourist, 1907

William Nanson and Walter Roman both served in the Boer War (South Africa Campaign) as rugby union players at Carlisle and Bridgewater, respectively. Nanson received the King and Queens medal for gallantry whilst in South Africa.

Players who also served in the South Africa Campaign (The Boer War)

1. Nanson, William (Carlisle RU)
2. Roman, Walter (Bridgewater RU)
3. Tobin, James (Leigh)

For many of the men, joining the forces may have represented adventure, of course before the full horrors of the war become a reality. Sergeant Frank Ganley played for his home-town club Leigh before joining up. He was part of the Dunsterforce led by Major-General Dunsterville. This mission took the theatre of war beyond the trenches on the Western Front. Ganley was a Sergeant in the Machine Gun Corps and was in the Armoured Car Brigade which included converted Rolls-Royce Silver Shadow cars. The Dunsterforce was dispatched from Baghdad to secure Baku from the Turkish army. Frank Ganley was killed during this offensive and is buried at Tehran War Cemetery in Iran having been killed on 17 September 1918 aged 38 years.

John Harrison is the only rugby league player to receive the Victoria Cross (VC), the most prestigious military award. He was a Second Lieutenant in the 11th Battalion of the East Yorkshire Regiment and died on the 3 May 1917. The VC was posthumously awarded "For most conspicuous bravery and self-sacrifice in attack." He also received the Military Cross (MC) a month earlier "For conspicuous gallantry and devotion to duty." Harrison also played for Hull FC with distinction. A poignant addition to this story is that Harrison's son, also named John, became a Captain in the Duke of Wellington (West Riding) Regiment in the Second World War and was killed in action during the chaotic scenes at Dunkirk on 1 June 1940.

Examples of Military Honours

1. John Harrison (Hull Football Club) Victoria Cross and Military Cross
2. James Tobin (Leigh) Military Medal
3. Douglas Clark (Huddersfield)

The exploits of John Ewart, who was a private in the 5th Battalion of the Cameron Highlanders, is indicative of a breed of brave men who also played in Northern Union. Unlike other rugby league players, he was signed from outside Lancashire and Yorkshire and returned home to enlist having signed for Halifax from Scotland. Another example is Fred Perrett who was a Second Lieutenant in the Royal Welsh Fusiliers having signed for Hull FC from South Wales. Interestingly, William Nanson, who is recognised at the War Memorial at Twickenham having played international rugby union for England before signing for Oldham and then Coventry, was also from outside Lancashire and Yorkshire as he was born in Carlisle. He was a Sergeant in the 1st and 10th Manchester Regiment and died aged 34 on 4 April 1915 at Gallipoli and in addition is remembered at the Helles Memorial in Turkey.

The overwhelming number of casualties in the Great War were either killed outright or received such severe injuries that they died shortly afterwards. There were some casualties who received injured and subsequently returned home to recuperate. This was known at the time as being 'Blightyed'. Unfortunately, even the medical care back home was insufficient for some of these courageous men and often they died of their injuries. This list includes the aforementioned Walter Roman who is buried in his hometown of Bridgewater in Somerset; George Thom who is buried in his hometown of Weaste in Lancashire and Ernest Swinton who is buried in his hometown of Widnes in Cheshire. Ernest Swinton, a Second Lieutenant in the Royal Field Artillery played for Widnes. He was injured on the Western Front, but died back home and is buried at St Luke's, Farnworth not far from the Queens Arms Hotel in Widnes, a public house which was run by his parents.

The same happened to George Thom who was an Armament Staff Sergeant in the Royal Army Ordnance Corps. He died on 30 December 1915 back home in Salford and is buried at Weaste Cemetery.

The majority of casualties were in France and Belgium which is testament to the vast scale of the conflict in these countries. There are a number of men who fell elsewhere reflecting the global nature of the conflict beyond the European Theatre of War. As mentioned William Nanson who was originally from Carlisle was killed during the Gallipoli campaign in 1915 and honoured at the Helles Memorial in Turkey. Tom Williams from Salford who played for Swinton and Salford was also killed in 1915 during the Gallipoli campaign and is honoured at the Lancashire Landing Cemetery in Turkey, where 1,800 Lancashire Fusiliers died.

Most of the players in Northern Union teams were working class. The men were coal miners, dock workers or operatives in the textile mills and engineering factories across the North of England. Unsurprisingly, the majority of the casualties were privates in the British Army. However, quite remarkably there was at least one General in the British Army who was a former Northern Union player. R. Edgar Sugden played 84 Northern Union games for Brighouse Rangers between September 1895 and January 1900, scoring five tries. He also played for Yorkshire Northern Union three times in 1895 and 1896. In the army he was a Brigadier-General and known simply by his initials 'R. E.'. The following soldiers were all killed in the Great War and had non-commissioned ranks.

Examples of Non-Commissioned Officers

1. Lieutenant W. L. Beattie (Border Regiment: 1st Battalion) was also a player at Wakefield Trinity.
2. Second Lieutenant J. Harrison VC (East Yorkshire Regiment: 11th Battalion) was also a player for Hull Football Club.
3. Second Lieutenant F. L. Perrett (Royal Welsh Fusiliers: 17th Battalion) was also a player at Hull Football Club.

Also, Gwyn Thomas and Lance Todd both of Wigan enlisted as officers and both survived the war. Many other players climbed the ranks beyond private. This list includes the following Northern Union players all of whom perished in the Great War:

Examples of players' rank other than private

1. Sergeant F. Ganley (Machine Gun Corps: Armoured Car Brigade) and Leigh.
2. Lance Sergeant J. Flanagan (South Lancashire Regiment: 11th Battalion) and St Helens.
3. Lance Corporal B. Lloyd (South Lancashire Regiment: 7th Battalion) and Leigh.
4. Sergeant W. Nanson (Manchester Regiment: 1st/10th Battalion), Oldham and Coventry.
5. Sergeant W. Roman (Somerset Light Infantry: 1st Battalion) and Rochdale Hornets
6. Armament Staff Sergeant G. Thom (Royal Army Ordnance Corps) and Salford.
7. Sergeant J. Tobin MM (Royal Horse Artillery: 15th Brigade) and Leigh.
8. Sergeant H. S. Turtill (Royal Engineers: 422nd Field Company) and St Helens.
9. Sergeant R. Twigg (Manchester Regiment: 16th Battalion) and Rochdale Hornets.
10. Sergeant S. Whittaker (Lancashire Hussars: 18th Battalion) and Leigh.

There were some remarkable stories of escape and survival, too. Douglas Clark of Huddersfield recovered from being blown-up at Passchendale and Jim Pollitt of Swinton survived when his troopship was torpedoed. Both players survived and retuned to play again for their clubs.

Conclusion

"On 4 August [1914] Britain had declared war on Germany. Warfare was no longer a metaphor for sporting endeavour but a bloody reality." Tony Collins (2006).

There is little or no mention of the 1914-1918 conflict in many contemporary rugby league club handbooks and players who were killed are not celebrated like those men from rugby union clubs who have been remembered rightly and properly. So why did rugby league tend not dwell on events once the Great War was over? There is little doubt that the game of rugby league after 1918 tended to look inward and generally wanted to forget about the Great War which had caused so much hardship and misery for all concerned. The game even forgot about domestic expansion for at least a decade as survival seemed to become the primary objective. The amateur base had been reduced, many players and spectators had been killed or seriously injured and rugby union had been promoted in the armed forces to the detriment of Northern Union which by 1914 had developed its distinctive characteristics of XIII-a-side, play-the-ball and no line-outs.

The experience of the Northern Union in the Great War shows there was precious little to celebrate, of course. Whole communities across the country had been shattered by the process of a modern, industrial warfare which included tanks and aeroplanes for the first time. In addition, there were many broken promises. Nearly one million British Empire soldiers, sailors and airmen perished, many from the industrial north who enlisted in Pals Regiments some from the heartlands of rugby league such as Bradford, Leeds, Salford and Swinton. In addition, the "war to end all wars" was not "over by Christmas" as promised and those men who were fortunate to come home did not return to "land fit for heroes". The primary task of the Northern Union was to ensure the long-term survival of a game that many had predicted would not even re-appear after the war. In fact, the Northern Union authorities did not take too long in re-branding the game and took a suggestion from the Australian administrators to even modernise its name and replace Northern Union with Rugby Football League in 1922. So out of necessary, the game of rugby league had to adapt quickly to a changing social and economic environment post 1918.

References
Bruce, Anthony (1989). *An illustrated companion to the First World War.*
Collins, Tony (2006). *Rugby League in the twentieth century: a social and cultural history.*
Fletcher, Raymond and Howes, David (1995). *Rothmans Rugby League Yearbook 1995-96.*
Gate, Robert (1989). *Rugby League: an illustrated history*
Gilbert, Adrian (1990). *World War One in Photographs.*
Mather, Tom (2005). *Missing in Action.*
Moorhouse, Geoffrey (1995). *The official history of Rugby League: 1895 to 1995.*
Tennant, John (2005). *Rugby: the golden age.*
Turner, Michael (1997). *Oldham RLFC: the complete history 1876 to 1997.*
Wild, Steve (1999). *The Lions of Swinton: a complete history.*

Champagne Rugby: The Golden Age of French rugby league

Roger Grime has been working on a translation of *Champagne Rugby* by Henri Garcia. Below he explains why the book will be of interest to rugby league enthusiasts in Great Britain, Australia and New Zealand.

Henri Garcia, one-time chief rugby correspondent of the prestigious French sports daily *l' Equipe*, crafted in 1961 a consummate account of the golden age of French rugby league. The book has not so far been accessible to the non-French speaker, but in August, this masterpiece will be available in English. Then, everyone will be able to share the trials, battles and ultimate elation of those three famous French Tours down under in 1951, 1955 and 1960.

Cleverly, Garcia traces the rise of the 'new' rugby from the time of the great schism in England in 1895, through the 'All Gold' tour of 1907-08 and via the surge of the game in Australia and New Zealand. The account, however, is rather different from what we have been used to and throughout his book he fearlessly gives the French slant on events — something which, to be honest, has often been overlooked through language and culture difficulties. When he comes to the seismic last day of 1933, when the Australia-England exhibition game in Paris changed the face of rugby in France, he takes up the story with a passion and insight which cannot help but engage Anglo-Saxon interest.

The early chapters do present a translation problem and the original style can feel awkward to our ears, but I aimed to stay close to the original without creating problems for the reader, and refused to water down or edit Garcia's essentially Gallic overview. Hopefully, the result is a refreshingly pertinent account. Jean Galia and Maurice Tardy figure prominently as the reader is taken with the central characters on the trip into the unknown and this section is rounded off with the telling statistic that in 1930, the French Rugby Union had 784 members whereas in 1939 they had shrunk to 471.

Even today, the Vichy decree which sought to destroy le rugby à XIII is regarded with contempt, especially in those parts of France which still feel the effects and, after expressing scorn for the unprincipled perpetrators of the ban, Garcia really picks up the pace with the post-war resurrection. Despite the Treizistes' well-documented stand against the collaborationist regime, promises were not kept (by De Gaulle in particular) and shamefully, it was not until 1949 that the game was granted membership of the National Sports Council. Thanks to the commitment of fantastic characters like Paul Barrière, the Resistance leader and force behind the first World Cup in 1954, the game was driven back into prominence. Every rugby league aficionado has heard of the iconic Puig-Aubert, but few will know how Barrière enticed him from the rival code. This roly-poly full-back with an acute aversion to training was the embodiment of French flair as the fabulous Tricolor stars gelled to be crowned World Champions in 1951.

This is where we can really appreciate Garcia's superb gift for making the past come to life. Now, for the first time, the English speaker can share the vicissitudes and ultimate triumphs as, far from home, the Tricolors' battle with strange surroundings, conflicting cultures and the challenge of the Australian superstars. Week by week, match by match, we can experience the highs and lows until that fabulous star-studded 1951

Gilbert Benausse
(Photo: Courtesy Robert Gate)

His obituary is in the Obituaries section.

team are welcomed home with wild scenes as tens of thousands choke the streets of Marseille.

More success follows in 1955, when Benausse, Merquey and Dop lead them to a repeat triumph against the likes of Churchill, Holman and Kearney. Record crowds and unprecedented interest seemed to suggest the fairy tale would continue for ever. The 1960 team made a hugely impressive effort to square the series with Jiminez, Mantoulan, Bescos and Barthe carrying on the proud traditions. Garcia's gripping account of the Third test is a superlative piece of sports journalism which captures the drama of a defining event. His final emotional paragraphs honour the fantastic comeback achievements of the party, but there is an element of sadness as he, and we, realise that this is effectively the end of a golden era. He puts his finger on the weakening pulse of the French game, for French rugby league had peaked and the future belonged to the Gasniers and Rapers.

Where did it all go wrong? Reading between the lines, one senses that essential steps were not taken, strategies were not initiated and the stars, quite simply, were not replaced. Rugby league in France just seemed to wither and lose its momentum until it is today virtually a village game. Bordeaux, Marseilles, Paris and Lyons have lost their former status and 20,000 crowds no longer throng the big city stadia. This, then, is a book which no rugby league supporter should be without. The English edition will include photos and researched statistics not found in the original version to make it a veritable work of reference, not only for the three tours, but for the French slant on history. No one who reads it can fail to answer the calls for help from present day French rugby league. We helped them once. We need to do so again. Like Henri Garcia, we must never forget.

The book will be available from London League Publications at the end of August 2007.

A short life – but a happy one!
Reflections on St Helens Recs

Alex Service and **Denis Whittle** look back at St Helens Recs.

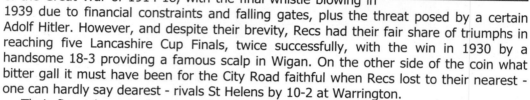

Over the sometimes chequered history of professional Rugby League the Recs of City Road - or more formally St Helens Recreation - enjoyed but a brief stay in the 'Greatest Game.'

It kicked off amid the inevitable sporting surge in the wake of the Great War of 1914-18, with the final whistle blowing in 1939 due to financial constraints and falling gates, plus the threat posed by a certain Adolf Hitler. However, and despite their brevity, Recs had their fair share of triumphs in reaching five Lancashire Cup Finals, twice successfully, with the win in 1930 by a handsome 18-3 providing a famous scalp in Wigan. On the other side of the coin what bitter gall it must have been for the City Road faithful when Recs lost to their nearest - one can hardly say dearest - rivals St Helens by 10-2 at Warrington.

Their finest hour as far as pot-hunting went came in the 1926-27 season. By then, from feet-finding beginnings in the Lancashire Combination, resilient Recs had established themselves as a team to be reckoned with. In a nutshell it was a campaign when little went wrong. They finished in pole position and, for once in a while, the Championship Final pairing ran true to form with top-dogs Recs facing runners-up Swinton in the play-off showdown, which was again staged at Wilderspool Stadium.

All went well for the local lads in the first 40 minutes when they led 5-2 thanks to a blockbusting try by prop Frank Bowen, one of five rugby-playing brothers and a conversion by Tommy Dingsdale, while a goal from Oliver Morris accounted for Swinton's early points. The second half proved to be Recs' nemesis however, as elusive Lion's half-back Bryn Evans jinked his way over the try-line. His partner 'Billo' Rees then put the finishing touch to a round of passing and then Fred Beswick pounced on a fumble by Dingsdale and Morris added the extra points. Centre Bob Innes notched a late consolation touchdown for Recs but a cliff-hanging 13-8 defeat was nonetheless a bitter pill to swallow, although it could be said that the men from City Road lost to one of the best teams ever to grace the rugby league code. The Swinton line-up that soared to a four-cups haul in that great season of 1926-27 fielded such time-honoured immortals such as Evans and his brother Jack, Chris Brockbank, Rees, Beswick and Frank Strong.

Reliving the Recs squad would have rekindled the memory banks of many City Roadites of yesteryear namely: Tommy Dingsdale; Jack Wilson, Joe McComas, Bob Innes, John Wallace; Jimmy Honey, Johnny Greenall (captain); George Highcock, Harry King, Frank Bowen, Tommy Smith, Albert Fildes, Billy Mulvanney.
The attendance was 24,000.

It is arguably a study of the absorbing annals of the Challenge Cup which triggered the fiercest arguments among die-hard Recs supporters, who were adamant that their heroes were 'refereed' out of the semi-final clash against Wigan in 1929. At stake was the most prestigious prize in the rugby league calendar, and that was to be one of the sides in the first-ever Final at Wembley Stadium. The decider was fought out in two stages: first a 7-7 draw at Swinton followed by a nerve-wracking 13-12 victory for Wigan in the replay at Leigh.

Legend has it that unlucky Recs were 'robbed' because the Rugby League authorities wanted a big name club for its Challenge Cup showpiece in the Metropolis. This, the powers-that-were decided, was of paramount importance because, with 'minnows' Dewsbury already booked for Wembley, it just had to be mighty Wigan to provide the opposition. But the sad fact was that this was the nearest rueful Recs got to realising their Wembley dream.

On a personality note the City Road club yielded up many household names, including the peerless back three forwards Tommy Smith, Albert Fildes and Billy Mulvanney. In their hey-day this tried-and-tested trio supplied weekly evidence of what teak-tough pack stars should be all about. Mention the name Greenall and the thoughts of Recs greybeards of 70 years ago would immediately focus on brothers Johnny and Billy, both of whom wore that famous red, amber and black jersey with distinction. Captain Johnny in particular was worthy of the accolade 'great', and would have soared to even loftier heights but for the immortal Jonty Parkin of Wakefield Trinity.

However, with due deference to a Duggie Greenall of later vintage, the most unforgettable character to bear that hallowed name in St Helens XIII-a-side circle was 'Mother' Ellen Greenall, was protective instinct manifested itself from the touchline whenever an unwary opponent took illegal liberties with her devoted sons. A forerunner to be sure of the petulant Minnie Cotton 40 seasons later, who meted out instant justice via her lethal umbrella when, at Swinton, a Dewsbury forward dared to transgress on Saints' forward John Warlow, who was Mrs Cotton's lodger. But those of more venerable years who remembered these rugby league 'suffragettes' remained convinced that Nellie Greenall was the most belligerent of them all, both at professional and amateur levels.

Family talent also abounded in those General Strike days of the 1920s, so dubbed the time of the Great Depression but not for the Recs regulars, who rejoiced in the diversity from hum-drum living which their heroes served up both at good old City Road and further afield. For, along with the Greenall clan, there were the Bowen and Dingsdale brothers, plus the original Jimmy Honey whose son of the same name, a generation on, maintained the family tradition, albeit with amateur giants Vine Tavern and Saints.

Just like Olde Father Tyme the Hall of Fame within the City Road pantheon rumbled on, for example John 'Tot' Wallace, a fine upstanding winger signed from Barrow; Jack Wilson from Hope Street, whose limpet-like tackling often kept the legendary Alf Ellaby in check and earned Wilson the pseudonym 'Durdock.' Add to all these Recs' favourites of the 1920s and 1930s Jim Pyke, tourist hooker Oliver Dolan who lived to a ripe old age after being torpedoed in the Dardanelles during the First World War; George 'Jumbo' Highcock, a front-rower of ramrod military bearing and waxed moustache; speed merchant Jimmy Owen... one could go on ...

As is the case today, rugby league held pride of place within the sporting life of the town during the halcyon days, if sometimes traumatic, times of the fondly remembered St Helens Recreation club. Long may it be so.

Alex Service and Denis Whittle are currently working on a history of St Helens Recs, which will be published by London League Publications Ltd in October 2007.

St Helens and Mal Meninga

Mike Critchley recalls a historic season.

The 1980s was a pretty dismal decade in St Helens. The scourge of mass unemployment and the decay of our once proud industrial heritage was compounded by a rugby team that played second fiddle to both Hulls, Widnes and then latterly Wigan.

Saints' diminishing ranks of loyal fans soldiered on as the young, largely locally recruited team did all it could to compete against the money clubs, but we lacked that extra bit of quality when it came to the crunch. No trophies had made their way to the Knowsley Road sideboard since 1977.

But in the summer of 1984, one signing made supporters pinch themselves with the news that Australian test centre Mal Meninga had signed a one-season contract. They say 'the darker the night, then the brighter the star' and none beamed brighter than Big Mal. Saints supporters were well used to our board's 'irons in the fire' transfer policy – irons which invariably went cold when it came down to the nitty gritty. Understandably there were more than a few saying, "We'll believe it when we see him!"

With the previous year's axing of the international transfer import ban it seemed as though every club had brought over Australians. Leeds had signed over half-a-dozen, including Eric Grothe. Wigan had brought over Brett Kenny and wingman Chica Ferguson, with Kangaroo tourists John Muggleton and Peter Sterling joining Hull. Halifax had signed virtually a full team of largely unknown Antipodeans – and they were joined shortly after the start of the season by player-coach Chris Anderson.

We could not wait for ours to come – but before Big Mal arrived with young full-back Phil Veivers in tow – our side had already lost two away games at Bradford and Hull KR. But when he rolled into town on a fine October afternoon, a week before our home game against Castleford, we just knew it was going to be all right.

Meninga's first match saw 7,500 roll up – not spectacular, but double Saints' previous home game's gate. We did not to go home disappointed as Big Mal thundered through for two tries in a convincing 30-16 victory.

When the ball was worked his way he was simply devastating as he brushed off the attempted tacklers. It was just like giving the ball to that oversized kid at under-14 level – with similar results.

Mal had penned the opening lines of another chapter in the history of St Helens RLFC, but never satisfied, unbelievably there were still grumbles from some supporters. 'He'll have to improve his bloody goal kicking!' mumbled one elderly fan coming off the ground. Meninga's style of pointing the ball towards the posts and then toe-bunging it was a bit suspect, but that was the least of our worries.

It was onwards and upwards from there, and Mal and his buddy Veivers helped Saints to the Lancashire Cup Final with a comfortable win over Leigh in the semi-finals.

The Saints bandwagon continued to roll, and as we rattled the points past Hunslet, Halifax and Oldham, other fans jumped on board. Some weeks it was just too easy, but there was always another talking point and other players in the spotlight. The crowds were up and the town walked with a collective spring in its step.

We faced Wigan in the Lancashire Cup Final, and lost the toss for venue. It was the only thing we lost as Saints' first half display went like a dream with Meninga scoring two and creating one for Sean Day, which combined with a blockbusting effort from Roy Haggerty, gave us a 24-2 half time lead.

Wigan mounted a ferocious second half onslaught with Graeme West, Henderson Gill and Nicky Kiss scrambling over for scrappy tries which stirred the Wigan fans in the 26,000 Central Park into raising their voices.

Saints held on for their first trophy win since May 1977. It was only the Lancashire Cup, but it meant so much and blokes in their 40s were welling up when proud skipper Harry Pinner raised the ornate piece of silverware.

The John Player Trophy was our next mission, and after we had beaten Bradford following a draw at Odsal we expected to progress all the way to the final. We felt bullet-proof. But the Meninga-mania bandwagon was derailed in such unlikely circumstances when Saints lost at home to Halifax in the John Player Trophy quarter-final. We all thought Halifax player-coach Chris Anderson was some Australian has-been, over in England for a career swansong at a slower pace. Nobody could have even imagined then what this Kangaroo coach in waiting was about to achieve at unfashionable Halifax. That afternoon they closed us down, and surprisingly went on to record a famous 14-8 knock out. It ruined our Christmas – a festive period that had Band Aid's *Feed the World* as its back drop. Apart from Anderson's coaching prowess, other explanations did the rounds as to why the wheels had come off Saints' season in such an unlikely fashion and in front of the BBC cameras.

Drink was top of the list. It is hard to know the truth because St Helens is a terrible place for gossip and Chinese whispers. Some players felt that the wild allegations that circulated across town blew matters out of all proportion. There were, however, sufficient grounds for the club to slap an alcohol ban on the players, saying those caught drinking within 48 hours of a match would be dropped. Saints' feeling of invincibility had slipped, with Wigan taking advantage four days later at Knowsley Road on Boxing Day.

Although Saints got back on the horse at Widnes with a New Year's Day win, thick snow brought the sporting programme to a grinding halt. A break in the season was the last thing we needed really, with January's league programme decimated Saints were unable to erase the memory of those Christmas defeats and recover from that mini implosion. All we had talked about since Mal's arrival was getting to Wembley, but champions Hull KR at home was a tough opening hurdle. The ice and snow had shunted this game back and it was eventually played on a Thursday night. It was as tense a tussle as you could imagine.

Saints held a 3-2 lead and were tantalisingly close to going through when the combined efforts of Gavin Miller and Gary Clarke sent us tumbling out. That result was not in the script back in those heady autumn days when we envisaged our date at the Twin Towers. If we couldn't get to Wembley with big Mal in the side, when could we?

The following Wednesday Saints suffered a 46-point drubbing at Hull and we were back to the early 1980s mode of thinking again.

Meninga copped most of the verbal flak from opposing fans, especially after his star billing of the autumn. The knives were out from Saints supporters too and at the Boulevard one irate and hoarse speccy kept yelling 'Do something Meninga, you fat pig!' After walking on air in autumn, the harsh winter had brought us crashing back down to earth. With spring on the way, Saints put their miserable mid season blip behind them and our return clash at home to Hull marked the turning point.

It was a cracking game, which did much to take the edge off the sour taste of winter. Skipper Harry Pinner played a blinder, and the team's overall passing and support play was tremendous. Leading 17-12 at the break Saints took complete control in the second half. The try of the match saw Neil Holding race from the base of the scrum, feed centre Phil Veivers, whose lobbed pass found Barrie Ledger. The nippy Saints winger cut inside four Hull defenders, on a diagonal inside run towards the posts, before releasing to Steve Peters. He combined with Big Mal to leave Sean Day with a walk in at the corner.

We were pipped for the title by Hull KR – and although it had been the best league campaign for 10 years, we really were left thinking of what might have been. At least Saints were coming good for a run in the Premiership.

Some days the rugby league planners made some barmy decisions, but the one to make Wigan play their Premiership semi-final against us three days after their Wembley win was perfect for us! Wigan were suffering from tired limbs and hangovers from Wembley, but surprisingly their adrenalin helped them in the opening stages roared on by a good section of a mammoth 20,000 crowd. The game was close for a spell but once the tired legs of the Wembley victors buckled, Saints coasted home 37-14.

Back-to-back champions Hull KR were the most consistent team of the season and had also won John Player Trophy. Fortunately, when they faced us in the Premiership Final they were missing their inspirational Australian loose forward Gavin Miller, who had done more than most to knock us out of the cup earlier in the year. Saints' key Australian Big Mal was there and had a crucial impact on the game.

Gary Ainsworth scuttled in to give us a great start, followed by a Phil Veivers try from a forward pass. There was no doubting the brilliance of our third with a surging break by Meninga only halted by a crunching, high, tackle by Rovers' full back George Fairbairn. However, quick hands, particularly from centre Steve Peters, saw the ball whiz across our back line for Barrie Ledger to score. Determined Rovers hit back, but Meninga's interception from a David Hall pass ensured that Saints went in at half time in front.

The opening of the second half saw Rovers test our defence, but crucially it didn't flinch an inch. Then came that pivotal moment – and one that is etched upon the memories of those Saints fans there that day. Meninga latched onto another loose David Hall pass before steaming fully three-quarters of the length of the pitch running towards us, holding off Fairbairn and Garry Clarke for a crucial try. It broke the Robins' resolve and Harry Pinner sold an audacious dummy to score by the posts and then the flying Ledger grabbed his second, sparked by Neil Holding, to seal the 36-16 win.

The victory was a perfect end to a season that had seen us finally escape from the doldrums. Much of our success was the due to our young local players maturing and the coaching of Billy Benyon, but nobody can ever underestimate the role Meninga played in the 'Return of the Saints'. Big Mal had completed his afternoon's work and his stint for the Saints with two crunching tackles. Unfortunately he hurt his own shoulder with the last tackle that lifted Kiwi Test centre Gary Prohm off his feet. Mal was left wincing, holding his shoulder. Surely he did not feel pain like a mere mortal? It was his last act for Saints, as he left the field a few minutes from the end to tumultuous applause. His all-too-brief 31 game stint at Knowsley Road will always be remembered - Mal earned his Sainthood, and the honour of being cast into clay in the form of Meninga gnomes!

Even though the following season was 10 times worse for his absence, at least we still had those memories and the wishful thinking that one day he would return sustained us during our darkest days of Wigan dominance in the late 1980s and early 1990s.

Mike Critchley's book *The Patience of a Saint – St Helens rugby league 1978 to 1996* will be published by London League Publications in May 2007 at £12.95.

To snuff out the Moon

Tom Mather reflects on the early days of floodlit rugby.

There is a tendency for the average rugby league fan to sit down on a Friday evening and watch the latest offering from the Super League on Sky. We may well moan and groan about Stevo and Eddie, or the referee or the quality of the rugby being played but we watch none the less. We have become so blasé about floodlit rugby, there is a danger of believing that this is how it has always been. That the game has been played during the evenings for so long that it is a natural part of the game. Nothing could be further from the truth.

In a book to be published by London League Publications in July of this year, entitled *To snuff out the Moon* the myths surrounding floodlit rugby are laid bare. The first myth to be dispelled is just when did floodlit rugby actually occur? It most certainly was not in the 1930s as many would have us believe. This was when the Australians first played under the lights in London, and the London Highfield experiment was played out. No it was much earlier than that, in fact almost 60 years or so earlier, in 1878.

The book, *To snuff out the Moon*, traces the developments that occurred from around 1700 up to 1878 which enabled the very first floodlit association football and rugby matches to be staged. It also looks at just why sport in general was selected to play such a huge part in the development of the fledgling electrical industry of the day, and allowed it to take on, then, dethrone the powerful gas industry as the major form of illumination in this country.

In the book there is a detailed account of the events which transpired that culminated in the worlds' first ever floodlit association football match in Sheffield. Some 30,000 or so, not all bothering to pay the entrance fee witnessed the magnificent spectacle that lit up Bramall Lane and it must be said most of the surrounding area.

The football was incidental to the average spectator, who was there to witness the whole area lit up as if it were mid-day in the middle of summer, rather than a cold autumnal evening. They turned up in their thousands, working class folk standing along side the gentry, along with the women folk of both classes. It was an experience which was repeated over the Pennines a couple of weeks later when Broughton entertained Swinton, albeit to a smaller crowd, this time playing the rival code of rugby football.

We see how the whole country became enveloped in the floodlighting phenomena with matches being staged in the most unlikely of places. The book has a vivid picture with the help of newspaper reports of the day of the floodlit matches in the heartland of what is now rugby league territory. It then looks at the first ever association football and rugby matches to be staged in Wales and debunks some of the myths with regard to just who did stage the first soccer match, and what part Thomas Edison played in the event, if any.

There is then a detailed account of the Scottish incursion into floodlit sport with an account of the Hawick Melrose encounter in 1879. All of these events had a number of common feature, the organisers of each event grossly underestimated the size of the crowd that would be in attendance. Secondly in almost ever case the number of supporters not paying to watch the events out numbered those who did.

Thirdly the reporters of the day were either violently opposed to the advantages offered by the lighting or were massively in favour of what the lights offered. There seemed to be no middle ground.

With the three countries covered the book looks at the events which were to lead to the rapid demise of floodlit sport, and just why it was to be another 50 years or so before it was seen once again.

Finally the book move into the 'modern' era with a detailed account of the first ever floodlit rugby league competition. This was staged in 1955 and was organised by Associated Rediffusion Television in the south of the country. This was a short lived competition involving eight of the top clubs, lasting only one year but provided the format for the very successful BBC2 Floodlit Trophy Competition that followed it some years later. The BBC2 competition is covered along with some of the innovations it spawned, the four tackle rule, later to become the six tackle rule we all know today, The introduction of floodlights to most of the clubs in the league, previously only Leigh and Bradford had shown any interest in the new fangled equipment.

A great deal of the material used in the book is previously unpublished apart from in the newspapers of the time. It covers an area of the sport which is now taken for granted but give a fabulous insight into just how society, technology and industry combined to produce floodlighting and hit upon sport as the best vehicle to take it forward. It also pays tribute to those early pioneers who made it all possible. Those socialists who conspired to give the working man more free time to watch and participate in sport. To those scientists who worked to produce electricity and the means of using it to light up sports fields. Finally those industrialists who recognised the potential the new medium had for society.

A short extract from the forthcoming book is reproduced below.

"History tells us that the first ever rugby match to be played at night by floodlights was between Broughton and Swinton. In truth that is not strictly the case. There were references in the press at the time to other 'illuminated matches' being played earlier but research failed to throw up any evidence to support these claims. One thing is sure, either Parker and Bury or the Broughton Club themselves, and we shall never know which, took on board the lesson from John Tasker in Sheffield. They decided to market the match not as an interclub fixture but as something far grander. The match was to be between Mr. A.T. Bowman's XV and Mr. W. Longshaw's XV. The intention was to create the impression that these two sides were in fact invitational sides. To the public that meant perhaps players from other clubs would actually be playing also, when in actual fact this was not the case. The team representing Bowman was in essence Broughton, whilst Longshaw's squad was really Swinton. Things like the Trades Description Act of today held no sway when it came to marketing rugby football in 1878. There could well be another explanation for this ploy, perhaps they needed to use such a deception in order to satisfy the demands made by the controlling Manchester and Liverpool clubs in order to allow the match to go ahead.

It would also be fair to say that perhaps the press and the club tended to exaggerate the actual size of the attendance at the game, mind you that tended to be the norm then as it is now. There is no doubt that Broughton fell into the very same trap that Sheffield F.C. did, and everyone else who staged similar matches around this time. They all vastly underestimated the size of the crowd that turned up to witness the spectacle of rugby and illuminated lighting. It is a theme which runs through the early history of floodlit soccer and rugby; clubs were totally unprepared to handle the vast crowds who did turn up. In the chaos that ensued I suppose it could be excused that people tended to over estimate the actual numbers at the grounds.

One thing is certain, this match failed to attract anywhere near the same newspaper coverage as did the soccer match played just over a week earlier. The two local newspapers of the time, *The Salford Weekly News* and *The Salford Chronicle*, sadly, both published on the same day, afforded the event around five column inches or so each. Both make interesting reading however, as they take slants on the proceedings. One concentrated more on the actual lighting arrangements put in place to illuminate the game, while the other did at least try to describe events that took place on the pitch.

Swinton who were to be the opponents in both of the proposed matches were by this time classed as a 'well established' club, having been formed way back in 1866, even before the Broughton club. Like many before them they had come into being as a result of the efforts of the members of St. Peter's Church Cricket Club. When formed they had officially been named Swinton and Pendlebury Football Club. When, in 1871 the Rugby Football Union had been formed, Swinton had been one of the clubs in the north that had joined this new governing body for the sport. Their headquarters were at the White Lion Pub, hence their nickname of 'The Lions'. Incidentally it is a nickname they carry even today. By 1874 they were playing their games on an enclosed ground on what is now Pendlebury Park.

The reporter for the *Chronicle* wrote:
'On Tuesday evening a football match was played at Broughton between the club of the district and Swinton. The ground was illuminated by means of the electric light and the novelty of the proceedings attracted a large number of spectators, it being estimated that not less than 10,000 persons were assembled within the enclosure, besides large numbers in the adjacent streets and houses overlooking the ground. The arrangements for the illumination were under the supervision of Messers Parker and Bury of Market Street, Manchester, and consisted of a portable steam engine and a dynamo-electric machine known as a 'Gramme'. Differing from previous occasions when this light has been used for the same purpose...'"

It is to be hoped that the brief extract has whetted the appetite of the rugby league lover and will stimulate them into wanting to learn more about the history of the modern day floodlit game we know and love.

To Snuff out the Moon will be published by London League Publications Ltd in July 2007.

Book Reviews

St Helens RLFC: 100 Greats
By Alex Service

Yet again, Alex Service has displayed his talent for converting immaculate research into a highly readable book which will fascinate many outside the boundaries of the glass town. By his own admission, his selection of the 100 players is subjective, but while there may well be quibbles around the town about who's in and who's not, it is undeniably a compilation of rugby league greats.

Which leads me nicely on to Alexander James Murphy. In his foreword, the peerless 'Murph' defines 'great' as being a match-winner or a man of character. I could not argue with any of his examples and especially liked the way he avoids the error too many of yesteryear's stars commit - thinking that only their contemporaries are worthy of consideration. That he doesn't include any recent players is, I think, because he confines himself those with whom he has played or coached.

Alex Service, on the other hand, has an empty canvas and an imperative to cover every era from pre Northern Union to present day. This is one of the book's strengths: the ability to include without facile comparison (which is never really useful anyway). For most of us who are not steeped in encyclopaedic knowledge of the 1890s, it is a joy to have the exploits and backgrounds of early Saints laid out so concisely and those who object to their inclusion on the spurious grounds that the game wasn't then as demanding, are missing the point of Alex's book.

Human nature might demand that later stars should take precedence, and here I can slip in a few of my candidates. There may be a very strong case for including the flinty Welsh back-rower of the 1950s, Ray Cale, that epitome of a covering second-row, Brian Briggs or my own number 1 candidate, Albert Halsall. Albert enjoyed a purple patch around 1966 and, in my view, gave the greatest display ever seen from a Saints' prop in scoring a hat-trick against Halifax in the Championship Final. There, I've had my whinge!

His choice of the 20 'Special Ones' worthy of two pages will bring few criticisms. Ask any Sintelliner and he will agree with 90 odd percent of them and, I suspect, the top five would be near enough unanimous. Vince Karalius, Alex Murphy, Vollenhoven, Keiron Cunningham and Cliff Watson would be my first five and few would argue with my next five either. What Alex has done, however, is to span the generations and explain to me why I should have included Alf Ellaby. Perhaps I should.

He conveys his information in a lively style which sidesteps the statistical wasteland that can sometimes overwhelm the reader. The text is splendidly spiced with photographs which are often new, and all the more welcome for that, especially the action ones. I particularly liked the way he linked the formative years of the 1890s via the pre-1914 War to the hard days of the 1920s and 1930s. His players and the way they were presented seemed to echo the times and allow the reader to grasp the context of the eras.

Bravely, he includes 'one season wonders' where the dogmatic would insist on a minimum of games over a period to establish the player as a great. Meninga, Fairleigh and Lyon are the obvious exceptions to the rule and surely no-one can leave these three out of a book like this. Others may have come, briefly, and with huge reputations, but failed to convince, like O'Connor or Vautin.

St Helens has always sought to excite its supporters with superstars from exotic places like Brisbane or Stanley, but 49 of those Alex includes were born and bred in the town.

Many of these can be rated just below those superstars, but will rank just as high, if not higher, in the fans' affections. Of them all, I would like to suggest Roy Haggerty as Saint incarnate: brave, faithful, honest as the day is long, hard as nails, flamboyant and prone to horrendous error. The Popular Side look for nothing else in their heroes.

Sometimes, books like these can regurgitate too much in the way of local gossip at the expense of genuine information. Alex Service crafts rugby-based potted histories so his subjects do not come over as cartoon characters in a plastic world and his book will, therefore, serve as a point of reference for anyone interested in the famous club.

With proceeds going to the Saints Heritage Society to source and preserve new material, by buying this book you will not only get value for money but help Alex and his band of helpers to preserve the history of a great sporting institution.

St Helens 100 Greats deserves a place in the bookcase of anyone with an interest in St Helens in particular and the game in general.

Published by Stadia, an imprint of Tempus Publishing Ltd in 2006 at £12.99. ISBN: 0752440799.

Roger Grime

Duggie Greenall
A Rugby League Saint
by Denis Whittle

When I was growing up as a young St Helens supporter in the late 1960s, one of the names from the past which my Dad used to mention frequently was that of tough centre and one of his great favourites, Duggie Greenall. I was therefore delighted to discover many years later that Denis Whittle, veteran of rugby league journalism in St Helens (and I hope he won't mind me calling him that), had written Duggie's biography and was to have it published.

Duggie enjoyed a marvellous career at Knowsley Road encompassing 484 games between 1946 and 1959 - only 11 others have made more than 400 appearances for the Saints - and tales of his heroic feats are legendary. They have been superbly related in this book. The author's memories, stories from the man himself about his life off the field as well as his experiences in a Saints jersey and thorough research all have prominent parts to play in the telling of the story.

The book covers Duggie's career chronologically, starting with his early days at the Saints in the immediate post war years when times were hard and ending with his brief spells at Wigan in 1959-60 - when, according to Duggie, he had not defected to the enemy but was merely on a carefully orchestrated spying mission - and at Bradford Northern in 1960-61.

The book tells how a successful Saints team was built in the late 1940s and early 1950s to become a power in the land, the arrival of Jim Sullivan as coach in 1952 being a major catalyst in the success.

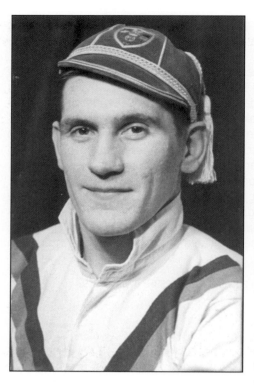

Duggie Greenall wearing his first test cap.
(Photo: courtesy Denis Whittle)

Duggie featured in many of the most significant matches in Saints history and the book brings contains many memories for supporters of a certain vintage as well as an insight into what the world of rugby league was like half a century ago. Today's younger supporters would find certain events surprising and, in some cases, scarcely credible.

Epic matches are mentioned such as Saints' Lancashire Cup final triumph over the 'Old Enemy' Wigan at the late, lamented Station Road ground in Swinton in 1953 when Saints overturned an 8-2 deficit to win the trophy, and the long awaited first Wembley win against Halifax three years later. Also given prominence is the Challenge Cup semi-final replay that year when over 40,000 people attended Wigan's Central Park on a Wednesday teatime to see an extra time win against the holders Barrow. The victory was inspired by a wonder try by Welsh union convert Steve Llewellyn, one of two great wingers to benefit from Duggie's superb centre play; the other was Tom van Vollenhoven who, after arriving at St Helens in 1957, was taken under Duggie's wing.

To retain the balance, less successful finals which ended in defeat against Leigh, Huddersfield, Oldham and Warrington are mentioned, all accounts being backed up by meticulous research with details of teams and photographs being very much to the fore.

Strongly featured as well are Duggie's feats in the international arena surrounding his legendary tussles with the New Zealanders and Australians among whom Duggie had a fearsome reputation. When Duggie was asked to "give them Mammy", the Australians were convinced that was a code for Duggie to unleash some thuggery against them, but thuggery was not part of his armoury; he played the game very hard, but fairly.

The book also confirms some of the hardly believable stories which my Dad used to relate. It is true, for instance, that punctuality wasn't always Duggie's strong point and that he wouldn't turn up at training before *Dick Barton Special Agent* had finished on the radio. It is also true that, during a match against Leigh at Knowsley Road, Duggie ran into the goal post and as a result of the collision the cone from the top of the post fell and hit him on the head. Of such tales are true characters made the likes of which, some say, are lacking in the modern game.

No book on Duggie would be complete without mention of Al Jolson and Duggie's fondness for "giving them Mammy". Duggie's rendition of the classic song at the launch of his book in October 2006 was particularly memorable. Duggie may be nearly 80, but he sang like a true professional.

Former team mates such as Austin Rhodes, Glyn Moses, Vince Karalius and Alex Murphy - all greats in their own right - have also made telling contributions in the book speaking about Duggie's character and the great contributions he made to the St Helens cause. It is obvious that their contributions are sincere, recognising that Duggie, too, is a St Helens all time great in his own right.

To receive the accolades of one's peers is perhaps to receive the highest possible compliment. Reading Duggie's story will show these compliments are more than well deserved.

Published by London League Publications Ltd in 2006 at £12.95. ISBN: 9781903659274

Peter Cropper

Captain Courageous
The Chris Hesketh Story
Chris Hesketh and Graham Morris

To those Salford fans of a certain age, Chris Hesketh is a man who will be remembered fondly. The Salford fans of the time called him 'the Wriggler' due to his unconventional movements when tackled. If you recall captains of the Great Britain test teams, his name may not be in the first list that you can think of. I was amazed to learn that Chris was also the first Wigan born player to captain Great Britain.

This book has brought back many happy memories of when I was a boy. It also recalls the upbringing of Chris Hesketh in Wigan. He was brought up near in Central Park and often went to the match as a small boy shouting for the Colliers from the Hen Pen. But it was at the Willows, that he had his greatest triumph. It is typical of the man that he comes across as he was as a player.

All the triumphs of the Red Devils great era of the 1970s are recorded in this book, all the great players of that side are recalled, including Paul Charlton, David Watkins, Colin Dixon and Mike Coulman to name a few. At the time the Reds were called the 'quality street gang' but the hard work of the centre and his integrity shine through the pages. Chris's greatest in achievements was probably all the 1974 tour of Australasia. Chris captained that great side.

While the Salford side he played in could be considered as underachieving this could not be said of Chris, the book lists his scoring achievements and his role in playing for and captaining Lancashire. Chris only played for two sides Wigan and Salford. His ability was underrated at Central Park. But his abilities were spotted by the Salford chairman Brian Snape; it was to be at The Willows where the rugby league world would see what Chris was made of.

He nearly never made it as a player, because tragically as a small boy he became ill with polio and only a long convalescence allowed him to return to school and his rugby. It was at a rugby union school that he learnt how to play. But he was very happy to sign for his own hometown club and make his way in the game.

Graham Morris lists all the great players that Chris played with including Billy Boston, Eric Ashton and of course all the Salford side that won the championship in 1972-3 and 1974-5, in fact there is almost a blow-by-blow account of each game. The love of the game comes out clearly in this well-written book.

The international games in which Chris played are well documented, but it is the slog that the players had to go through in those days that hit home. Following one tour Chris arrived at the airport and was asked to play for Salford in a Sevens competition at St

Helens next day. There was also a time when Chris played twice in two days, and four games in five days - tell the modern Super League players that and they would not believe you! The shear durability of Chris's career is fantastic when you also consider he had a full-time job as well. There is a very interesting section in the book where Chris lists two sides for his dream test match, which should set a few arguments going.

Chris was awarded the MBE in 1976, but such was his modesty that when his company suggested putting the title on his business card Chris refused. However, like all great players his deeds on the pitch will always be remembered by those who saw his exploits, and his achievements for Salford and Great Britain surely deserve the appellation 'great'.

Published by Vertical Editions in 2006 at £10.99. ISBN: 9781904091196

Dave Farrar

A Pastel Revolution
Harlequins Rugby League – The Inside Story
Paul Fletcher and Philip Gordos

One of the big stories of 2005 to 2006 was the long running saga of London Broncos. The clubs financial problems, battle for survival and final change in to Harlequins RL made headlines in the national as well as trade press.

A Pastel Revolution tells the story of Harlequins RL's first season from the point of view of the players, coaching staff, supporters and board of directors as well as giving a good incite in to the battle to keep London Broncos alive when many thought the club was dead and buried.

The book has quite obviously had official blessing from the club and the benefits of this are quickly seen as all the way through the narrative contains quotes and stories from amongst others Tony Rea, Nic Cartwright, Ian Lenagan, David Hughes, Rob Purdham and Danny Williams to name but a few.

As a long standing supporter of rugby league in London who has seen first hand many of the trials and tribulations of the last 25 years the book in many ways offers much encouragement for the future.

New chairman Ian Lenagan comes across as massively ambitious for the club and unlike one of his predecessors, Richard Branson, seems to be in it for the long run. A combination of business acumen, knowledge of the game and most importantly empathy with the supporters lead to a belief that finally the club have found the right man to lead them forward. Many of the players including Paul Sykes, Mark McLinden, Rob Purdham and Lee Hopkins seem to show a real belief and passion for the club.

One of the more interesting sections covers Wigan's attempt to sign Hopkins after the Broncos dire financial situation was revealed. London fans had often had a soft spot for the cherry and whites but the Hopkins saga and confirmation that Wigan were one of the clubs that voted to exclude the Broncos from Super League have certainly added spice to recent clashes.

In a season of many surprises, when Quins RL kicked off against St Helens on 11 February not many spectators would have believed you if they'd been told that by the

Harlequins RL at the end of the 2006 season (Peter Lush)

end of the season Henry Paul would be a regular and the Tony Rea era would have come to an end with a new coach Brian McDermott filling the hot seat. Both these stories are again covered in some detail.

Much of the narrative with regards to how the season progresses refers to Tony Rea's thoughts. Rea has split the club's fans Broncos for some time. The pro-Rea camp point to the fact that with one of the smallest budgets in Super League in one of the most expensive cities in the world he kept the club in Super League and led the team to two play-off appearances.

Others will point out that with some of the players at the clubs disposal recently such as Jason Hetherington, Jim Dymock, Richie Barnett, Dennis Moran and others he should have done a lot better.

My gripe with Tony Rea has been that in my opinion although he is undoubtedly a great thinker on the game, he is not necessarily a good man-manager or coach and I think all the way through the book this is quite clearly shown. When the team is struggling he knows what they are doing wrong but doesn't seem able to carry these thoughts over in to actually changing things on the pitch. That said, his contribution to the club over the last ten years has been monumental.

All in all this is a good account of a momentous time for rugby league in London. However possibly due to the fact that the book has had official blessing from Quins RL some areas are left untouched.

A number of readers will want to know how London Broncos got themselves in to such a poor financial state and why were there no checks in place to stop this happening. There is a quote from Nic Cartwright in one of 2006's match programmes where he says that this season for the first time the club has a proper business plan. To me that is an appalling fact if true and deserved more investigation.

Ian Lenagan is quoted as saying that when he came on board he was not in favour originally of the name change and link with Quins. Would a debt free London Broncos with his backing have been sustainable?

Early days of 2006 also saw a decent amount of hard feeling from many fans who whilst embracing the new name were very uncomfortable with a number of things off the pitch. It would have been nice if the book had delved further in to this as well.

That being said Harlequins RL have a great chance to fly the flag for rugby league in the capital for years to come. Let's hope this book will one day be seen as chronicling the first tentative steps of a major new force in the game and not those of another false dawn.

Published in 2006 by London League Publications Ltd at £12.95. ISBN: 9781903659298

Giovanni Cinque

RUGBY
The golden age
By John Tennant

As someone who has little interest in rugby union on the field, any Christmas present about 'rugby' should be treated with suspicion. But *Rugby - The golden age* was a tome that I was thrilled to receive and had indeed requested.

Suitably subtitled 'extraordinary images from 1900 to 1980', it is a coffee table book for rugby fans of either code who appreciate gritty beauty. Almost 400 large pages of black and white photos from any array of sources, almost all British either side of the second world war and courtesy mainly of Getty, Popperfoto and Empics agencies. Visual delights abound but I shall highlight the league ones.

Tennant is keen to show rugby as a game of the people: Our Game. There are more photos of players with fans or fans watching matches than any other subjects. A close-up of a Wigan fan yelling at a game reveals teeth like Stonehenge, all the more startling as she is a middle-aged woman beneath scarf and bonnet. It is as far from our image of swinging England in 1968 as possible. A few pages later are the pursed gums of old men in flat caps in 1954. Leeds skipper Jim Brough shows off the Challenge Cup to hundreds of schoolboys in blue and yellow berets at Wembley in 1936, thousands peer over each others' caps to catch a glimpse of Brian Bevan outstripping Jack Cunliffe to touch down in the corner of Central Park during the Great Britain versus The Rest game in 1950.

The quality and clarity of the pictures is stunning, given the supposedly antiquated equipment. Close-ups and huge panoramic stadium shots are equally detailed. No digital camera now could capture those images as beautifully. Most of the action shots are sharp but the relatively small number confirms that Tennant was more interested in the context of the performance but also suggests that high speed play was extremely difficult to capture. The swathe of photos from supposed training sessions – clearly PR exercises before major matches – show an adventurous initiative so often absent now from professional rugby league. Great Britain's class of '62 train in a Brisbane beach in tight trunks and Puma trainers and nothing else; Salford, in smart kit but an array of tatty footwear, have a training run beneath the tower on Blackpool beach; Warrington's canine mascot heads a football towards a line of players at Wilderspool; England toss a ball around on HMS Indomitable en route to Australia in 1946 wearing shirts, ties and braces; Widnes train at Park Royal Stadium before the 1937 Challenge Cup Final; and Swinton practise passing a rotund balloon-like ball through a hole in a wooden dummy defender in a gym in 1937. Black Olympic sprinter Emmanuel McDonald Bailey looks understandably baffled holding a ball after signing for Leigh on a strangely clear day at Hilton Park in December 1953.

There is fun, honesty and community coursing through the book rather than fame, glory and greed. One cracking shot shows Wigan forward Ted Slevin humping furniture for £7 a week in 1950, another Gus Risman showing the Challenge Cup around Wembley in 1938 as schoolboys almost spill over the wall while the doctor, fag in mouth, lugs his case and sponge on the lap on honour!

Perhaps two of the finest shots show the down-to-earth nature of league, even at its peak. Wakefield legend Neil Fox lies of his hotel bed, shoes off, gazing up at the ceiling, while a team-mate gazes at his dirty match shirt, seemingly struggling to take in the enormity of his achievements. Sitting on the bedside table is the enormous gleaming Challenge Cup. A job well done, which is exactly how Tennant should feel.

The coup de grace is the photo chosen for the back cover: Leigh players Bill Kingdon and Ces Ryan walk with a group of tickled kids in shorts across wasteland to Kirkhall Lane ground. Behind them are allotments, behind them smoke-belching chimneys and pit wheels against a charcoal sky.

The hardback original is well worth the £30. His 2001 football version is now out in paperback but has lost much of its beguiling quality. Go for the original if you can find the money and the book.

Published by Cassell Illustrated in 2005 at £30.00. ISBN: 9781844032907

Gavin Willacy

A Game for Hooligans
The History of Rugby Union
Huw Richards

For those interested in the history of rugby league this is a must-read book. Huw Richards is not just a union loyalist; indeed he was the Fulham RLFC programme editor in the 1980s and regularly writes about rugby league. If you think about it, the history of union prior to 1895 is our history also, and it is a period we need to reclaim. Huw dives into this period with gusto and torpedoes the William Webb Ellis myth with the fact that by the end of his life the story of him inventing the game of rugby were not taken seriously. I was a little disappointed that he did not point out that it is now believed that Ellis was born in Salford, certainly he was christened there. I also learnt that the top schools such as Eton and Harrow did not originally play rugby, but played association football and the issues of professionalism did not really threaten the ruling classes as they did not feel threatened by the lower classes earning shillings for playing a sport in their spare time.

The spilt between the codes is well documented in two chapters and the RFU do not come out with any credit in the matter, indeed Richards states that the Northern Union played a positive role, as an outlet for those who wanted to make money out of their talents, to quote the book "if league hadn't existed it would need to have been invented"! The book also shows how the creation of the Northern Union destroyed union in the north: the Lancashire Union was down to 13 clubs and the Yorkshire Union Cup was down from 132 to 11, even the total number of union clubs was down from 481 to 244. Union lost not only clubs but also some of their best players such as Dewsbury's Dickie Lockwood.

The book is well researched and has lots of curiosities, did you know that Che Guevara played scrum-half in Argentina and that Eamon de Valera played union for Munster; indeed some of the most interesting parts of this book is how rugby developed worldwide with some reference to league as well.

One of the important aspects of this book is that it is the first serious history of union since the game went professional. Richards analyses the inevitable road to professionalism and the impact that it has had. He deals with the 'shamatuerism' period which showed the head in the sand attitude to professionalism could no longer be applied and that when the wall fell it did so quickly and everybody wondered what the problem was. One of the most interesting chapters is called 'Journey without maps' which identifies the fact that union is still feeling its way in the modern era. The southern nations have adapted better with the Super 12, and borrowing of league styles of play. In the professional era, as league has always known, it is adapt or go under, and union has paid a high price with the demise of a lot of its junior set-up and the with famous names such as Moseley, London Welsh, Blackheath, and Waterloo slipping down the leagues.

After reading this book, my attitude to the old enemy has changed slightly, I now see union as an estranged parent rather than the empire of evil! If you want to understand where we came from and what union is about – read this book.

Published in 2006 by Mainstream Publishing at £16.99. ISBN: 9781845960162

Dave Farrar

Rugby League: Back o' t' Wall
The history of Sharlston Rovers ARLFC
Graham Chalkley

These days we are used to having a wide range of books on rugby league appearing on publishers' lists each year. Included in the London League Publications list for 2006 was Graham Chalkley's history of Sharlston Rovers, members of the Pennine League Premier Division. In what was obviously a labour of love, Chalkley describes very clearly the highs and lows in the long life of Yorkshire's oldest amateur rugby league club. Although the amateur game is a crucial part of rugby league, books about it are rare. Why that should be is unclear for there is much for an amateur club like Sharlston Rovers to be proud of.

For most of its life rugby league provided few ways for an amateur club to grab the whole game's attention. One of the hardest, but most rewarding ways open to an amateur club was to work through the qualifying rounds of the Challenge Cup and earn

Sharlston Rovers 1923-24 (Photo courtesy Sharlston Rovers ARLFC)

a crack at one of the professional clubs. Not many amateur clubs can even claim the distinction of reaching that lofty stage, but Sharlston have managed it on five occasions. Although no surprises are really expected at that stage Sharlston actually managed to beat the professional new-boys, Workington Town, in February 1946 to join a very select band of amateurs. Unfortunately at that time the first round was played over two legs and that was only the first. Town restored professional honour by winning the second leg by a sufficient margin to go through on aggregate. More recently, Sharlston beat Dewsbury Rams.

Outside the Cup many followers of the game have only become aware of the good work being done by the leading amateur clubs through news reports of their players signing on for professional clubs – and the list of names contained in the first appendix of Sharlston's history of those who have made the grade is certainly very impressive. In both cases, however, the amateur game's achievements were defined through its involvement with the professional game. Yet for those involved in the amateur game there was much more to it than a loyal nursery.

Because Rovers have such a long history, reading this book makes you realise just how rich amateur rugby league's history is and probably how little you know about it. Some of that lack of knowledge can be ascribed to the very local nature of amateur rugby league. Almost immediately after joining the Northern Union in 1901, Sharlston Rovers became members of the Wakefield and District League and the club has spent most of its life in that district league's competitions.

So while Sharlston Rovers' achievements in tackling the professionals in the Rugby League Challenge Cup have made their way into various record books and annuals there is no place for many of their achievements in other, purely amateur, competitions.

Although the advent of BARLA enabled the amateur game to regain its momentum, it has not seen fit to rescue its past from obscurity. BARLA chooses to start its records from its foundation, ignoring the years when the RFL was the governing body for the amateur game. That means that the records for the Lancashire and Yorkshire Cups on the BARLA website start in 1973-74. So while Sharlston's victory in the 2005-06 Yorkshire Cup can be found there, there is no acknowledgement of the club's previous victories, the last 57 years ago in what was then the old Yorkshire Junior Cup. This is hardly an ideal situation as it tends to devalue pre-BARLA success.

Unlike soccer and cricket, rugby league has not enthusiastically embraced the possibilities offered by the major anniversaries of its amateur clubs and competitions as a way of raising profiles and revitalising traditions. That attitude has meant that opportunities have been missed, such as the centenary of the Oldham Standard Cup in 2004, a competition whose finals have regularly attracted thousands, which could have been publicised far beyond the boundaries of the town.

It is practically 10 years since the last anniversary books on the amateur game were published. Then, Don and Dave Kirkley's celebration of 50 years of Keighley Albion, *Seasons to Remember*, published in 1998, and Steve Pyrah's 75 year history of the game in Silsden, published in 1996, brought valuable publicity to the amateur game in that part of West Yorkshire. Through their work and that of Graham Chalkley the amateur game is slowly beginning to get its own history at last. Let's hope that it will not be another 10 years before the next histories of the amateur game appear.

Published by London League Publications Ltd in 2006 at £12.95. ISBN: 9781903659281.

Graham Williams

Rugby League Journal Annual 2007
Edited by Harry Edgar

The third annual produced by Harry Edgar and *Rugby League Journal* is excellent value at £12.95 for those who enjoy reading about the history of the game. One of the best features is a page on each of the game's 'favourite clubs of old' with favourite players, match photos and programme covers.

There are wonderful old photos, including some of the game's great venues that no longer exist, such as Central Park. Some of the game's old publications are recalled, such as Eddie Waring's *Rugby League Annuals*, *Rugby League Gazette* and *Rugby League Review*.

However, it is not all nostalgia. There are reviews of the 2006 seasons in France, New Zealand and Australia, a two page review of British amateur rugby league which mainly concentrates on BARLA, and a review of New Horizons in 2006 which looks at student rugby league, the rugby league conference and the Powergen Champion schools competition.

For the modern-day fan, one of the most interesting articles is a review of the Championship Finals, when the top four teams competed to decide the champions. The play-offs are not a Super League creation after all.

Published in 2006 by Rugby League Journal Publishing at £12.95. ISBN: 9780954835521.

Peter Lush

Gillette Rugby League Yearbook 2006-2007
Edited by Tim Butcher & Daniel Spencer

For those supporters who want a comprehensive record of the most recent season in rugby league, League Publications' annual Yearbook is invaluable, and also very good value at £15.99 for 319 pages.

The traditional statistics are supplemented by the Opta Index Analysis for the Super League clubs, with even the number of penalties for different offences recorded. Curiously, or maybe reflecting the heat of a relegation struggle, Castleford Tigers both were awarded the most penalties for dissent and conceded the most. And Wigan conceded the most for not playing the ball correctly. Harlequins were awarded the least penalties, 163, 23 behind Catalan Dragons, which confirms Quins supporters' longstanding suspicions of referees.

Apart from voluminous statistics, there is also much to read in this book, with a month-by-month account of the season, coverage of the National Leagues, the tri-nations tournament, the season in Australia and much more.

Well illustrated, every rugby league follower will enjoy this book.

Published in 2006 by League Publications Ltd at £15.99. ISBN: 1901347168.

Peter Lush

The Story of the 1958 British Lions Tour
Joe Holliday

The 1958 British Lions tour to Australia and New Zealand was one of the most important and historic Lions tours down under. It included the famous 25-18 victory in the second test in Brisbane when Alan Prescott broke his arm, but continued to play as Dave Bolton had gone off with a broken collar-bone, and other players were carrying injuries. Great Britain had played poorly in the first test in Sydney, going down 25-8. So defeat in the second test would have see Australia win the Ashes. As it was, Great Britain returned to Sydney for the third test to win 40-17, with Mick Sullivan scoring three tries and Eric Fraser eight goals to win the Ashes.

The Great Britain party played 18 matches in Australia, then nine in New Zealand and then three more in Australia. Twice there were matches on consecutive days, and as the tourists gradually accumulated injuries, they were at times struggling to put out a team. The sheer stamina needed to survive this tour was incredible, given the amount of travelling involved, and the somewhat basic standards of hotel accommodation.

The book is a mine of fascinating information. There is a report on every match, and background information, including a profile of each place the tourists visited. However, it was also a difficult tour because of disagreements between the business manager, Barney Manson, the tour manager Tom Mitchell and the coach Jim Brough. When the party returned to England, there was an enquiry into the management of the tour by the RFL, and the book includes the interviews with all three, and the enquiry report.

There are also profiles of all the players who faced the Lions on the tour, although some of these say little more than that they played against the Lions. However, to be fair, some were quite obscure players from country teams.

This book is well worth reading, and provides some fascinating insights into the tour, and the conditions the players faced at that time on a long tour. However, from a historian's point of view it is also frustrating. The match reports clearly are from newspaper reports of the time, as often Great Britain are referred to as 'England', which would have been the norm in Australia, but not here. However, no sources or references are given for them. The tour managers also submitted reports, and some of the material may be from them. Also, the book relies on the RFL's official documents, which are very interesting, but Barney Manson wrote his own book on the tour, and it is unclear whether the author read that book and used Manson's version of events from it. Also, some of the players on the tour are still alive, and their memories of it would have provided more insights into the challenges and conditions they faced.

Finally, although much of the information, such as tour itineraries and travel arrangements give an insight into the tour, these documents would have been better as appendices.

However, Joe Holliday deserves much credit for bringing a great deal of information to light, and providing much that will fascinate readers as we approach the 50th of this dramatic tour. A book well worth reading.

Published in 2006 by Richard Matthew Publications at £18.00. ISBN: 0952830109.

Peter Lush

Celtic Crusaders Yearbook 2007

Celtic Crusaders made a very successful debut in National League 2 in 2006. Finishing third was the highest ever position by a Welsh club in a professional league. Tony Duggan scored 37 tries, a record for a Welsh club in one season. They missed out in the play-offs, losing at home to Swinton by a point in extra-time. Every match is covered in this booklet, a great record of a successful debut season.

This publication would put many a Super League club to shame as it not only gives a report of the Welsh club's first season but has an excellent guide to the club, club records and pen pics of its players. The club have made no bones that they are keen on a SL franchise and this yearbook shows why, the backing of benefactor Leighton Samuels and the professional style of the club's administration will go a long way to getting them there.

There is also a handy guide to all the clubs the side will meet in the season, including a page on each of their opponents' histories, and travel details, which shows a serious attitude to the culture of the game. There is also excellent material on the game in Wales, including the international matches and the Welsh Conference.

It says quite a lot for the club when their first few fixtures are against Widnes Vikings, Brisbane Broncos, London Skolars and Leigh Centurions, who said the game below Super League was parochial? Well done Ian Golden and the Crusaders.

Dave Farrar

Obituaries

Robert Gate recalls those lost to the game in the past few months.

Trevor Allan
(26 September 1926 – 27 January 2007)

The signing of Trevor Allan by Leigh in 1950 was a devastating blow to Australian rugby union. Trevor was the captain of the national XV and had played in 14 of their 15 post-war internationals. In 1984 Jack Pollard described him in his book *Australian Rugby Union – The Game and the Players* thus: "One of the best footballers Australia has produced. He was a boy prodigy who fulfilled all expectations. Dramatic in attack with fast, incisive running, and a match-winning tackler, his positional play was uncanny, and his avoidance of mistakes in play remarkable. There was in his play a quality which inspired team-mates, yet he remained modest and courteous, with a disarming smile and an infectious sense of humour... Allan received more publicity than any Rugby player of his time, and with 'Dally' Messenger, he was probably the biggest drawcard Australian Rugby has known".

Trevor Allan had played rugby league as a schoolboy and had captained a schoolboy league team as late as 19 but he had made a wonderful reputation for himself as a rugby union centre at North Sydney Technical High School. Although the Sydney rugby league clubs, Norths in particular, were desperate to sign him, there appeared little chance that he would turn professional. Trevor's father, 'Slab' Allan coached the Gordon RU team and was apparently a vitriolic defender of the amateur faith. Trevor, naturally enough, joined Gordon and was a Sydney Premiership winner with them in 1949.

His career in union was meteoric. On 14 September 1946, 12 days before his 20th birthday, he made a try-scoring debut for Australia against New Zealand at Dunedin and went on to play further tests against the Maoris at Hamilton and the All Blacks at Auckland. On 28 June 1947 he landed three penalties and a conversion against New Zealand at Sydney, displaying a skill with the boot which was hardly called upon in rugby league. Trevor was never on a winning side in any of those tests. He would put that right soon enough, however. Still aged 20, he was selected as vice-captain of the Wallabies for the 1947-48 tour of Europe, along with future rugby league converts Ken Kearney (Leeds), Bob McMaster (Leeds), Alan Walker (Leigh) and Neville Emery (Whitehaven). Six games into the tour Bill McLean, the tour skipper, broke a leg playing against Combined Services at Twickenham and Trevor found himself as the Wallaby captain – the second youngest captain of Australia by five months, behind Jimmy Flynn, who set the record against New Zealand at Brisbane in 1914.

Trevor led the Wallabies to victories over Scotland by 16-7, Ireland by 16-13 and England 11-0, but they were defeated 6-0 by Wales and 13-6 by France. Uniquely, none of the four home countries managed to score a try against Trevor's side, which was always prepared to play the open game. Trevor played in 32 of the 41 fixtures played in Europe, Canada and the United States – more than any other member of the party. He was also the second leading points scorer with 86 from 17 tries, 10 conversions and five penalties.

On returning home he continued to lead Australia and was in charge for the three match series against the Maoris in June 1949, which ended all square, each team winning once in Sydney and drawing 8-8 in Brisbane. Later that season he led a tour to New Zealand, his side winning 11 of their 12 matches. The tour was crowned by a 2-0 series victory over the All Blacks at Wellington 11-6 and Auckland 16-9, as the Wallabies reclaimed the Bledisloe Cup. Trevor took his captaincy of the national XV to a record 10 tests, kicking a penalty and a conversion in his final international. A new colleague in those Bledisloe Cup triumphs was Rex Mossop, a forward who would team up with Trevor in Leigh and make his own name as a rugby league legend.

Trevor's brilliant performances with the Wallabies alerted English rugby league to his talents and there was still a queue of Sydney clubs wanting to sign him – he was one very hot property. The prospect of his forthcoming marriage in November 1950 had mollified any hesitancy about the wisdom of turning professional and he secretly agreed to sign for Leeds. He had wanted the announcement to be delayed until the end of the Australian season but his agent had failed to impress that fact upon Leeds, who went public. It caused an absolute storm in Australia, Trevor declared he had not signed for Leeds, which was true, and he carried on playing union. Leeds's loss was Leigh's gain. Trevor signed for the Lancashire club for a fee reported, frustratingly, at £5,000 or £6,250, and sailed for England on 15 November 1950, two days after his wedding.

At Leigh, a progressive, big-spending club and captain-coached by Joe Egan, he became an instant hero. He invariably played at right centre, his unusual habit, for a back, of wearing headgear making him all the more distinctive. English fans warmed to his direct straight running, his wonderful acceleration and his magnificent tackling. He made his first team debut on 13 January 1951 in an 8-3 home win against Halifax before 11,153 spectators. The following Saturday he scored his first try for the club in a 16-15 win at Wakefield Trinity. His try-scoring abilities were pretty pronounced, as he finished his Leigh career with 52 in 97 appearances. In his time at Leigh he bagged a four-try haul against Hull and registered hat-tricks against Latchford Albion and Bramley in the Challenge Cup, Liverpool Stanley and Hunslet. At the end of his first season Leigh finished fourth in the league but lost 15-9 at Warrington in the Championship semi-final before a crowd of 26,000.

In 1951-52 Trevor appeared in Leigh's Lancashire Cup final team which lost 14-6 to Wigan at Swinton and had the opportunity to make a trip to Wembley, when Leigh fought their way into the semi-finals of the Challenge Cup. Although red hot favourites, Leigh disappointed by going down 6-2 to Featherstone at Headingley before a crowd of 35,621. In 1952-53 Trevor led the Leigh try-scorers with 30 in 38 appearances, just one short of Jack Wood's club record set the previous season. One of those 30 touchdowns came at the close of his second Lancashire Cup Final. On that occasion, at Swinton before another crowd of almost 35,000, Leigh completely crushed St Helens 22-5 to lift the trophy for the first time in their history, having lost in six previous finals. Prior to the game a previewer in the *Rugby Leaguer* had written of Trevor, "He will be a marked man before he steps on to the field. Allan is now playing better than ever he did. His brilliant swerving runs and wonderful anticipation have won him golden opinions from the writers and his tackling – copybook tackling at that – is known to every opponent who meets him".

The Other Nationalities selectors made good use of his talents, awarding him five caps. His debut, on 31 March 1951, brought him a try at Swansea, where Wales were beaten 27-21 in a splendidly entertaining match. He went on to represent Other Nationalities, usually as partner to Brian Bevan, against England in 1951 and 1952, scoring two tries, France in 1952 and Wales in 1953. He represented Australasia when they beat Great Britain 23-20 at Headingley on 19 May 1951, when Ken Kearney bowed out of English rugby league (see obituary on Kearney). On 23 January 1952 he was a try-scorer at Stamford Bridge, Chelsea for a British Empire XIII which defeated New Zealand 26-2.

Trevor Allan's sojourn at Leigh ended on 19 December 1953 with an 18-10 victory over Rochdale Hornets at Hilton Park. He returned to Sydney, where many pundits expected him to make a big impression in rugby league. For two years, however, injuries kept him out of the game. Norths finally got their man in 1956 and he became their captain-coach until 1958. Unfortunately, he continued to have wretched luck with injuries and played only 11 games in first grade, scoring four tries and one goal. That goal, kicked in a 39-17 victory over Parramatta at Cumberland Oval, on 12 April 1958, was the only one he ever landed in first class rugby league. For some reason he was nicknamed 'Tubby' in Australia – probably because he wasn't, as the power he exhibited in his tackling and running came from a frame which measured 5 feet 10 inches and hardly reached 12 stones. Trevor worked in car sales and later became a well known rugby commentator for the Australian Broadcasting Commission.

Gilbert Benausse
(21 January 1932 – 24 November 2006)

When English speaking rugby league history buffs start talking about the true greats of the game, the usual suspects spring readily to mind – the members of the Rugby League Hall of Fame and the Australian Immortals. New Zealanders hardly get a mention and Frenchmen might as well not exist, unless someone suggests Puig Aubert. It may well be because of the language barrier that so little has been recorded of French league in British rugby league literature. Whatever the reasons we are diminished by the lack of significance accorded to the greatest of our Gallic opponents. Harry Edgar and Mike Rylance have endeavoured to remind us that French rugby league continues to exist and has produced players of exceptional talents – without their literary contributions our knowledge of the trans-Channel game and its history would be next to nothing.

Certainly one of France's most brilliant players was Gilbert Benausse, a stand-off, who possessed the full panoply of skills required for the position. As an attacking, creative player he had few equals. He made tries and scored tries, he could dictate the pattern of play and he kicked unerringly from hand or ground. Gilbert was immensely durable too, as a career which stretched over 13 years at representative level is monumental in anyone's language.

Born in Carcassonne, he gravitated to his hometown team AS Carcassonne and by the time he was 19 he became a test player, making his debut as partner to Jean Dop in an 8-3 victory over New Zealand at the Parc des Princes in Paris on 23 December 1951. A week later he was in the team which completed a 2-0 series win against the Kiwis with a 17-7 success at Bordeaux.

His international career did not end until 1964 and just as the Brits and the French speak different languages, they also have differences when it comes to counting international and test appearances. Gilbert is credited with being the most capped French player in history with 49 appearances. British record keepers would reduce that figure to 43, discounting games against Rugby League XIIIs in 1958 and 1961, the United States in 1954, Welsh XIIIs in 1955 and 1959 and an Eastern Division XIII in

1962. Those 43 international and test matches accepted by British statisticians are, however, more than enough to put Gilbert in the very top rank. Thirty-three were full-blown tests, of which France won 15, drew five and lost 13. Put into perspective, it there are only four British players have won more test caps than Gilbert Benausse – Mick Sullivan, Garry Schofield, Ellery Hanley and Shaun Edwards. When his 10 international games against England, Wales, Other Nationalities and Great Britain (non tests) are thrown into the equation he is right up there in the Jim Sullivan, Gus Risman, Ruben Wiki, Mick Sullivan, Garry Schofield, Mal Meninga and Gary Freeman bracket.

Gilbert played in all three tests against Australia in 1952-53. The French won the series 2-1. He scored his first test try in the decider on 25 January 1953, a 13-5 win at Lyon. The following year saw him in France's World Cup squad, when he figured in a 22-13 triumph over New Zealand in Paris and a 13-13 draw against Great Britain at Toulouse. Antoine Jimenez, one of his great rivals, played stand-off in the final, however. In 1955 Gilbert went to Australasia with France's second touring team, when he demonstrated his wonderful goal-kicking ability at test level for the first time. Being a team-mate of the incomparable Puig Aubert at both club and international level, he had learned much from the master, but had not been called upon to exhibit his own skills in the kicking area. Having missed the first test, which France lost 20-8, he came into the stand-off spot for the Brisbane test on 2 July, and gave his own master class in goal-kicking with six successes as France overturned a 28-16 deficit with a dazzling six minute burst of rugby which ended in an incredible 29-28 victory. He and skipper and centre Jackie Merquey were the stars of the show, which astonished a capacity crowd of 45,745. Five of Gilbert's goals were landed after he had been laid out by a savage tackle from Clive Churchill. The final test in Sydney, an all-ticket 62,458 sell-out, was an equally exciting but low scoring affair in heavy conditions. Gilbert gave the final pass to a 28th minute try-scoring move finished by winger Raymond Contrastin, which levelled the scores at 3-3 but France had to pull out all the stops to finally overcome the Australians 8-5, thereby emulating the success of their 1951 pioneering predecessors.

In the up-country games Gilbert produced some phenomenal goalkicking, including 12 in a 66-21 win against Far North Queensland, followed by nine when North Queensland were defeated 42-26. At one point in Australia he landed 40 goals from 47 attempts. An Australian reporter noted that he kicked in a relaxed style, similar to Puig Aubert, always taking six steps for short kicks and eight for longer efforts. The New Zealand series was drawn 1-1 but when the Kiwis toured Europe in 1955-56 Gilbert was again on the winning side, playing stand-off in all three tests, which were all lop-sided affairs. France won the first 24-7 at Toulouse, lost the second 31-2 at Lyon and won the decider 24-3 in Paris.

Australia had their revenge on France in 1956-57, winning all three tests, Gilbert landing a couple of goals in his only appearance at Bordeaux in the second, which was lost 10-6. He was restored to the side for the three tests against Great Britain in the winter and spring of 1957, contributing eight goals and a try in a series which the French lost 2-0 with heavy defeats at Leeds and St Helens, although drawing 19-19 at Toulouse. In 1957 he returned to Australia with the French World Cup squad, playing and scoring in all three games France lost to Australia and Great Britain but Gilbert's four goals won the game against New Zealand 14-10 at Brisbane. He was a try-scorer in the tournament's final fixture at Sydney, when a Rest of the World side lost 20-11 to champions Australia. After the tournament the French and British squads played a series of exhibition matches in New Zealand and South Africa, where three fixtures were staged, but Gilbert only figured in one, a 61-41 romp for the British at Benoni.

On 5 April 1959 he played one of his best games against Great Britain, claiming 12 points from two tries and three goals in a 24-15 win at Grenoble. The goals he landed that afternoon were his last test goals for three years. In his next test, a 20-19 loss to Australia in Paris on 31 October 1959, full-back Pierre Lacaze booted eight goals and for a time Gilbert's position in the test teams became haphazard. He came back into favour for a clash with Great Britain at Toulouse on 6 March 1960, turning out at centre in test match rugby for the first time as France won a famous 20-18 victory. He was subsequently selected for the 1960 French tour of Australasia but had a disappointing time, playing only one test, again at centre – an 8-8 draw at Sydney in the series opener. France lost the second test 56-6 at Brisbane but remarkably squared the series with a 7-5 win in the third at Sydney.

Left out of the squad for the 1960 World Cup in England, many thought his days at top level were over but such was his class that the selectors could not ignore him. In 1961 he played against Britain and in all three tests against the touring Kiwis. Uniquely, two of the latter, at Bordeaux and Paris, were drawn but New Zealand were 23-2 victors in the second test at Perpignan. In 1962 Gilbert enjoyed three consecutive wins against Great Britain, with his points scoring contributing mightily, France winning 20-15 at Wigan, when he bagged two tries and four goals, 23-13 at Perpignan (five goals) and 17-12, again at Perpignan (four goals). His test career finally came to a halt on 18 January 1964, appropriately enough where it had commenced, at the Parc des Princes. The game was the deciding third test against Australia and Gilbert turned out at centre for the fourth time in his 33 tests, the remainder having been at stand-off. France, under captain Jean Barthe, gave a good account of themselves but succumbed 16-8.

At club level Gilbert, whose employment took in hairdressing and the civil service, was equally successful, playing for Carcassonne, Toulouse and Lezignan. He appeared in his first Cup final (Coupe de France) in 1951, when Carcassonne defeated Lyon 22-10 at Marseilles. The following year he was a double winner, Carcassonne beating Marseilles 14-6 at Stade Chapou, Toulouse, in the Championship final (Championnat de France) and XIII Catalan 28-9 in the Cup Final at Marseilles. In 1953 his four goals helped Carcassonne to retain their hold on the championship, when they beat Lyon 19-12 in the final at Toulouse. A third Championship Final at Toulouse in 1955 ended in a 7-6 defeat by Lyon.

A move to the Toulouse club brought Gilbert no domestic honours but his next stop at Lezignan rectified that. He played in three more Championship Finals, scoring in them all, as Lezignan fell 24-16 to Villeneuve in 1959, but overcame Roanne 7-4 in 1961 and St-Gaudens 20-13 in 1963. He also played in three Cup finals for Lezignan. He was a winner in 1960, when Carcassonne were pipped 7-4 at Perpignan, but was a loser the following year when Carcassonne reversed the result with a 5-2 win after extra time. His last Cup final in 1966, fittingly enough in his hometown of Carcassonne, ended in a 22-7 victory for Lezignan over Villeneuve.

In all six of his Championship finals and in the Cup finals of 1952, 1960 and 1961, Gilbert played in the company of his older brother René, who was a winger of distinction. René also toured Australia with Gilbert in 1960 and won test status. Gilbert's son Patrice, a French international winger, has followed in the family tradition and is currently a Carcassonne player.

David Brook

(Died 21 November 2006, aged 76)

David Brook received the MBE in 1987 for services to business and sport in Yorkshire. That was soon after Halifax had won the Challenge Cup at Wembley after beating St Helens 19-18 in a heart-stopping final – their first Challenge Cup since 1939. In 1985-86 Halifax had astounded the rugby league world by taking the Championship. In 1988 they returned to Wembley but were well beaten by Wigan. By 1989 they had been relegated to Division 2 and on 22 June 1990 the club found itself taken into administration with debts running to £649,000. 'Brookie', as he was genuinely affectionately known to the Halifax faithful, had joined the club's board on 17 May 1984 and was immediately made club president. His six years at Thrum Hall provided Halifax fans with just about all the emotions it is possible to experience in following a rugby league team. The highs were almost celestial, the lows positively infernal. Those of us 'Fax followers who lived through this period will always be grateful to Brookie for the good times, even if they did end in tears. One thing that can be said about his stewardship of the club is that there really was never a dull moment.

Son of an engineer, David Brook's working class roots were in Halifax and he never lost his love for his native town, helping to bring unimagined success to both its rugby clubs over the last 20 or so years. David had supported Halifax since 1938, from the age of eight. The family had not been able to afford a trip to Wembley in 1939 but the memory of the blue and whites' homecoming with the Challenge Cup to Halifax Town Hall never faded for him.

He attended Holy Trinity Junior School and Heath Grammar School, the latter for many years one of Yorkshire's most productive rugby union nurseries. At Heath he became a member of the First XV and an adept cricketer. As a union player went on to become a member of the Halifax RU club.

Brook won a scholarship to Cambridge University, where he studied English and economics. He also played for the Cambridge University XV but did not figure in a Varsity Match, although every interviewer who tackled him reported that he did and was consequently a Cambridge Blue. He did, however, much more impressively, turn out on 83 occasions for Leicester, following his debut on the wing against Bedford on 4 September 1954, when he was a try-scorer in a 17-8 victory. He proved a versatile performer at wing, centre and fly-half over three seasons, appearing for the Tigers against many of the game's major clubs, including the Barbarians and both Oxford and Cambridge Universities. In 1955-56 he topped the Leicester appearances with 39. He scored 16 tries in his career for Leicester, which ended on 29 December 1956, when he played centre in a 3-0 home defeat by Headingley.

It was in Leicester that David began his career in management with the British United Shoe Machinery Company. Within a few years he returned to Yorkshire and set up his own company in Knaresborough. He is reported to have founded Modern Maintenance Products (MMP) with capital of just £412. The company, which produced a wide range of compounds, adhesives and anti-rust materials, moved to Harrogate and by 1984 employed a work force of over 100 and had an annual turnover in excess of £4 million.

Having become a successful businessman, he became a major sponsor of rugby league through MMP. In 1984 MMP was the first company to sponsor a British Lions tour. Although the Lions, under skipper Brian Noble, lost the Ashes in a whitewash, their performance against the Australians was an improvement on the disasters of 1979 and 1982. It was also the first time that a sponsor's logo had appeared on a Great Britain jersey and at least it was tastefully incorporated into the classic red and white chevron. Unfortunately, subsequent sponsors have not been as restrained.

David took a novel hands-on approach to making Halifax successful. In the summer of 1984 he accompanied the Great Britain Lions to Australia, taking in the Los Angeles Olympics on the return home. Before leaving Australia for the United States he had spent much time in signing up a clutch of eight Australian players for £20,000 – a bargain in anyone's terms, especially as among them were future internationals and State of Origin players such as Martin Bella, Paul Langmack and Michael Hagan. Many more Australians would arrive at Thrum Hall in the next couple of years, a trend which has, of course, accelerated throughout rugby league ever since and may now have reached such proportions that our international credibility is seriously compromised. His greatest capture was Chris Anderson, a Kangaroo winger, to whom he handed the coaching reins. The coach Anderson replaced was Welshman Colin Dixon, the former test second-rower, one of Halifax's greatest players and one of the town's most popular adopted sons. The decision caused fury but Brook was vindicated entirely. Everything he and Anderson touched seemed to turn to gold.

On the field Anderson proved to be a masterly player-coach, transforming himself into a wonderful stand-off. Crucially, he had an intimate knowledge of the personnel in Australia and the ability to spot good up-and-coming youngsters, as well as the contacts and charisma to attract more experienced men at bargain prices. Off the field David provided endless copy for the back pages of the *Halifax Evening Courier* and for the rugby league trade press. Halifax were never out of the news and Brookie was never short of a good line or shy of a publicity stunt. There was always a new player in his pipe-line, even if some turned out to be phantoms. Some of his proposed captures would have certainly been eye-poppers, especially from rugby union, for he bandied the names of Wales's winger and captain Ieuan Evans and France's legendary centre Phillipe Sella as likely Halifax acquisitions. In the event Thrum Hall supporters were happy enough to enjoy the skills of Joe Kilroy, Graham Eadie, Keith Neller, Cavill Heugh, Grant Rix and the incomparable Geoff Robinson, to name just a few of the Australians who materialised. Brook and Anderson were, however, not blind to the British market and made some astute signings in the likes of Colin Whitfield, John Pendlebury, Paul Dixon, Les Holliday and Gary Stephens.

David always appreciated the importance of keeping the club in the public eye and while he was in charge there was always a sense of anticipation – anything could happen. He obviously wanted the club's name to stand for good values – 50 odd years of supporting Thrum Hall made him qualified to judge such things. One of my major memories of David Brook is the occasion of an unsavoury incident at Thrum Hall. Halifax, because of their success on the field, attracted big crowds. Unfortunately, for a time they also attracted considerable numbers of National Front (sic) supporters. On the occasion in question Wilf George scored a try at the Scratching Shed end of the ground. The try was greeted by a shower of bananas and abuse from the moronic element. To his everlasting credit, David Brook was on the public address system within seconds telling the idiots that they were not wanted at Thrum Hall and advising them just what they should do with themselves.

Good decision-making, super team spirit, imaginative playing tactics and inspired management on and off the field kept Halifax in the limelight and in the hunt for trophies until 1988. At that point mistakes began to be made and David Brook was the first to admit that. The loss of Anderson was incalculable but his successor as player-coach, the phenomenally popular Graham Eadie, was disastrously ditched in favour of another Australian, Ross Strudwick, as coach. Strudwick broke up the team and presided over 'Fax's relegation, leaving Alan Hardisty to see out the last couple of months of their nightmare. Another Australian player-coach, John Dorahy took over for the 1989-90 season, steered Halifax to the final of the Regal Trophy but, unforgivably, failed to win promotion. Administration followed and the Brook years at Halifax ended.

David had certainly brought glory years and untold excitement to the club but he recognised that it was now time for him to leave. When he was interviewed in the *Halifax Evening Courier* a few months after his departure, he was typically candid, saying, "I'm a high profile guy. I'm not a financial brain or a money-maker. My responsibility was to put rugby back on the map". He definitely did that.

David's interest in sport continued with his chairmanship of Harrogate Cricket Club but he declined approaches to become involved with both the Huddersfield and Leeds rugby league clubs in the 1990s, preferring to take a role at Harrogate rugby union club. In 1997 he joined the committee of Halifax rugby union club, who like Halifax rugby league in 1984, had seen much better days. He became chairman and president at Ovenden Park and his Midas touch returned as Halifax rose through the leagues and are now in National League 2, having also twice won the Yorkshire Cup ('t' owd tin pot') and lifted the Intermediate Cup at Twickenham in 2002.

Peter James Flanagan
(22 January 1941 – found dead 8 January 2007)

In the olden days, when scrums were scrums, rugby league's hooking fraternity always had more than its fair share of characters. Even in the oldest of olden days, contrary to what some people might say, there were always hookers who could play a bit, as well as do their dark deeds in the scrimmage. Peter 'Flash' Flanagan was definitely a character and a hooker, who could play, as well as getting the ball, although it might be fair to say that he played better than he hooked.

No one who saw Flash play is likely to forget him. He looked like Elvis Presley but he had more moves. Reading match programmes and press cuttings of the 1966 and 1970 Lions tours, it is obvious that the Australians were fascinated by him. They routinely commented on his Teddy boy haircut, his spectacular sideburns, his status as the tourists' major vocalist and his blindingly bright red shirts. They also recognised the same qualities that British rugby league fans were familiar with – the alarmingly effective side-step, which could throw defences off guard in the twinkling of an eye, the quick scurries from the play-the-ball, the persistence of his support play and the stamina to keep tackling. What's more, Flash was fun to watch and even those who sometimes judged his *modus operandi* a little risky were always entertained.

A native of Hull, where he worked on the docks and later ran a pub, Flash signed for Hull Kingston Rovers in May 1960 from the Craven Street Youth Club side. He was still only aged 19 when he made his first team debut on 15 October in an 11-11 home draw with Oldham. He scored the first of his 69 career tries on 28 January 1961 when Rovers beat Pilkington Recs 56-8 in a Challenge Cup-tie at Craven Park. By the time he retired in 1978 he had clocked up 486 first class matches.

Flash had to wait a couple of years to cement the hooking position at Hull KR, who had the vastly experienced Alvin Ackerley doing the job for them in his twilight years and then had to face competition from Alan Lockwood, a Yorkshire county hooker signed from Dewsbury. Flash, who looked physically as much like a half-back as a hooker, did appear once at scrum-half in a Yorkshire Cup-tie at Headingley on 2 September 1961 but Rovers were demolished 46-13 and the experiment was never repeated.

By 1962-63 Rovers were beginning to establish themselves as contenders for honours after a long period in the doldrums but Flash was still in and out of the first team. He picked up a Yorkshire Cup runners'-up medal after playing in all three rounds of the competition but was left out of the final, which Rovers lost 12-2 to Hunslet at Headingley. A fortnight later he displaced Lockwood for the inaugural Eastern Division Championship Final at the same venue, where Rovers beat Huddersfield 13-10 to lift their first trophy for 33 years. Later in the season Rovers lost to Wigan in the semi-finals of the Challenge Cup but again Lockwood was preferred. It must have seemed strange to Flash that he could not nail down a regular place with Rovers, when the selectors chose him to hook for a star-studded Eastern Division XIII against France at Carcassonne on 1 November 1962. Although the game was lost 23-16, Flash did well enough to win an England cap at Headingley on 17 November, when France were beaten 18-6. Two weeks later he was awarded the first of 14 test caps, when Britain went down 17-12 in Perpignan, a match universally condemned for the appalling intimidatory tactics of the French and some equally inept refereeing by Edouard Martung. Flash retained his place for the return at Wigan on 3 April, when Britain turned in a glorious performance in winning 42-4.

In 1963-64 Flash played 40 games for Rovers but lost his test place. He did, however, win a place in the Yorkshire team, which lost the Roses match 45-20 at St Helens on 11 September. If the test selectors were a mystery to Flash, the Yorkshire selectors were simply baffling. He would only win two more Yorkshire caps – in 1966, a 17-17 draw against Cumberland at Workington and a 22-17 loss to Lancashire at Headingley, when the floodlights were inaugurated. The selectors seemed to prefer the proven ball-winning skills of men such as Don Close (Huddersfield), John Shaw (Halifax) and the Castleford pair, Johnny Ward and Clive Dickenson, while later on Mike Stephenson was a hard man to displace.

Rovers won their way to Wembley for the first time in 1964, but lost to Widnes. It was to be the only time Flash would appear at the Empire Stadium and it was not a happy experience. George Kemel beat him 19-11 in the scrums and Flash picked up a stomach injury in making a try-saving tackle on Widnes winger Billy Thompson. Rovers continued to challenge for honours for the next decade but fell short on many occasions. Flash did participate in Yorkshire Cup Final successes in 1966, 1967 and 1971 and also picked up a winners' medal for 1974, although he did not play in the final. There were, however, no other major trophies for Flash and the Rovers, who lost in the Championship Final to Wakefield Trinity in 1968, and suffered defeats in Championship semi-finals in 1966, 1967 and 1970, while they also lost in the Challenge Cup semi-final against Wigan in 1970 and the Players Trophy semi-final against Salford in 1972. Among the highlights of his career at Craven Park were victories against the 1967 Kangaroos, 27-15 and the 1971 Kiwis, 12-10, when he scored a try. Another great day was 28 August 1972, when he scored his only hat-trick in a 58-5 home mauling of Hunslet, a game in which Roger Millward claimed 31 points from three tries and 11 goals.

At representative level Flash won back the selectors' approval for the 1966 Lions tour with a series of eye-catching displays. He had a tremendous tour, winning the test jersey ahead of Wigan's Colin Clarke, another very quick and mobile hooker. Britain won the first test 17-13 in Sydney, but lost agonisingly 6-4 at Brisbane and narrowly 19-14 in the decider at Sydney. Flash missed the first test against New Zealand, which was won 25-8 but played in the remaining test, when the Lions repeated the dose 22-14. He made 16 appearances on tour, scoring three tries. Flash, at 5 feet 7½ inches and a mere 11½ stones, was by far Britain's smallest forward − heavier in fact than only the Lions four half-backs − but his dash and industry meant that he could not be overlooked when it came to who got the hooker's role. In 1967-68 Flash played in all three Ashes tests, which were lost 2-1, but also figured in both tests against France, which ended in victories − 22-13 in Paris and 19-8 at Odsal.

In the summer of 1968 Flash went on Great Britain's World Cup trip to Australasia, by which time he had put on half a stone, but not lost any zip. Leigh's Kevin Ashcroft hooked in Britain's first game, a disastrous 25-10 loss to Australia at Sydney. Flash superseded him in the remaining two fixtures − a 7-2 defeat by France in the mud and rain of Auckland and a face-saving 38-14 thrashing of New Zealand at Sydney. He also appeared in all four of Great Britain's tour fixtures in Queensland, all of which were won.

The European International Championship was revived in 1969-70 and Flash hooked in all four of England's games, home and away against France and Wales, although both the Welsh matches were staged at Headingley. England won the tournament on points difference over France. His swansong at representative level came with the 1970 Lions tour, when he and Bradford Northern's Tony Fisher earned the hooking berths. Flash played in the first Ashes test at Brisbane on 6 June, scored his only test try and edged Elwyn Walters 15-13 in the scrums. Unfortunately, Britain went down 37-15 and Fisher played in all the remaining tests of a record-breaking tour. Flash figured in 13 matches, scoring eight tries and a goal, the latter being kicked in a 57-2 victory against West Coast in New Zealand. Since his death some obituary writers have claimed that Flash was the first hooker to make three trips to Australasia with Great Britain (1966, 1968 [World Cup] and 1970) but they are mistaken. Hull's Tommy Harris (1954, 1957 [World Cup] and 1958) had already achieved that distinction.

Flash shared a joint benefit with Colin Cooper in the 1972-73 season. Hull Kingston Rovers were relegated at the end of the 1973-74 season and Flash made the last of his 414 appearances, having scored 57 tries and 13 goals, for the Robins on 11 October 1974 in a 10-5 home reverse to Whitehaven. There was, nonetheless, still mileage in Peter Flanagan's rugby league life, even if he had passed 33 years of age. He began to play amateur rugby league with Hull Dockers, until Second Division Hull persuaded him to help them out when regular hooker Tony Duke received a long term injury. So Flash changed his Robin's red and white plumage for an Airlie Bird's black and white. He made his debut for Hull on 21 October 1975 in an 18-11 victory over Bramley at The Boulevard in a Floodlit Trophy fixture. Flash helped Hull astonish the rugby league world by reaching the Players Trophy Final on 24 January 1976. Hull gave mighty Widnes a good run for their money at Headingley, losing only 19-13 and displaying some fine football.

Flash retired for a second time from the professional game in 1976 and Hull won promotion in 1976-77. The following season they found life tough in the First Division and another injury crisis prompted them to send for Flash once more. He responded to their plea and played seven consecutive games between December and January. Sadly, even for Flash, this was one miracle too far − all seven games were lost and Hull eventually went down. Flash made his 21st and last appearance for Hull on 29 January 1978 in an 18-12 home defeat by St Helens, one week after his 37th birthday.

Keith Holden
(31 July 1937 – October 2006)

Before he ever played a game as a professional Keith Holden had caused an unholy rumpus in the corridors of rugby league power. An outstanding schoolboy stand-off in his native Wigan, he had contrived to sign professional forms for both Wigan and Leigh, who were both desperate to obtain his services, when he became 16 in July 1953. The Rugby League Management Committee refused to accept both clubs' claims to Keith and the dispute rumbled on for a year. In March 1954 the Management Committee declared that he was free to sign for any club he chose. More complications then arose when Swinton also claimed to have a written promise from Keith that he would sign for them and that he had actually been training at Station Road for a time. History shows that Keith finally signed for Leigh to begin a long and successful career, which took him on a wide peregrination around Lancashire and cost several clubs big transfer fees.

Three days after playing in the 'A' Team at Barrow, Leigh gave Keith his debut at stand-off in a 21-10 home victory over Bramley on 24 March 1954. During the 1954-55 season he was a regular first-teamer, playing 30 games at centre and one on the wing, scoring 15 tries, including hat-tricks against Hull KR and Belle Vue Rangers. In 1955-56 he was shifted to the wing for 22 of his 27 games. His 13 tries included one in a 14-13 victory over the New Zealanders, four against Hunslet in a 46-20 win at Queen's Park Rangers' ground in the experimental Rugby League Television Trophy and one in the final of that competition, when Warrington beat Leigh 43-18. By the time he was 20, Keith had clocked up a century of games for Leigh and was one of the brightest prospects in the game. His displays in Leigh's centre catapulted him into contention for a Lions tour place in 1958 and he was brought on as a substitute for Syd Lowden (Salford) in the 47th minute of a tour trial at Headingley on 19 March 1958. However, Great Britain were not short of top class centres with more experience than Keith.

Keith played his 142nd and last game for Leigh on 11 October 1958 in a shock 26-25 home defeat by Blackpool Borough, having scored 58 tries. Wigan had finally got their man, four years after they thought they had him. He cost them a whopping £6,666 and made his debut on 25 October in a 17-8 loss at Leeds. Wigan did not lose many more games in his time at Central Park, where he became a vital cog in the great three-quarter line which comprised Billy Boston, Eric Ashton, Keith Holden and Mick Sullivan. That was a tough quartet for opposing teams to control and Keith did not look out of place in combination with three of the greatest players the game has produced. At 5 feet 10 inches and over 14 stones, he provided solidity and strength and his bustling, forceful style caused plenty of problems for opponents.

At the end of his first season with Wigan he appeared at Wembley, where he scored the opening try after eight minutes as Wigan swamped Hull 30-13. He also picked up a Lancashire League Championship winners' medal for 1958-59. The following season he scored 20 tries in 41 games for Wigan – the best returns of his career – and was at left centre in Wigan's terrific 27-3 beating of Wakefield Trinity in the 1960 Championship Final, which drew a Championship record crowd of 83,190 to Odsal. Six months later

Keith joined Oldham for a fee of £7,500, after making 87 appearances for Wigan in which he claimed 36 tries.

Keith made his debut for the Roughyeds, scoring a try from the left wing, in a 16-2 win at Whitehaven on 26 November, 1960. In 62 games for Oldham, he was used on the wing 17 times and 45 times at centre, scoring 31 tries. Oldham were struggling to maintain the high standards they had achieved in the 1950s but to little avail. The nearest Keith came to winning more honours at Watersheddings ended in a 10-8 home defeat by St Helens in the Lancashire Cup semi-final on 2 October 1962. At the season's end they were relegated but Keith had been sold to Warrington for £3,500 just before the Challenge Cup register closed. He made his debut for the Wire on 30 January 1963 at Castleford, where a 12-9 victory was gained. Injury kept him out of Warrington's Challenge Cup semi-final team against Wakefield Trinity, which was lost 5-2, and he only made seven appearances in his first season at Wilderspool.

However, 1963-64 saw Keith hit a rich vein of form. He scored 17 tries in 33 games, including two touchdowns in the opening fixture of the Kangaroos' tour, when the Wire lost 28-20. The Australians hammered Great Britain in the opening tests at Wembley and Swinton and the British selectors completely reshaped the side for the third test at Headingley on 30 November 1963. Keith was one of seven debutants, partnering Swinton's Alan Buckley in the centres. It was not a test for faint hearts and Keith was anything but faint-hearted. In the first 15 minutes referee Eric Clay issued cautions to four Australians and Keith, and he also cautioned Keith in the second half. Three players - Britain's Cliff Watson and Australians Brian Hambly and Barry Muir - were dismissed, as the game developed into one of the roughest tests ever played. Keith and Alan Buckley did their jobs manfully in shackling their illustrious opposing centres, Reg Gasnier and Graeme Langlands, and victory went to Great Britain 16-5. Perhaps surprisingly, Keith never played another test and was unfortunate to have won no more representative honours than a couple of caps for Lancashire against Cumberland in 1958 and 1964.

After 47 appearances and 22 tries for Warrington, Keith was on the move again. He returned to Wigan for a £3,000 fee, making his first appearance at left centre on 6 February 1965 in a 16-0 home win against Barrow in the Challenge Cup first round. The return to Central Park took Keith back to Wembley, where, as he had done in 1959, he scored the opening try in a fabulous final against Hunslet, which Wigan won 20-16. Wigan returned to Wembley in 1966, losing to St Helens, but Keith missed the last six months of the season. He was back, however, for the Lancashire Cup Final at Swinton on 29 October 1966. Along with Billy Boston and Eric Ashton, who had never won a Lancashire Cup, he completed his collection of the game's major medals as Wigan beat Oldham 16-13. He continued as a Wigan player until 1968, adding another 65 tries and 22 tries to his career record.

Keith's final club was Blackpool Borough for whom he made his first appearance on 17 August 1968 in a 16-11 win against Hunslet at Borough Park. He played at the seaside for over two years, 12 of his 41 appearances (three tries) for Borough being made in the pack. However, he played his last professional game on the right wing, scoring a try in a 10-10 draw at York. By then his career had stretched over 16 years and yielded 448 games and 173 tries.

Trevor Allan

David Brook at Wembley as Chris Anderson
holds the Challenge Cup

Left: Peter 'Flash' Flanagan

Above: Ken Kearney

Left: Keith Holden playing for Wigan versus Oldham in 1960.

Middle: Berwyn Jones playing for Wakefield Trinity.

Bottom: Alan Kellett playing for Oldham versus Salford.

Left: Jimmy Ledgard playing against France in 1954. Above: Jim Lewthwaite

Above: Tommy Lynch and Arthur Daniels in 1952.

Right: Emlyn Richards.

All photos in this feature supplied by Robert Gate.

Thomas Berwyn Jones
(13 February 1940 - 12 January 2007)

On 30 March 1964 something extraordinary happened at Fartown. Nobody had warned the 5,472 members of the crowd, which included me, at that time still a schoolboy. We were watching a tense but not particularly thrilling game between Huddersfield and Wakefield Trinity. To say that defences were on top would be an understatement, as the only score of the match proved to be a penalty goal by Fartown full-back Brian Curry in the 65th minute. Trinity fielded a trialist winger from Wales, dubbed 'Walker', on their left wing. He was partnering Neil Fox but because the game had developed into a forward battle, 'Walker' had had precious little to do. Then in the 70th minute he finally got the ball. The crowd was palpably shaken when he clicked into gear. Fartown had seen some pretty quick wingers but this chap was something else. He streaked down the left touch-line toward the score-board end. Time seemed to stand still, because he was the only one moving at that rate. Just as it seemed he must score Brian Curry, running a much shorter distance, managed to push the human lightning streak over the touch-line.

The following afternoon Trinity won 44-3 at Doncaster in an Eastern Division Championship fixture. 'Walker' displayed his startling pace when he scored in the corner after 19 minutes but then took a spectator's role as Gert Coetzer on the other wing rattled off five touchdowns. The Trinity board had seen enough, however, to sign up the trialist, and the reported fee was a massive £6,000. When it was revealed that 'Walker' was in fact Berwyn Jones, the fastest man in Britain and Europe in 1963 and fourth fastest in the world, the sensation was felt throughout the British sporting scene and it became one of the biggest news events our sport has seen.

Jones was the Welsh sprint champion, the British 100 metres record holder (10.3 seconds) and had won four out of five international races in 1963. He was a member of the Great Britain 4 x 110 yards relay team which had set a world record, he had won bronze in the Welsh 4 x 110 yards team in the Commonwealth Games in Perth, Australia, in 1962, a bronze for Great Britain in the European Championships at Belgrade the same year and he was the AAA 100 yards champion in 1963. He could cover 100 yards in 9.4 seconds. Who knows what he might have done in the 1964 Tokyo Olympics, if he had not decided to play rugby league – to literally take the money and run.

This signing was seriously big news. It was also a seriously big gamble for Berwyn and for Trinity. There is no doubt that it paid off. The publicity was enormous, the BBC televised Berwyn's first game after his signing was made public and Trinity immediately reaped the benefit of their first £1,000 league gate of the season at Belle Vue, when they beat Halifax 38-10 on 4 April.

Athletes such as Trinidad's MacDonald Bailey, an even faster man than Jones, and shot-putter Arthur Rowe, had tried and failed at rugby league in the preceding decade, but Berwyn proved an exception to the rule. A PE teacher in Birmingham, he had played rugby union at school and on occasions for his native Rhymney. He was not therefore a complete novice. Of solid build – 5 feet 9 inches and a little over 12 stones – he soon showed he had the courage to go with his amazing pace, and he eventually proved that he could take the knocks, handle the ball well and run in more than just straight lines.

These were the days when subterfuge was still required in dealing with potential converts to the game. Eddie Thomas, a Welshman who was Trinity's secretary, had been alerted to the possibilities of Berwyn as a rugby player by Idris Towill. Idris, a Cup

Finalist with Huddersfield in 1935 and Keighley in 1937 and a Welsh league international stand-off in 1932, lived in Bridgend but was still well connected with the north. Eddie arranged for Idris to visit Berwyn's family home under the pretext of asking him whether he would consider turning out for Bridgend! The conversation then took other directions.

Berwyn soon settled to rugby league and was quickly scoring spectacular tries, picking up 20 in 43 appearances in 1964-65, his first full season. Trinity soon realised that Berwyn was more effective on the right wing than the left because he tended to sidestep to the left and was consequently taken more easily into touch on that flank. Opponents also realised quickly that if he got a clear field or was chasing a kick no one on Earth was going to catch him in a straight race. He subsequently became the victim of a lot of blatant obstruction, taking considerable physical punishment. Berwyn's phenomenal speed was a bonus in defence, as he saved many tries through his ability to overhaul opponents who thought they were in the clear.

Trinity won the Yorkshire Cup in 1964, beating Leeds 18-2 at Fartown. Berwyn hared over for two tries, while Neil Fox claimed the remaining 12 points. His progress was such that he was in the Great Britain team which lost 18-8 to France at Perpignan on 6 December 1964, scoring one of his side's two tries. He had better luck in the return test at Swinton on 23 January 1965, a game notorious for the fiasco surrounding the dismissal of French skipper Marcel Bescos. Britain won 17-7, largely because Neil Fox booted seven goals, with Berwyn scoring their only try.

The 1965-66 campaign saw Berwyn claim 19 tries in 29 games for Wakefield, who lifted the Yorkshire League Championship but surprisingly fell in the Challenge Cup semi-final to Hunslet. He represented a Commonwealth XIII which lost 15-7 against the New Zealanders at Crystal Palace on 18 August 1965, but was overlooked for the test series against the Kiwis, when the selectors preferred to use Geoff Wriglesworth, Ken Senior, Bill Burgess and John Stopford on the wings. He was reinstated for the test match against France at Perpignan on 16 January 1966. Britain scored three tries to two, Berwyn claiming one, but lost 18-13. He had obviously done enough, however, to win a place in the Lions squad for the 1966 tour – a sharp smack in the face for those who doubted his ability to make the grade in his new sport.

Despite failing to break into the test side, Berwyn had a good tour. He made 15 appearances, failed to score in only four matches and led the try-scorers with 24 – 17 in Australia and seven in New Zealand, topping the list in both countries. He scored four tries against Queensland and against Western New South Wales, and claimed three against Far North Queensland and Taranaki. His most significant contributions in terms of winning matches, however, came against Newcastle and Auckland. At Newcastle he raced 65 yards to score in the 68th minute after Peter 'Flash' Flanagan had intercepted from what everyone on the ground considered a deeply off-side position, enabling the Lions to win 5-2. In the final game of the tour at Carlaw Park he was a scorer, but Britain, who had won all their games so far in New Zealand, trailed Auckland 11-10 as the game entered its last minute. Berwyn made a desperate effort to score from a kick and, as so often had become the case, was gratuitously obstructed to prevent a try. A penalty was awarded, however, from which full-back Arthur Keegan landed a last gasp winning goal.

Wakefield Trinity won the Championship for the first time in 1966-67 and Berwyn qualified to receive a medal, having played in six league fixtures during the season. He had, however, parted company with Trinity after playing in a 31-6 victory at York on 18 February 1967. That had been his 89th game for the club, for whom he had scored 47 tries. Berwyn transferred to Bradford Northern, the transfer fee being £3,000. He was among the scorers on his debut on 25 February in a 24-0 home win over Huddersfield. Injuries restricted him to a mere seven games for Northern that season. He was back to fitness and form for 1967-68, roaring over for 26 tries in 35 games, bagging five tries against both Batley and Bramley. On his day Berwyn was capable of scoring wonderful tries but his days at Odsal and in rugby league were approaching their end. He scored his last try - his 35th - for Northern, ironically enough, against Wakefield in a Challenge Cup-tie which was drawn 7-7 at Odsal. The replay, a 10-0 defeat at Belle Vue, on 27 February 1969 was his 63rd and last for the club.

A £3,000 move to St Helens saw Berwyn score a try on his debut on 16 August 1969 in a 27-3 home win against Castleford. Less than a fortnight later, on 29 August, his rugby league career ended after a 14-7 victory at Warrington. He had some problems with injuries, and took up a teaching post in Hertfordshire.

He had played just four games, scoring two tries for Saints. His first-class career brought Berwyn 111 tries in 175 appearances. He died in Ross-on-Wye after suffering from motor neurone disease.

Kenneth Howard Kearney
(3 May 1924 - 18 August 2006)

Ken Kearney — 'Killer' to his friends and enemies — enjoyed an extraordinary career in both codes of rugby, on both sides of the globe.

The youngest of eight children, Ken was born in Penrith, New South Wales, where he played some junior rugby league. However, on attending Parramatta High School, his path took him into rugby union as a reluctant hooker, a position he decidedly did not want to fill. By 17 he was playing for the senior Parramatta RU club — at hooker, where he remained for the rest of his career.

He made his first trip to Great Britain in 1943 while serving in the Royal Australian Air Force (RAAF) as a radio operator on Lancaster bombers. He managed to play quite a bit of Services rugby in the process. After the war he had developed so well that he was selected to play for Australia in two tests against the All Blacks in June 1947, which were lost — 13-5 in Brisbane and 27-14 in Sydney. He had acquitted himself well enough to gain a tour place with the 1947-48 Wallabies, who were the first rugby union tourists to visit Europe in the post-war period. The tourists left Sydney on 19 July 1947 and did not return to their homeland until late March 1948. The tour took in 41 games, of which only six were lost. It included five fixtures in France and six in Canada and the United States. Ken made 22 appearances, scored four tries and hooked in all five internationals. Scotland, Ireland and England were beaten but the Wales and France games were lost.

Ken attracted considerable attention while playing in Britain and took up Leeds's offer of $2,000 plus match fees and a job, returning to England on a three-year contract in time for the start of the 1948-49 season. He made his debut on 21 August in a 7-7 draw with Bramley at Headingley. As an illustration of how history repeats itself, the Leeds team contained just three Englishmen — Dennis Warrior, Sammy Newbound and Reg Wheatley. Three Australians, a New Zealander, two Scots and four Welshmen assisted them. Ken's compatriots were Arthur Clues and prop Bob McMaster, the latter a fellow Wallaby on the 1947-48 tour. Despite all the imports, Leeds finished 14th, Ken making 29 appearances and scoring a solitary try at Hull KR. The following season Leeds rose to sixth and Ken experienced the heartbreak of losing in the semi-final of the Challenge Cup against Warrington. In 37 appearances he again bagged one try – his last for Leeds - in a 63-3 home demolition of York. On 19 September 1949 at Borough Park, Workington, he had the distinction of playing for the Other Nationalities in their inaugural game in the European International Championship, when they beat England 13-7. He went on to represent the Other Nationalities four times, twice against Wales and once against France.

His last season with Leeds brought him a Yorkshire League winners' medal and another disappointment at the semi-final stage of the Challenge Cup. On that occasion Leeds drew 14-14 with Barrow but collapsed to a 28-13 defeat in the replay. Ken played his 95th and last game for Leeds in a 15-14 loss to Bradford Northern at Odsal on 25 April 1951. He ended his three year stint in England, however, on 19 May, at Headingley in the Australasia team which beat Great Britain 23-20 in a game staged as part of the Festival of Britain celebrations. Ken had played exactly 100 games in his English career and, more importantly, he had learned enough revolutionise the Australian game.

As a hooker he had received a thorough education in England. When he arrived at Headingley he knew how to cope with rugby union scrummaging but winning the ball in rugby league was an entirely different matter. In Larry Writer's wonderful book, *Never Before, Never Again*, Ken remembered, "As a lilywhite union player I played by the book and that made me a lamb to the slaughter. Things went on in those north-of-England scrums I'd never dreamed of. Loose arms, the opposing half would throw the ball either in his second-row or right at my face, I was punched from the second-row, head butted, bitten, scratched, had mud rubbed in my eyes. I didn't stand a chance" After a few drubbings in the scrum counts and a lot of painful lessons from the likes of Dave Cotton, Alvin Ackerley, Harry Bradshaw, Vic Darlison, Mel Meek and Joe Egan, Ken wised up pretty quickly. He set about learning all the dark arts of winning possession and the even darker arts of getting in his retaliation first. Apart from becoming an expert in self-preservation, Ken also realised that the British were miles ahead of Australia in individual skills, defensive structure and tactical know-how. He was determined to put his new knowledge to good use on his return to Sydney.

On his rugby first trip to England with the Wallabies Ken had stood 5 feet 7 inches tall and weighed a paltry 12 stone 2 pounds, being the lightest forward on tour. As he matured he put on a stone and a half and ultimately topped 14 stones. Sporting crew-cut hair, he began to look like the old fashioned archetypal hooker – squat, low to the ground, bandy-legs swathed in voluminous shorts and by no means the fastest thing on two legs. He was once graphically described as "toothless and ruthless". He was certainly tough, a hard man to best in the scrum, dominating around the play-the-ball, a fearsome tackler and he always had a perfect understanding with his scrum-half. He was also a severe trial to referees in Australia, who were not as content as English referees to put up with his bending of the scrummaging laws. His forwards knew that his priority was to subdue the opposing pack before the backs could do their work.

Ken joined St George on returning to Australia – because they made him the best offer. He was an immediate success and won selection for the 1952 Kangaroos tour at the end of his first season. He went away as second choice hooker to Manly-Warringah's Kevin Schubert, who played in the first two Ashes tests, which were both lost. He was drafted in for the final test at Odsal on 13 December – a game which has gone down as one of the ugliest and nastiest in test history. Ken won the scrums against Tom McKinney, despite losing his prop Duncan Hall, who was dismissed in the 52nd minute and Australia won the test 27-7. Ken did not miss another test or World Cup game for the next six years, rattling up a staggering 31 consecutive matches in the green and gold, captaining the side in nine tests and claiming three tries.

The 1952-53 Kangaroos were almost as busy as the 1947-48 Wallabies, fulfilling 40 fixtures, of which Ken played 20, including all three tests in France, which the Australians lost 2-1. Apart from losing both test series the 1952-53 Kangaroos had a brilliant record, winning 33 games and drawing once, while piling up a record 1,117 points and conceding 373 – all for £8 a week. In the 1953 season he toured New Zealand, playing in all three tests, another series the Australians lost 2-1. In 1954 he was at last in a victorious series for Australia, when the Lions were defeated 2-1. Later that year he was in the Australian team in all three of their games in the inaugural World Cup in France, scoring tries against Great Britain at Lyon and New Zealand at Marseilles. In 1955 he was on the wrong end of a dramatic series against France on home soil but was appointed captain for another home series against New Zealand in 1956, when he presided over a 3-0 win.

Ken, aged 32, retained the captaincy for Australia's tour of Europe in 1956-57, when he was also the coach. The Kangaroos played only 28 games, winning 18 and drawing once. Ken made 18 appearances, scoring a couple of tries and a goal. He played in all six tests, the French being beaten 3-0 but the Ashes were surrendered rather tamely – 19-0 at Swinton in the decider. Ken got something he had not anticipated in the game against his old club Leeds, when, with 15 minutes left, he was kicked in the head, was taken off, received six stitches and saw his team go from leading 13-8 to losing 18-13.

His wound turned septic and he missed the next four matches. It was not a great tour, the Australians did not measure up to their post-war predecessors and Ken lost the captaincy to Dick Poole, when the 1957 World Cup was staged in Australia. He did, however, play in all three games as Australia won the trophy with some ease. His last test appearances were also on home soil against the 1958 Lions. Ken out-hooked Tommy Harris in all three matches, but Australia were no match for Great Britain in the second and third tests, after an initial 25-18 win at Sydney.

Distinguished as his record at test level was, Ken's achievements at domestic level with St George put everything else into the shade. Ken became captain of the side in 1953 and held the position until he retired in 1961. He coached the side from 1954 to 1961, with the exception of 1956. In that period he indelibly stamped his mark on Australian rugby league. St George became more disciplined, they trained harder and they adopted Ken's tactical theories learned from the English. He introduced circuit training and he developed a straight line of defence, which the Australians christened the "Brickwall defence". In *Never Before, Never Again*, he recalled, "I was able to inspire my men's loyalty because I worked at my football as hard as they did, if not more so. And we won, and the more we won the more they respected me and the harder they tried. I've been blessed with a good tactical brain... People always asked how I could read a game with my head stuck in a scrum, but I saw everything, don't worry about that. People were amazed because I saw everything going on – in the scrum, in the backs, all over the field. I had 360-degree vision. Players couldn't hide from me and if I caught them loafing or making mistakes or defying my instructions I'd hurry them up, very smartly."

Between 1952 and 1955 St George never finished below third but they never won the Premiership. From 1956 onwards they became the great unbeatables, winning 11 Grand Finals in a row. There is no doubt that Ken Kearney was the catalyst for St George's absolute domination of the competition and the knock-on effect their success had on the wider Australian game in subsequent years. He was captain in 1956 when Balmain were defeated 18-12 in the Grand Final – Norm Tipping was coach - and he was captain-coach for the next five years, although he had retired from playing before the Grand Final of 1961 when Wests were despatched 22-0. In 1959 St George went through the league programme undefeated, Balmain being the only team to take a point from them in a 20-20 draw at Kogarah Oval. Norm Provan took over as player-coach, when Kearney stepped down, and added the next four Premierships to the Dragons' honours board, before their eleventh consecutive title was gained under Ian Walsh.

Ken remains the oldest player to have figured in a Grand Final, being aged 36 years and 123 days in 1960, when Easts were humbled 31-6. He shares with Souths' Jack Rayner the distinction of winning a record five Premierships as captain and jointly held the record for most Grand Finals as coach with Jack Gibson and Wayne Bennett until 2006 when Bennett won his sixth with Brisbane Broncos. In 2006 he was elected to the Australian RL Hall of Fame. After finishing at St George he coached Parramatta from 1962 to 1964 and Cronulla from 1967 to 1968.

Alan Kellett
(6 October 1937 - 10 October 2006)

Although Alan Kellett was undoubtedly one of the outstanding stand-offs of the 1950s and 1960s, he never attained the representative honours he might have expected in almost any other era. In his time in the game he had to contend with the likes of Ray Price, Gordon Brown, Dave Bolton, Lewis Jones, Austin Rhodes, Brian Gabbitas, Frank Myler, Harold Poynton, Alan Hardisty, Willie Aspinall, Roger Millward, Phil Kitchin and Cliff Hill and they were only the number sixes who earned test caps. Even so, Alan made nine appearances for Yorkshire between 1958 and 1965, was named in test 'shadow' teams and was one of the reserves for the 1960 World Cup squad.

His career for the county began on 24 September 1958, when he partnered Jeff Stevenson in a 35-19 drubbing of Lancashire at Craven Park, Hull. Five weeks later, on 29 October, Yorkshire met Lancashire again under floodlights at Leigh in a play-off for the County Championship. This time his partner was Don Fox and a thrilling 16-15 victory to the Tykes brought Alan his first County Championship winners' medal. Just over a year later at York, on 28 September 1959, he bagged a hat-trick, while Neil Fox scored a record 23 points, as Yorkshire butchered the Australians 47-15. He followed that with two tries in the Roses Match at Leigh on 11 November, picking up a second winners' medal as Yorkshire won 38-28. He was a try-scorer in the Roses Matches of 1961 at Wakefield and 1965 at Swinton, as well as figuring in Yorkshire's victories over the 1961 and 1965 Kiwis.

Alan was a native of Halifax and was playing for Ovenden when he was invited to play in trials at Thrum Hall in 1954. He made his first class debut at Wakefield in a 20-13 loss on 13 November and was a try-scorer the following week when 'Fax beat Hunslet 26-10 at Thrum Hall. Unfortunately for Alan, the resident stand-off at Halifax was the great Ken Dean, whose partnership with Stan Kielty was unshakeable. Alan consequently signed for Oldham, making his first team debut in a 34-8 win at Belle Vue Rangers on 12 March 1955. By the end of the 1957-58 season he had established himself at stand-off in the formidable and entertaining Oldham side, one of the best in the league, and he had earned his first medal as the Lancashire League Championship was won.

His first big game, however, ended in disappointment when Hull gained a surprise 20-8 success at Watersheddings in the 1958 Championship semi-finals. The following season saw another defeat in the Championship semi-finals at St Helens but earlier in the season Oldham had beaten Saints 12-2 in the Lancashire Cup final, when Alan scored a try and dropped a goal – the first goal of any description he had landed in senior rugby.

Alan's half-back partnership with the zippy Frank Pitchford caused no end of problems for opponents, the stand-off scoring 18 tries for Oldham in 1958-59, followed by tallies of 19, 19 and 13 in the following seasons. Oldham had finished winning trophies, however, the nearest Alan ever got to Wembley being a 12-9 semi-final defeat by Hull at Swinton in 1960. He played for Oldham in games against the touring Kangaroos in 1959, lost 25-14 and against the Kiwis in 1955, lost 15-13, while in 1961 he was in the combined Oldham-Rochdale Hornets XIII which beat the New Zealanders 10-8 at Watersheddings. Alan played his last game for Oldham at Castleford on 27 April 1963, having rattled up 76 tries and four goals in 196 appearances.

By August he had signed for Halifax, who had to fork out £4,500 for a local boy they could have had for next to nothing, had Ken Dean not been such a fine player. However, it was money well spent as Alan and second-rower Ken Roberts, who signed from Swinton at the same time, became the catalysts which turned Halifax into a trophy-winning team. Alan, hitherto noted for his devastating try-scoring and upright running action, had lost some of his pace but more than compensated for it by his guile and tactical awareness. A natural at many sports and a very fine fast bowler in the local cricket leagues, Alan could do just about anything on the rugby field. Tall for a stand-off at 5 feet 10½ inches and 12½ stones, he was blessed with subtle handling skills, took the right options and was a superb link between the forwards and three-quarters. He was brave and tough too, did not shirk defensively and was a good kicker. He proved his versatility by shining at centre, full-back and, late in his career, at loose-forward.

Within months of his arrival at Thrum Hall Alan had earned a Yorkshire Cup-winners' medal, although injury kept him out of the team in the final, when Featherstone were beaten 10-0 at Wakefield. At the close of the season he was in the Halifax centre when they beat Castleford 20-12 at Fartown in the Eastern Division Championship Final. In 1964-65 he became vice-captain to John Burnett and the pair played a big part in Halifax's defeat 15-7 of St Helens in the Championship Final at Swinton on 22 May. Halifax reached the Championship Final again in 1966, but Alan was in dispute with the club and missed the game. In October he had been transfer listed at £8,000 and had then accepted the post of secretary at Bradford Northern – a decidedly novel move for a player. Two weeks later he resigned and returned to play for Halifax but again went on the list. He eventually signed as a player for Northern for the start of the 1966-67 season, Halifax receiving £1,250. In his second spell at Halifax he had made 107 appearances, claiming 21 tries and 12 goals.

Alan's subsequent career followed a Byzantinely bewildering path. He made 51 appearances for Bradford, scoring 14 tries and a goal, before moving as player-coach to Keighley, where he made a try-scoring debut in a 7-2 Challenge Cup-tie victory over Batley on 3 February 1968. Keighley got 64 games, with nine tries and three goals, out of him before he returned to Odsal for 11 games, with one try and one goal, for a second spell, this time as player-coach.

A third sojourn at Thrum Hall followed in 1970-71, with 19 games, one try and six goals, and he ended his days as a professional at Oldham, for whom he made nine appearances in 1971-72, scoring a couple of goals. Fittingly, his last game was at stand-off on 5 February 1972, when Oldham defeated Bramley 15-12 at Watersheddings, the scene of many of his greatest triumphs.

Alan Kellett's first-class career encompassed 469 games, 130 tries and 29 goals. He had not finished as a player, however, and continued to turn out as player-coach for Siddal.

He then coached Keighley from January 1975 to May 1975 taking his side to promotion. He returned to Halifax for a fourth time as coach in May 1976 remaining for a year, before coaching again at Keighley from April 1979 to April 1980. He finally called it a day after coaching at Carlisle for four months from February to May 1986.

Away from the game life Alan was a partner in a printing and stationery business in Halifax – just along the road from Thrum Hall. For many years he organised an annual sportsman's dinner in aid of various charitable organisations at Elland Cricket Club.

James Arthur Ledgard
(9 June 1922 - 26 January 2007)

Jimmy Ledgard's professional career lasted just one day short of 17 years. When he retired in 1961 he had kicked 1,560 goals and scored 3,279 points. No Englishman had scored more and only two Welshmen – Jim Sullivan and Gus Risman – stood ahead of him in the all-time lists. That stupendous statistic alone should really have made Jimmy a bigger name in the game's history. Our sport's inability to lionise its major stars and Jimmy's own natural diffidence has probably served to make us underestimate his gigantic achievements and significance.

A brief summary of some of his accomplishments gives an indication of Jimmy's prowess. He topped the league's points scorers with 374 in 1954-55 and led the goal-kickers in four seasons with 89 in 1945-46, 142 in 1951-52, 178 in 1954-55 and 155 in 1955-56. Even now, 46 years after he played his last game, he stands eighth in the all-time goal-kickers' and ninth in the all-time points-scorers' lists. He repeatedly broke club records at Dewsbury and Leigh, holding some simultaneously at both clubs. He was a Lion in 1950, was Great Britain vice-captain when they won the inaugural World Cup in 1954 and captained Yorkshire and England.

Jimmy's position was always full-back and he was a past master in the arts and crafts of the old-time number one. Completely cool and steady, he caught, tackled and kicked superbly and he could join the line effectively if the opportunity arose, although running the ball was not his forte, nor was it expected of full-backs through most of his time. While there were some fine running full-backs such as Martin Ryan (Wigan), Johnny Hunter (Huddersfield) and Joe Phillips (Bradford Northern) about, Jimmy epitomised the finest of the old style practitioners. His kicking skills were exceptional and despite not being a big man, at 5 feet 8½ inches and 11 stone 6 pounds, he could give the ball an almighty wallop. He invariably came out on top in the kicking duels which developed between rival full-backs as they played cat and mouse with each other in trying to manoeuvre their sides into favourable field positions. Jimmy always reckoned he could beat or match anyone in that particular activity, but admitted that Freddie Miller (Hull and Featherstone) gave him plenty of trouble and was the biggest punter of a ball he ever encountered. At a time when goal-kicking conditions were so much more difficult than today, Jimmy Ledgard was worth much more than his weight in gold to his teams.

Jimmy hailed from Sandal in Wakefield, attended Sandal Council School and Manygates School and was good enough to win a Yorkshire Schools rugby league cap before playing with Wakefield Trinity Supporters 14-16 year-olds team. He then tried his hand at rugby union with Sandal and Wakefield Old Boys before returning to rugby league. He was invited to trial at Leeds, for whom he made his first team debut on 26 February 1944 in a 14-0 defeat at Huddersfield. Jimmy played five games for the Loiners and landed five goals but was not retained. Dewsbury, one of the most successful of clubs during the Second World War, had more sense and snapped him up. He made his first appearance for them on 2 September 1944 in a 20-5 loss at Castleford and at the end of his first season had scored 39 goals and a try in 31 matches. He had also landed a couple of goals for Bradford Northern, for whom he guested in a 13-0 victory against Hull on 10 March 1945.

After the war Dewsbury continued to prosper, Jimmy being one of the main reasons. In 1945-46 he broke Joe Lyman's club records of 70 goals and 158 points set in 1926-27, extending them to 86 goals and 184 points. He also made his county debut, kicking one goal in Yorkshire's 45-3 drubbing of Cumberland at Headingley on 31 October 1945. He played in the first of eight Roses Matches when Yorkshire lost 17-16 at Swinton 10 days later. Perhaps surprisingly, Ron Rylance was given the goal-kicking duties in those games. Jimmy's form was impressive enough to earn him a place in both tour trials in 1946 at Wigan and Leeds but he was overlooked in favour of his opposing full-backs in those games – Martin Ryan and Barrow's Joe Jones. Jimmy had the minor consolation of a brief tour to France in late May 1946, where he played games for a Rugby League XIII against St Etienne and Roanne.

In 1946-47 he picked up his first winners' medal as Dewsbury took the Yorkshire League title, finishing second to Wigan in the league and qualified to meet them in the Championship Final at Maine Road. Dewsbury went down 13-4 with Jimmy and Jack Holt dropping goals. Jimmy would never figure again in a Championship Final, nor did he ever participate in a Challenge Cup Final. The 1946-47 campaign did, however, bring him the first of three County Championship winners' medals, as Yorkshire beat Cumberland 11-9 and Lancashire 13-10. At the season's end, on 17 May, he made his debut for England in a 5-2 win over France at Headingley, which earned England the International Championship title, the first of four International Championship medals Jimmy won.

The 1947-48 season brought Jimmy a Dewsbury club record when he booted 10 goals against Yorkshire Amateurs in a first round Yorkshire Cup-tie on 13 September. Within the next few weeks he represented Yorkshire, England, for whom he notched four goals in a 20-15 win over France at Fartown, and Great Britain. The latter brought him the first of 11 test match appearances and ended in a thrilling 11-10 victory over New Zealand at Headingley on 4 October. That game was the first time the test side had been styled 'Great Britain'.

Jimmy's brilliant displays had drawn admiring attention from many of the game's pundits and it was not surprising that he was coveted by other clubs. However, it took a world record fee of £2,650 before Dewsbury transferred him to Leigh, for whom he made his debut on 14 February 1948, helping his new side to defeat Featherstone Rovers 10-6 at Hilton Park in a first round, second leg, Challenge Cup-tie, a crowd of 14,000 attending. He kicked a couple of goals – the first of 1,043 he would provide in Leigh's cause over the next decade. Thirty-six tries brought his points tally to 2,194 for the club in 334 appearances. The estimable John Woods eventually overtook Jimmy's points total but no one has yet matched his aggregate goals record for Leigh.

Appointed captain for 1948-49, his first season at Leigh was pretty unsuccessful as the team finished 18th in the league, with his personal contribution being 55 goals and two tries in 34 appearances. Even so, Jimmy had created a new club goals-in-a-season record, passing the 51 set by Fred Farrington in 1935-36, while his 116 points equalled the club record of Jack Wood, created in 1947-48. The sure-footed full-back would go on to break his own records in 1948-49 (92 goals, 202 points), 1951-52 (125 goals, 262 points) and 1954-55 (165 goals, 345 points). The 1948-49 season also provided a couple of personal highlights for Jimmy, who made his first appearance in an Ashes test on 9 October, when Australia were beaten 23-21 at Headingley in a spellbinding match. He only played once at Wembley, on 12 March, when England lost 12-5 to France.

In 1949-50 Jimmy captained Leigh to the Lancashire Cup Final – an all-ticket 35,000 sell-out at Wilderspool. He kicked two goals but Wigan took the trophy with a 20-7 score-line. Four Lancashire Cup Final appearances proved to be Jimmy's only domestic honours with Leigh. He was in their beaten side in 1951 at Swinton, Wigan again being their nemesis. In 1952 he had better fortune, kicking five goals in a 22-5 beating of St Helens at Station Road. He skippered Leigh to a 26-9 win over Widnes at Central Park in his fourth and last final in 1955. He contributed a record seven goals and 14 points on that occasion. When the Lancashire Cup was abolished in 1992, Jimmy's record of seven goals in a final was intact, having been emulated only by Steve Hesford for Warrington in 1980 and David Stephenson for Wigan in 1985. Hesford also broke Jimmy's points record with 17 in the Wire's 17-10 victory over Wigan. The nearest Jimmy came to realising his dream of playing in a Challenge Cup Final came in 1952 and 1957, when Leigh lost to Featherstone Rovers and Barrow in the semi-finals, the latter after a replay.

Jimmy captained Yorkshire for the first time on 5 October 1949, kicking two goals in a 22-13 defeat by Lancashire at Warrington but had lost his England place after Other Nationalities beat them 13-7 on the latter's international debut at Workington on 19 September. Martin Ryan had definitely edged ahead of Jimmy in the selectors' eyes but when the Lions tour party for 1950 was announced Jimmy and Martin were both included. Great Britain surrendered the Ashes for the first time since 1920 but Jimmy had the satisfaction of ousting Ryan from full-back for the second and third tests and held the position for the first test against New Zealand at Christchurch. Unfortunately, that was his solitary game in New Zealand, as he suffered a severe back injury, retired in the second half and did not play again on tour. He made 12 appearances on tour, totalling 80 points from 37 goals and two tries. Against Wide-Bay & Burnett in an 84-9 romp on 28 June, he scored 33 points from 15 goals and a try, the best of his career.

Between 1950 and 1954 Jimmy only played one more test, when he kicked four goals in a 20-19 win against New Zealand at Swinton in 1951. He did, however, continue to be a regular in England sides, earning the captaincy against Wales and France in 1951, while his Yorkshire career did not end until 1955. He won 18 caps with 31 goals and a try for Yorkshire, a figure bettered by just a handful of great players, his first 11 being consecutive. Those figures are truly exceptional, as county selectors seemed to vacillate even more than international selectors.

His greatest triumph was the 1954 World Cup. He had been overlooked for the 1954 Lions tour, perhaps not too surprisingly as he was 32. A controversial tour, replete with tales of misbehaviour on and off the field and the loss of the Ashes, provoked the British selectors to pick a largely untried 18-man squad for the newly created World Cup tournament in France in the autumn. Dave Valentine captained this makeshift combination and Jimmy, the oldest man in the squad, was appointed vice-captain. His selection was certainly a bit of a surprise, but his form in 1954-55 was quite outstanding. His kicking had been metronomic. A week after the World Cup concluded, on 20 November, he landed his 100th goal of the season in a home win over Huddersfield and became one of a select band of men to post a century of goals before Christmas. By the end of the season he had amassed 178 goals – the nearest approach to Jim Sullivan's record of 194 set in 1933-34.

The tale of Britain's against-the-odds winning of the 1954 World Cup is well enough known to all avid followers of the sport. Jimmy's own contribution was tremendous. Up against the two most celebrated full-backs in the world game – Clive Churchill of Australia and the amazing Frenchman Puig Aubert – Jimmy outshone them both. He and Puig Aubert shared the spoils as leading goal-kickers in the competition with 13 each, but Jimmy's try in a 26-6 win against New Zealand at Bordeaux made him the leading points scorer. However, it was more than his ability to land goals which enabled Jimmy to enjoy such an outstanding tournament. His ability to make Puig Aubert run about the field with his long punting, took the edge of the French genius's play at Toulouse and in the final in Paris. Moreover, his calmness, great anticipation and sound tackling transmitted good vibrations throughout the team, who knew that they had someone totally reliable as their last line of defence. In the opener against Australia at Lyon – a 28-13 victory – he set the standard, creating the opening try for Phil Jackson after nine minutes and went on to kick five goals, albeit from 11 attempts. However, it was other aspects of his play which took the *Daily Mail's* Derek Marshall's eye. He commented: "He often sidestepped his man with ridiculous ease before sweeping play upfield. His handling and tackling were faultless".

A 13-13 draw with France followed at Toulouse – a rough, tough and ugly but thrilling game. Jimmy and Puig Aubert both kicked two goals but Jimmy's touch-line conversion of Gerry Helme's 58th minute try, which gave his side a 13-10 lead, was the most crucial of the four. Jimmy's contribution to the victory over New Zealand was four goals and a try. His was Britain's sixth and last touchdown. Derek Marshall described Jimmy's dummy before touching down as "one of the sauciest I have ever seen". Another journalist, Frank Taylor wrote: "The New Zealanders started to follow Kitchen, but there was Ledgard laughing his head off as he crossed the line. I had to look twice myself to make sure that Ledgard really had the ball". Just for good measure Jimmy kicked the touch-line conversion.

Jimmy had a perfectly good penalty goal disallowed by a French touch-judge in the final against France at the Parc des Princes. Most people thought it passed at least two feet inside the post. It failed to unnerve him though, as he landed a couple of goals in a 16-12 victory. Jack Bentley wrote in the *Daily Dispatch*: "Ledgard's touch-finding was splendid and he had the tubby Puig Aubert... puffing and blowing. Ledgard's backing-up was also first-class, and it was a neat, jinking run of his which paved the way for [Gordon] Brown's second try." Davis Nicholls of the *Daily Express* summed up the reasons for Britain's winning of the World Cup thus: "Every player on this tour has done a tremendous job. But this British triumph has been moulded round Valentine, Helme, Jackson, and the tactical kicking of full-back Jimmy Ledgard. That was what beat the French. They were driven back by the length of Ledgard's kicking, harassed into errors by Valentine and his five eager forwards, bewildered by the wiles of Helme."

Jimmy's international career ended on 12 September 1955 when he kicked five goals but finished a loser as Other Nationalities slew England 33-16 at Wigan. It was his twelfth England cap.

He continued to play for Leigh until 1958, all the while piling up records. Just before the World Cup he had finally set a new goals-in-a-game record for the club. Sam Johnson had landed 10 goals against Keighley in 1908 and Jimmy had equalled that record three times in August and September, 1954. He finally cracked it on 16 October with eleven successful shots in a 58-3 thrashing of Hull KR at Hilton Park. Even in his last season, when approaching his 36th birthday, Jimmy landed 101 goals in 30 matches for Leigh – his sixth century for the club. He played his last game for Leigh on 5 April 1958 in a 15-6 defeat at Widnes.

Dewsbury, who had fallen from the heights to the depths of the league in Jimmy's time in Lancashire, re-signed their old match-winner and made him team captain in January 1959. He made his second debut for them on 31 January, when they went down 24-0 to Featherstone Rovers at Crown Flatt. It was certainly no sinecure at Dewsbury, who finished next to bottom (29th) in 1958-59 and 1959-60 but rose to 27th in 1960-61, Jimmy's last season as player. His capacity for kicking goals, even in such a poor side, hardly diminished. In 57 games for Dewsbury in this period he potted 158 goals and scored three tries. His last season saw him kick 70 goals in 28 matches and such was his consistency that he scored in 27 of them. Those last three seasons at Crown Flatt nudged his career record for Dewsbury to: 182 matches, 399 goals, 11 tries and 831 points. He landed two goals in his finale – a 16-7 home win over Doncaster on 25 February 1961. It was his 574th first-class appearance.

Jimmy was persuaded to take on a three-year contract as team manager at Bradford Northern at the start of the 1961-62 season - a poisoned chalice, if ever there was one. Northern would have been happier if he had agreed to play on, even though he was heading for 40. The Odsal club was in terminal free-fall and his time there was unhappy and he left after one season – never more to coach.

Although his best years were spent at Leigh, perhaps one of the best compliments paid to Jimmy came in March 1998, when, in a Dewsbury Supporters' poll, he was placed second behind Mike Stephenson in Dewsbury's all-time top 10 players.

James Lewthwaite
(10 November 1920 - 23 December 2006)

Jim Lewthwaite scored more tries in first class rugby league than any other Cumberland-born player – 383, between 1943 and 1957. Only two other Cumbrian legends have broken the 300 tries barrier – James Lomas with 310 from 1902 to 1923 and Ike Southward with 374 between 1952 and 1969. That places Jim firmly among the gods. Yet, of those 383 tries, a mere dozen were claimed in Cumberland. Amazingly, he actually scored more touchdowns in Australia. That, of course, is because he played his entire professional career down the coast at Barrow, a path trodden by hordes of talented Cumbrians from the north-west of the county.

Jim was a native of Cleator Moor and as a schoolboy he was a noted sprinter and played both association football and rugby union at county level. Later he briefly played amateur rugby league for Clifton and for Moor Row in the Cumberland Rugby League. It looked as if he was lost to rugby league, however, when he went to work at an aircraft factory near Reading and thence to the shipyards at Barrow, and concentrated on football as a prolific goal-scoring centre forward. He was good enough to earn trials for Blackburn Rovers and Preston North End. Fortunately, he changed codes in 1943 and subsequently established a reputation as one of the most outstanding wingmen rugby league has seen.

His debut in a first round, first leg Challenge Cup tie at St Helens on 13 March 1943 ended in a 13-2 defeat for Barrow but Jim was immediately picked out as a rising star. The *North-West Evening Mail* reporter was in no doubt about his potential, observing: "He sidesteps easily, changes pace cleverly, accelerates brilliantly, and shows some of the marks which originally distinguished Alf Ellaby when he joined St Helens. With a centre to bring him out Lewthwaite might develop into something clean out of the ordinary". To be compared to Alf Ellaby was praise indeed but the words proved prophetic.

Jim was pretty big for a winger at 6 feet and around 13 stones. His style was direct, his creed "get to the line as soon as possible", and he could score from any distance. He could swerve unnervingly and possessed a devastating hand-off, allied to which he was an expert cross-kicker. He was a rare handful as an attacking force but, almost as importantly, he was a rock in defence. Just for good measure, Jim had an unsullied reputation for sportsmanship.

Jim - a one club man - played with Barrow in the days when they were in their pomp. Almost throughout his career with them Barrow were in the hunt for honours, played a clean and open style of rugby and nurtured a host of wonderfully gifted players. Their names are now merely echoes of halcyon days in Furness, but what memories are evoked for those they charmed – notables such as Joe Jones, Bryn Knowelden, Jack Grundy, Ted Toohey, Phil Jackson, Dennis Goodwin and the man who led them, the sublime Willie Horne.

Playing in such company and with talent to burn, it was not long before Jim was winning honours. In his first season of peace-time football Jim won the first of 20 caps for Cumberland on 31 October 1945 against Yorkshire at Headingley. He struck such good form that he was selected for both trials, at Wigan and Leeds, for the 1946 Australasian tour. His performances were impressive and he was duly chosen to tour alongside his Barrow team-mates, Horne, Knowelden and Jones. His fellow Lions wingers were Arthur Bassett (Halifax), Eric Batten (Bradford Northern) and Albert Johnson (Warrington) – all more experienced than Jim

Although he did not play in any of the tests, he finished as the tour's leading try-scorer with 25 tries in 15 outings, failing to score in only three games - a magnificent achievement. Moreover, he created his own piece of Lions history when he became the first tourist ever to score seven tries in a game, a feat which he achieved in a 94-0 victory over Mackay on 2 July. Only Jack Hilton, in 1950, and Mick Sullivan, in 1958, have emulated Jim. He also bagged hat-tricks against Canberra and South Island.

Despite his success on tour, Jim was destined never to win a test cap and to this day he remains the British player who scored most tries in a career without winning test selection. At club level, however, Jim was indispensable to Barrow. His value to the club is clearly illustrated in the statistics of 500 appearances, 352 tries, 21 goals and 1,098 points over 14 years. No one has played more games or scored more tries for Barrow.

From 1949-50 Barrow had two of the deadliest wingers in the sport for on the left wing was the flying Frank Castle, signed from Coventry RUFC. Between them they scored over 600 tries for the club but they only appeared together once in an international. That was at Huddersfield on 18 October 1952, when Jim belatedly won his solitary international cap against Other Nationalities. Jim scored a try that afternoon but was injured early in the second half and England succumbed 31-12. It remained a mystery to many why Frank Castle, a Lion in 1954 and winner of four test caps, was more favoured than Jim by the test selectors. Frank was a match-winner and definitely faster than Jim – indeed he was widely regarded as the fastest man in the game – but, arguably, he was neither as good a footballer, nor as good a defender as Jim.

At a domestic level Barrow won the Lancashire Cup for the first time in 1954, beating Oldham 12-2 in the final at Swinton. Jim hardly missed a game in his time at Craven Park but was unfortunately injured for that red-letter day and was absent. He did, however, figure in all three of Barrow's Wembley appearances in the 1950s, playing outside the great Phil Jackson, his long-time centre partner. Jim was on the right wing in 1951, when Wigan beat Barrow 10-0, and in 1957, when Leeds scraped home 9-7. His greatest triumph was reserved for the 1955 final, when Barrow defeated Workington Town 21-12, an unforgettable occasion in the sporting history of the North-West.

Jim Lewthwaite defied logic and the laws of nature by becoming more prolific as his career approached its close. In 1955-56, when past 35 years old, he posted a personal best of 41 tries for Barrow. His last season, 1956-57, was even more productive. It began with him being awarded the captaincy of Cumberland for his last game with the county XIII, which he led to a dramatic last minute 15-14 victory over Yorkshire at Whitehaven on 19 September 1956. He scored a try and, unusually, appeared at right centre. Remarkably, Jim had played at county level every season since 1945-46, with the exception of 1954-55. By the end of the 1956-57 season he had scored 50 tries for Barrow in only 43 games, eclipsing Frank Castle's club record of 47 scored in 1951-52. Jim's record has never been beaten. His last game for the club – his 500th – was the Challenge Cup final at Wembley against Leeds on 11 May 1957. Barrow may have lost, but Jim certainly went out in style.

Jim became coach at Barrow for the 1968-69 and 1969-70 seasons but golf claimed his active sporting life thereafter, while away from sport life he was an inspector for the local water board. It came as no surprise when Jim, along with Willie Horne and Phil Jackson, became the first inductees into the Barrow Rugby League Club's Hall of Fame.

Note: This obituary is a slightly amended version of an article from Robert Gate's book, *100 Cumberland Greats* (Tempus Publishing, 2002)

Thomas William Lynch
(20 July 1927 – 29 December 2006)

People who are ancient enough often say everyone can remember where they were or what they were doing when they heard of President Kennedy's assassination. I am ancient enough, but I can't. I will always remember, however, when I heard about the death of Tommy Lynch, one of the great heroes in the history of Halifax RLFC. Stepping out of the village newsagents, I was accosted by a long-time Thrum Hall enthusiast, who immediately said, "Pity about the bad news about Tommy, init?" I did not need to be told we were talking about rugby and that Tommy Lynch had passed away. To Halifax fans of a certain generation there is, and always will be, only one Tommy.

147

Tommy Lynch had never even seen a game of rugby league when he left New Zealand to play for Halifax, where he arrived on 21 December 1951. By the time he left on 11 December 1956 he had convinced a good many people that Halifax had never possessed such a wonderful centre threequarter.

Born at Naseby on the South Island, Tommy came from a family steeped in rugby union. His grandfather, also named Tommy, had played provincial rugby for Otago and represented South Island against the pioneering 1888 British touring side. His father, another Tommy, nicknamed 'Tiger', was an All Black threequarter, who won four caps in 1913 and 1914, and scored 37 tries in 23 games for New Zealand. Tommy junior's cousin, Tom Coughlan, won an All Black cap as a forward against Australia in 1958.

It was hardly surprising that Tommy Lynch should become an outstanding player. He specialised at second five-eighth, represented Otago in 1947 and 1949, Canterbury in 1950 and 1951 and South Island, also in 1950 and 1951. His club rugby was spent with Southern (Otago) and Marist (Christchurch). In 1951 he was selected to tour Australia with the All Blacks and was one of the major successes of the trip, scoring eight tries and a drop-goal in 10 appearances. Tommy played in all three tests, making his debut in an 8-0 win at the Sydney Cricket Ground on 23 June, when Rex Mossop figured in the Australian pack. In the second test, also at the SCG, Tommy scored a try and dropped a goal in a 17-11 victory, and was a try-scorer in the third test at Brisbane, where the All Blacks triumphed 16-6.

Halifax pursued Tommy, along with fellow Canterbury backs and future All Blacks, John Hotop and Allan Elsom, who both declined the offers. He signed a five-year contract on 26 November – just in time to beat a ban agreed two weeks later between the RFL and the NZRL, which extended by three years an existing ban on English clubs signing New Zealand league players, which was now to include New Zealand union players. Halifax paid Tommy £5,000, which equalled the world record transfer fees that Leigh had spent on Wigan's great hooker Joe Egan and Wigan's own capture of Dewsbury loose-forward Harry Street, both deals done in the 1950-51 season.

Halifax's gain was the All Blacks' loss. In 2004 Huw Richards wrote in his book *Dragons and All Blacks*, commemorating Wales's 1953 defeat of New Zealand at Cardiff, "The man they needed was in Britain in 1953, but as unavailable as if he had been climbing Everest". He went on to quote the All Blacks captain Bob Stuart, who still believed Tommy to have been the All Blacks' missing link, saying, "He could play second five, centre or wing, tackled like a demon and could kick. He would have been our midfield anchor".

Tommy made his debut for Halifax at right centre against Rochdale Hornets on New Year's Day 1952, when Thrum Hall threw some of its foulest weather at players and fans with snow on the ground, freezing wind and periodic sleet. Tommy scored the opening try for Halifax but crashed into the post in touching down and a few directors doubtless had palpitations that their record signing might have irreparably damaged himself. He survived the weather and the woodwork, however, as Halifax won 18-5. His try was the first of 111 he would score in 188 appearances for the club. No other centre had scored as many career tries for the club at that time. He also landed nine goals.

Tommy was a quick learner but was very anxious when he found out that in only his fourth game he was to face Bradford Northern's Ernest Ward in a league fixture at Thrum Hall, which 'Fax lost 6-5. Ward, captain of Great Britain and one of the game's all-time greats, was renowned for his exemplary character and sportsmanship. In the dressing-room Tommy asked his team-mates what to expect from Ernie. To a man they all assured him that Ernie was a brilliant, but scrupulously fair, player, who never caused any bother. At half-time Tommy limped into the dressing room all black and blue, complaining, "What was that you lot told me about Ernest Ward being a gentleman. Every time he tackles me I get a clout from him!"

Halifax were developing into one of the game's top teams in the early 1950s and Tommy Lynch was one of the main reasons for their rise. As a centre he had all the skills. He was quick and penetrative, robust at 5 feet 10½ inches and over 13 stones, a willing and damaging defender, who could wreak havoc with his ball-stealing and he had a deadly instinct for try-scoring. His greatest glory, however, was his sublime understanding with his winger Arthur Daniels, who was a Wales and Great Britain cap. Daniels and Lynch played together as 'Fax's right wing pair on 142 occasions and between them produced 185 tries, Tommy scoring 89 and Arthur 96.

Together they mesmerised opponents, who often had no clue as to which of them had the ball, so clever were their feints, scissors movements and dummy scissors. Tommy would often slide towards the wing characteristically holding the ball in both hands in front of him, while Arthur would come inside taking the cover with him, only for them to find out too late that Tommy had carried on running with the ball to score at the corner. Their machinations were so well disguised that it was not just opposing players who were bamboozled – the fans were also often at a loss as to what had actually happened. What is certain for those who witnessed the wiles of the pair is that the memory of them remains a thing of beauty.

Tommy played in all of Halifax's big games in the mid 1950s – three Championship Finals, two Wembley Finals, plus the 1954 Odsal replay, and two Yorkshire Cup Finals, one of which also required a replay. In addition he earned winners' medals for the Yorkshire League Championship in 1952-53, 1953-54 and 1955-56.

In his first full season, 1952-53, Halifax rose from 21st to second in the league table, won the Yorkshire League, were semi-finalists in the Yorkshire Cup and lost to St Helens in the Championship Final, when Tommy was a scorer in a 24-14 defeat at Maine Road. He also topped the Halifax try-scorers with 26 in 44 games. In 1953-54 Halifax finished top of the league, were Yorkshire Champions and contested both the Challenge Cup and Championship Finals against Warrington. Tommy scored 19 tries in 38 games but would have traded the lot to have had his disallowed try count in the Odsal replay. He always remained convinced that it was a legitimate try but the referee ruled Daniels' pass to his centre partner forward. Halifax lost 8-4 and Warrington completed the double in the Championship final, winning 8-7 at Maine Road. Tommy, of Irish extraction, would have been pleased to score three tries in Halifax's two victories over the Wire in Belfast and Dublin three weeks later.

In 1954-55 Halifax finished fourth and fell to Warrington again in the Championship semi-final, but Tommy got a winners' medal from their 22-14 victory over Hull at Headingley in the Yorkshire Cup Final. He played in all 44 of the side's fixtures and topped the try-scorers with 33 – a club record for a centre until Greg Austin eclipsed it in 1990-91.

Tommy's last season, 1955-56, saw Halifax go within 160 minutes of winning all four cups. The Yorkshire Cup was retained with a 7-0 win over Hull at Odsal, after a 10-10 draw in a bloody encounter at Leeds, and the Yorkshire League was won in a canter. However, Halifax stumbled at the last two hurdles, losing in the late stages of both the Challenge Cup final and the Championship final to St Helens and Hull respectively. Tommy racked up 25 tries in 45 games and helped Arthur Daniels to a post-war club record of 34 tries. He had the pleasure of scoring Halifax's winning try against the New Zealanders on 17 September, 1955 when the Thrum Hallers won 18-17 – his most memorable try, in his own view. He also had the unique experience of playing for the Kiwi touring side on 12 December 1955 in a match against a Rugby League XIII at Castleford in aid of the dependents of Dennis Norton, a forward who had collapsed during Castleford's fixture against the New Zealanders on 16 November and died shortly afterwards.

There was no doubt that Tommy Lynch was a centre of the highest class but his opportunities for representative honours in England were strictly limited. When he arrived the celebrated Other Nationalities side was fully stocked with brilliant centres, who had a head start on him – notably the three Australians, Pat Devery (Huddersfield), Tony Paskins (Workington Town) and Trevor Allan (Leigh). Tommy broke into the side for the 15-10 victory over France at Bordeaux on 18 October 1953, when the threequarter line read Brian Bevan, Tony Paskins, Tommy Lynch and Lionel Cooper. No Other Nationalities internationals were played in 1954-55, because of the inaugural World Cup in France, but Tommy played for a Rugby League XIII which lost 25-13 to Australasia at Odsal on 17 November 1954. The Other Nationalities team was resurrected for one final season in 1955 and won the International Championship, crushing England 33-16 at Wigan on 12 September and France 32-19 at Leigh on 19 October, when Tommy was a try-scorer. Tommy starred in both games in a threequarter line which must have been a dream for him, or anyone else – Bevan, Lynch, Lewis Jones and Billy Boston.

Tommy's last first-class game for Halifax was the Championship Final 10-9 loss to Hull at Maine Road on 12 May 1956. He started the following season by appearing in the traditional Charity Cup game against Huddersfield at Thrum Hall on 11 August, which was won 23-13, Tommy scoring Halifax's last try. Unfortunately, he sustained an eye injury, which was sufficiently serious to end his career – four months before the end of his contract. He had just turned 29.

When Tommy returned to New Zealand he settled in Gore on the South Island, where he started to coach a schoolboy team, which could not find any other coach. A radio station broadcast the story, the wrath of the Eastern Southland Rugby sub-Union fell on him and he was banned from any involvement in the game. In later years he was offered forms to apply for re-instatement with the NZRU but refused, believing "they would have knocked me back". In New Zealand he worked as a stock agent for a wool and meat exporter and then for a farm servicing company before retiring to Christchurch. In England he had worked at the Ajax Machine Tool Company in Halifax and as a clerk for the Moderna Company in Mytholmroyd.

Tommy returned to Halifax briefly in May 1993 to be inducted into the club's Hall of Fame as one of the inaugural 24 entrants, an occasion relished by Tommy and the hordes of admirers who turned up to renew acquaintances with one of the blue and whites' most revered icons.

Emlyn Richards
(30 June 1921 - 4 December 2006)

I corresponded with Emlyn Richards for over 20 years before he decided to scribble down his memoirs. He sent me his manuscript in January 2005 to see what I thought. In his accompanying letter he wrote, "If you think it's a waste of time trying to get it published at least you will have some information when and if you decide to write my obituary". Emlyn did self-publish his story, *To Hull and Back – Memoirs of a Rugby Renegade*, in July 2006 – it was not a waste of time – and here I am writing his obituary, as he anticipated.

Emlyn's career in rugby league was relatively short – six years as a professional with Leeds, Hull KR and Cardiff – but he never lost his interest in the game, even though he spent the last half century and more back in his native Mountain Ash, where his house was named 'Kingston'.

The son of a miner, who abandoned the pits to work in the milk delivery business, Emlyn attended Mountain Ash Grammar School. The school was a prolific producer of rugby talent, including union *alumni* such as Les Manfield and Haydn Morris. It also supplied rugby league with Dickie Williams (Leeds and Hunslet), Terry O'Brien (Keighley) and Brian Juliff (a Challenge Cup finalist with Wakefield Trinity, Wigan and Halifax). Williams, who was best man when Emlyn married, was one of rugby league's finest stand-offs, making Lions tours in 1950 and 1954, the latter as captain. The old enmity of rugby unionists first struck Emlyn when he found that the school had removed its portrait of Dickie in his Welsh Schools rugby union cap and jersey as soon as he joined Leeds. It would not be the last time he encountered such prejudice.

Emlyn at various times played union for Mountain Ash, Aberaman, Cilfynydd and London Welsh. He continued to play union when he went to Birmingham in 1939 to train as a teacher at Saltley College. By 1941 his teacher training had been disrupted by his call-up to the RAF. His services rugby included an appearance for an RAF Select XV against a Northern Command XV at Central Park, Wigan, while in 1943 he represented Welsh Academicals against a New Zealand Army XV at his home ground in Mountain Ash, scoring two tries from the wing in a 17-7 win.

Dickie Williams suggested to Eddie Waring, who was managing Leeds, that he should take a look at Emlyn. Consequently, Emlyn trialled for Eddie, and made his debut as a league player at centre in a 10-4 defeat at Castleford, on 17 February 1945. He represented Leeds five times in all (twice each at stand-off and centre and once on the wing) and scored a try at Wigan on 3 March 1945. Eddie did not sign Emlyn but recommended him to Hull KR, who did.

Emlyn made his debut for Rovers in a 17-3 loss at Batley on 29 December 1945 at stand-off. His second game brought him four tries in a 26-7 rout of St Helens at Craven Park on 5 January 1946. Although he had only appeared in five games for Rovers Emlyn made such a good impression that he was ear-marked for a place in the Wales team to meet France at Bordeaux on 24 March 1946. However, Emlyn was still in the RAF, which decided to transfer him to Dortmund and his chance of a Welsh cap disappeared.

Demobilised in August 1946, Emlyn's career with Rovers took off and he established a first team place immediately. There were complications, however, as he resumed his teacher training course and found himself up against the rugby union hierarchy. As a professional rugby league player he was banned from even training with the college rugby union team and had to train with the college soccer team.

Rovers were among the game's also-rans in the immediate post-war years so there were no medals for Emlyn. He did, however, enjoy the thrill of being on the wing when Rovers beat the 1947 Kiwis 13-7, and fulfilled another ambition when he played stand-off against Dickie Williams in Rovers-Leeds clashes. He made his 109th and last appearance for Rovers at Batley on 18 March 1950, having amassed 47 tries for the club. His subsequent connections with rugby league included a brief spell on the RFL's first coaching scheme under Trevor Foster and a three match (two tries) spell for the short-lived Cardiff club in October 1951.

Returning to Wales Emlyn enjoyed a successful teaching career, his specialities being PE and music, and became a head teacher. He was also a magistrate, treasurer of the local Mencap Society, and found time to write a history of Mountain Ash RU Club.

In 1973, even though he was in his fifties and 20 years had elapsed since his days as a professional rugby league player, Emlyn found the dead hand of rugby union on his shoulder. At that time he was vice-chairman of his local Cynon Schools Rugby Committee, while his friend Don Devereux, the former Huddersfield and Leeds forward, was coach and selector for the Welsh Secondary Schools XV. Both suddenly found themselves "in breach of the amateur laws" and relieved of their posts. Someone had obviously decided to use their past against them. Until then they had been allowed to serve schools rugby union without a problem, when it was hardly likely that the authorities did not know of their previous connections with rugby league.

The *Aberdare Leader*, in an article headlined "Apartheid in Rugby", wrote "…And Emlyn Richards is outstanding a citizen and educationist enough to be made a Justice of the Peace, but not a sporting figure fit to sit in the seats of Welsh schools rugby! … If we Welsh rugby lovers are a radical, fair-minded, tolerant lot, as we like to say we are, we should not put up with such bigotry and hypocrisy in our national game. The Welsh Dragon ought to be ashamed to look sport in the eye after this!"

Thankfully, Emlyn lived to witness more enlightened days.

(N.B. An extract from Emlyn's memoirs appeared in *Our Game* issue 13)

London League Publications Ltd

PO Box 10441, London E14 8WR. www.llpshop.co.uk

Rugby League and football books in print

A Dream Come True By Doug Laughton with Andrew Quirke.	£5.00	Special Offer
A Pastel Revolution By Paul Fletcher and Philip Gordos	£12.95	
A Westminster XIII Edited by David Hinchliffe MP. (hardback)	£12.95	
A Westminster XIII	£9.95	
Beyond the Heartlands By Julian Harrison	£5.00	Special Offer
Cougars Going Up! By David Kirkley.	£5.00	Special Offer
Duggie Greenall – A Rugby League Saint By Denis Whittle.	£12.95	
Fan's Eye City By Gareth Phillips.	£5.00	Special Offer
From Fulham to Wembley Edited by Dave Farrar & Peter Lush.	£5.00	Special Offer
From Great Broughton to Great Britain By Peter Cropper.	£5.00	Special Offer
Give it to Kelly By John Vose.	£5.00	Special Offer
I, George Nepia By Sir Terry McLean.	£5.00	Special Offer
Keeping the Dream Alive By Stuart Williams.	£9.95	
Kiwis, Wigan and The Wire By Ces Mountford.	£5.00	Special Offer
Neil Fox By Robert Gate.	£18.95	
Newlove By Paul Newlove with Andrew Quirke.	£5.00	Special Offer
Play to Win - Rugby League Heroes By Maurice Bamford.	£5.00	Special Offer
Rugby League Back o' t' wall By Graham Chalkley. £12.95		
Rugby League Bravehearts By Gavin Willacy.	£5.00	Special Offer
Rugby Rebellion By Sean Fagan.	£16.95	
Rugby's Berlin Wall By Graham Williams, Peter Lush & David Hinchliffe.	£11.95	
The Fulham Dream By Harold Genders.	£5.00	Special Offer
The Great Bev By Robert Gate.	£5.00	Special Offer
Trevor Foster By Simon Foster, Robert Gate & Peter Lush.	£14.95	
Tries in the Valleys Edited by Peter Lush & Dave Farrar.	£5.00	Special Offer
We'll Support You Evermore By David Kuzio.	£11.95	

Australian rugby league books:

Don't Die with the Music in You by Wayne Bennett	£12.95
Billy Smith by Graham Langlands & Helen Elward	£11.95
Shielding the Truth by Michael Panckridge & Laurie Daley	£8.50
The ABC of Rugby League by Malcolm Andrews	£16.95

Cheques payable to London League Publications Ltd.
Please send to LLP, PO Box 10441, London E14 8WR.
Credit card orders via our website: www.llpshop.co.uk

N.B. Special offer prices are only available direct from London League Publications Ltd. All British books can be ordered through bookshops, but at full price.

New and forthcoming books from London League Publications Ltd

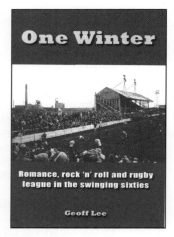

One Winter
Romance, rock 'n' roll and rugby league in the swinging sixties

A new edition of Geoff Lee's first novel.

£9.95 post free

The Patience of a Saint
St Helens rugby league 1978 to 1996
By Mike Critchley

A personal memoir of St Helens RLFC and growing up in the town. £12.95 post free – to be published in May 2007

To snuff out the Moon
The development of floodlit rugby league
By Tom Mather

Fascinating material from the early days of floodlit rugby, and the modern day development of league under lights.
£12.95 post free – to be published in July 2007

Champagne Rugby
The golden age of French Rugby League
By Henri Garcia

Roger Grime's translation of a rugby league classic on the 1950s French tours to Australia & New Zealand.
£12.95 post free - to be published in September 2007.

Also look out for Denis Whittle & Alex Service's book on St Helen's Recs, Geoff Lee's One Autumn, and Keith Macklin's autobiography.

All the books will be on our website, www.llpshop.co.uk at least one month before publication.

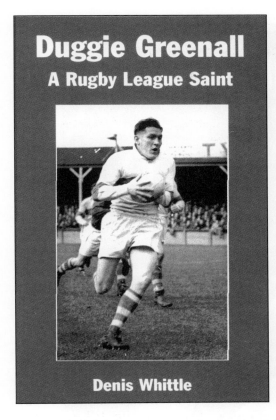

Biography of St Helens and Great Britain legend.

Well illustrated.

Published September 2006.

£12.95 post free

History of famous amateur rugby league club from a mining village that has produced many famous players.

Published in November 2006

£12.95

Both books available from London League Publications Ltd, PO Box 10441, post free. Cheques payable to London League Publications Ltd, credit card orders via www.llpshop.co.uk

A PASTEL REVOLUTION

Harlequins Rugby League - The Inside Story

Paul Fletcher & Philip Gordos

Based on interviews with players and key people behind the scenes, a fascinating new book about rugby league in London. Published in November 2006 at £12.95. Available from London League Publications Ltd, PO Box 10441, London E14 8WR. Cheques payable to London League Publications Ltd, credit card orders via www.llpshop.co.uk